ISSUES IN CANADIAN SMALL BUSINESS

THERE HAS BEEN a growing movement within colleges and universities in recent years to integrate more issues and applied skills into the traditional business curriculum. Industries have commented in business magazines and newspaper articles that today's business graduates lack the practical skills and know-how to be successful in the rapidly changing business world of the 1990s. Teachers have responded by providing a heavier focus on business applications and by making the students more aware of what to expect in the business workplace.

The Dryden **Applied Business Series** has been developed to provide resource material for these teachers and students. The series emphasizes real-world applications through the discussion of current events and issues in the business world.

DRYDEN is committed to developing a broad spectrum of quality new educational resource products. If you have ideas for projects that might suit the Dryden **Applied Business Series**, or if you are interested in reviewing or writing a book in the series, we would like to hear from you. Please contact Donna Muirhead, Editor and Marketing Manager for the **Applied Business Series**. Telephone: (416) 255-0177, or Fax: (416) 255-5456.

ISSUES IN CANADIAN SMALL BUSINESS

Ron Knowles

ALGONQUIN COLLEGE

Debbie White

CARLETON UNIVERSITY

DRYDEN

Harcourt Brace & Company, Canada

TORONTO   MONTREAL   FORT WORTH   NEW YORK   ORLANDO
PHILADELPHIA   SAN DIEGO   LONDON   SYDNEY   TOKYO

CANADIAN CATALOGUING IN PUBLICATION DATA

Knowles, Ronald A.
    Issues in Canadian small business

(Applied business series)
ISBN 0-03-922963-7

1. Small business – Canada – Management. 2. Small business – Canada.
3. New business enterprises – Canada.   I. White, Debbie. II. Title. III. Series.

ND62.7.K56 1995   658'02'2'0971   C94-932775-5

Publisher: Heather McWhinney
Editor and Marketing Manager: Donna J. Muirhead
Projects Manager: Liz Radojkovic
Projects Co-ordinator: May Ku
Director of Publishing Services: Jean Davies
Editorial Manager: Marcel Chiera
Production Editor: Louisa Schulz
Production Manager: Sue-Ann Becker
Production Supervisor: Carol Tong
Editor: Shirley Tessier
Copy Editor: Scott Mitchell
Design, Typesetting, and Assembly: ECW Type & Art
Printing and Binding: Best Book Manufacturers, Inc.
Cover image: Tony Stone Images

DRYDEN

This book was printed in Canada on acid-free paper.
1 2 3 4 5   99 98 97 96 95

Table of Contents

A NOTE
from the
PUBLISHER

Thank you for selecting *Issues in Canadian Small Business* by Ron Knowles and Debbie White. The authors and publisher have devoted considerable time and care to the development of this book. We appreciate your recognition of this effort and accomplishment.

We want to hear what you think about *Issues in Canadian Small Business*. Please take a few minutes to fill in the stamped reply card at the back of the book. Your comments and suggestions will be valuable to us as we prepare new editions and other books.

Preface

According to the Canadian Federation of Independent Business, a small business is defined as any firm that is independently owned and operated and is not dominant in its field of endeavour. For the past decade, our small business community has created jobs, generated wealth, and provided satisfying careers for Canadian entrepreneurs. As for the future, a number of studies have concluded that small business is the engine that will fuel the Canadian economy into the next millennium.

In tomorrow's economy, we believe that you will have two choices of employment: (1) create your own job, or (2) create your own job. Small business may very well be your only option to make a living.

It is within this context that Harcourt Brace asked us to write this book on the current issues facing the small business community. Like true entrepreneurs we jumped at the opportunity.

In our classroom lectures, public seminars, and on radio, we are constantly referring to the stories in *The Globe and Mail* of successful entrepreneurs. Realizing that small business people learn best through stories and examples, we decided to partner with *The Globe and Mail* to make current issues in small business come alive with case stories of successful Canadian entrepreneurs.

Entrepreneurs are opportunists who seek out a problem or an unfulfilled need and find creative ways to solve the problem or satisfy the need. The entrepreneur becomes a small business person when he or she is able to translate a *market opportunity* into a *financial benefit*. So, from *The Globe and Mail*, we gathered some of the more lively and colourful stories of entrepreneurs who had transformed their ideas into successful small businesses.

Our next step was to pose the fundamental questions: "Why are these small business entrepreneurs successful?" "What can be learned from their experience to help others start and run their own business?" Our response to these questions resulted in the development of several key issues or themes, which are individually addressed in separate chapters of this book. These issues can be collapsed into several broad categories.

The first and perhaps most important is the personality or character traits that drive an entrepreneur. These are discussed in the introduction, chapter 1, and to some extent in chapters 2 and 6. To get started, we strongly encourage you to complete the Entrepreneurial Questionnaire contained in the introduction. Whether you are just thinking about starting a business or even if you are already self-employed, it is important to continually assess your strengths and weaknesses.

We also hope you will learn from our cases in each chapter that small business entrepreneurs are mainly driven by the "pull" factor. They have an internal desire to create and succeed. Like mountaineers, they want to climb the mountain because of the challenge. Those who are "pushed" into the market because they need money or they lose their jobs, for example, soon learn that these types of external factors are only a trigger. Most entrepreneurs succeed in the long run when they are driven to action by an internal flame.

In every organization, whether large or small, the human element is crucial for its success. Entrepreneurs must be able to treat their employees and business partners with respect, provide leadership, recognize that they are not loners, accept their own limitations, and be receptive to other people's ideas. Growth and surviving it depend on the entrepreneur's human skills.

The second theme, and one that is of extreme importance, is that no one should start or operate a business in today's economy without a business plan. Thus, we have provided a basic framework for creating your own business plan in the introduction. Specific issues related to the business plan are contained in chapters 3 to 6. We start with the financing issues in chapter 3 because we know that this will be a major concern for most of you. In chapters 4 and 5 we move the discussion into marketing and customer service. In chapter 6 we urge you to start thinking now about the changes your business might face in the future.

Another emerging issue in small business is education. We deal with this critical topic in chapter 7. Our main point in education is that

Canada is now deeply entrenched in the knowledge-based or information era, and small business entrepreneurs therefore will not be able to thrive and succeed unless they are continuously learning. In the economy of the future, a grade five education will no longer "cut the mustard."

Lastly, but of course never the least important, is the theme of globalization or the global market. In the export market, the competition for any small business will no longer be "down the street." Chances are, entrepreneurs will be competing with a business nestled in another country half-way around the world. Our small business community must be export-ready and be able to compete on a global basis. This is the theme of chapter 8, and you will notice that in each of the case studies, "going global" is either a major goal for entrepreneurs or a force that they cannot ignore.

Not only do we discuss the major themes or issues in small business, but we also include a number of exercises for you to test your business readiness. For example, in chapter 7 you can evaluate your entrepreneurial skills and abilities, and in chapter 8 you can test your "export quotient." We have also dotted the book with a number of Small Business Notes. They provide tips, information, and food for thought.

Entrepreneurs learn from the experiences of others; *we all* learn from the experiences of others. We learn from real-life stories. The stories of Paul L'Heureux, Cindy Eeson, Thom Santos, and many others are intended to give you a sense of the entrepreneur's experiences, both failures and successes. In this text, you will find real-life stories about Canadians who took or were forced to take their future into their own hands. They created their own security by starting their own business. They shared their experiences in the form of articles printed in *The Globe and Mail*. Some articles do not tell a story, they provide information and facts — very real facts. They may be very uncomfortable facts, but you must be aware of them. Knowledge can be uncomfortable; however, lack of it can be a painful cause of failure. Gaining knowledge can mean you have gained the tool of power to succeed in your own business venture. Following the articles are thought-provoking questions based on the stories that you have read. They provide a framework for group discussion or instructions for a preparatory exercise.

We are truly fortunate to be surrounded by strong family and friends who constantly supported us as we spent many long hours ploughing through articles and writing and rewriting the manuscript. On a number of occasions, it seemed as though we would never make our deadline. But we made it. A special thank-you must go to our children — Stephen, Jennifer, Christina, Frederick, and Joseph — who waited patiently, and without complaint, for their time to be with their mom and dad. The term "quality time" seemed to come up often in our parental discussions.

We could not have completed this book without the support and leadership of our editors and colleagues at Harcourt Brace, especially Donna Muirhead and May Ku. They had the patience, tolerance, and understanding to listen to our excuses and screams of frustration when it seemed we would not meet deadlines. But with their strength and direction, the job got done on schedule. We deeply thank them for being true partners, and we hope we rose to their level of excellence.

Lastly a special thank-you must go out to Gordon Pitts and Ellen Roseman, the editors of *The Globe and Mail*'s Change Page and Entrepreneur's Page. Our success stories and Small Business Notes are based on articles from these special sections. Without the help and wisdom of these editors, we doubt very much whether we could have completed this book.

On that note, we encourage you to read, enjoy, and learn from the success stories of some of our entrepreneurial leaders.

Ron Knowles
Debbie White
Ottawa, Canada
January 1995

INTRODUCTION

The Current Economy

The restructuring of the world economy during the late 1980s and early 1990s has touched everyone and left many with little hope. Yet new businesses have started and thrived during the recession. Some existing businesses did survive and grow despite a record-setting number of business and personal bankruptcies. Economists' assessments and recommendations vary; however, all agree that Canada and the world economy will continue to experience unprecedented change.

The attitude of Canadians must also change. We have no choice: either we move forward and join the new economic revolution with passion and optimism or we will move backward and be left far behind. If we are to preserve our commitment to sharing the very things we hold sacred (our health care, social programs, education, equalization payments, day care, and so on), we must understand the world changes and position ourselves to take advantage of the new opportunities. Change is painful for most, but there will be no gain without first enduring pain.

Historically we have blindly depended on our governments, who have not listened or responded to the economic advice of our leaders. No wonder respected economists and business leaders warn that there is no political strategy for the future of Canada. Average hourly wages and average annual salaries have declined since the 1970s after inflation and will continue to do so unless Canada can rise to the challenge of the new economic order. Despite this, our labour costs still remain high and many companies have moved manufacturing off shore, leaving only the corporate offices here.

The new economy does not need our raw materials, it needs technology and knowledge. To move successfully into the next millennium, we have to change from a raw-materials-based economy to a knowledge-based economy. We have the potential to be well positioned to do this with a highly educated workforce. Now is the time to focus on education and alleviate the costly expense of high school drop-outs.

The issue of the 1990s for Canada will be education, starting with the three R's. A 1991 survey conducted by Towers Perrin and the Hudson Institute of Canada found that 60 per cent of Canada's major employers were having difficulty recruiting new employees. It was not because Canadians were unavailable to work — unemployment was in excess of 1.3 million people. Employers were looking for supervisors, managers, professionals, and technical and skilled trades people, but inadequate writing and verbal communication skills, not lack of experience, forced these companies to hire from abroad. In direct contradiction to the needs of the marketplace, we have continued to cut our spending on education. This trend has to stop.

Unemployment has reached a startling high and shows little sign of recovering to acceptable levels. We cannot return to a society where people have dignity in their work unless we improve our education and training and focus on entrepreneurship.

▮ The New World Economic Order

The fall of communism and the spread of liberal economic ideas to developing countries means new players and new markets in the world economy. Over three billion new people are entering the world trading market. After an absence of 40 to 80 years from the world marketplace, China and other Asian countries with large populations have re-entered the world economy and are aggressively looking for capital and goods. They are also providing the market with natural resources and their own manufactured goods for sale at a price we can never hope to compete with. The developing nations, like Mexico and South American countries, are providing natural resources and cheap labour, while experiencing a crash course in business development. These countries will also be the major source of increase to the world population. With hope and vision, these countries are rapidly formulating a strategy for the future.

The European Community policies to create a stronger economic base took effect January 1, 1993. The treaty prepares the countries for economic, monetary, and political union with the foremost goal of improving competitiveness through science and technology. As well as opening the trade borders, the plans include a social charter which standardizes work standards, skill levels, and education accreditation. They have a vision and a strategy for the future. For example, the Eureka program was established in 1985, linking together the twelve member states of the European Community and the five members of the European Free Trade Area. David Crane, a Canadian economist, states that Eureka will enable Europe to master and exploit the technologies that are important for its future, and to build up its capability in crucial areas by encouraging and facilitating increased industrial, technological, and scientific co-operation on projects having a world-wide market potential.*

To cite another example, Japan has a single-minded vision of becoming the world's science superpower for the next century. Japan's goals and overall directions for their future are set by the Prime Minister's Council for Science and Technology, which is composed of leading business and scientific figures, and recommendations from the Ministry of International Trade and Industry (MITI). MITI is advised by private industry experts as well as a host of government agencies and organizations.

Canada's Free Trade Agreement (FTA) with the United States and the North American Free Trade Agreement (NAFTA) have been opposed by many who predict a resulting loss of jobs. That prediction could not be further from the truth. For Canada to compete worldwide, steps had to be taken to open the borders to goods, services, and labour. Among other things, our population is ageing. That factor alone will put Canada in a precarious position over the next 12 to 20 years. If Canada is to compete in the new economic order, our vision must be to create associations and partnerships with other trading blocks. With a population of less than 30 million people, we will be only a drop in the ocean of the world's population in the twenty-first century. We must establish our niche with the guidance of a well-focused vision and aggressively learn to compete. The world is changing and Canada must also change or ours will become a new Third World economy.

---

* David Crane, *The Next Canadian Century: Building a Competitive Economy* (Toronto: Stoddart, 1992).

11 *Trends*

The future of the Canadian economy will be affected by tidal wave–type trends that will continue into the next century. Our small business community must recognize these trends and flow with the currents. Each trend represents opportunities for the Canadian business community. Following are the major opportunity trends emphasized and well documented by many Canadian economists:

- The world-wide loss of middle management and consequent chaotic restructuring of large business organizations. We know now that old-style bureaucracies do not work and will not be part of the new economic order.

- A global trend by large business to contract out their service requirements to small efficient companies, rather than carry the burden of employees themselves.

- An unprecedented growth in home-based business starts. By the next century it is predicted that 30 per cent of Canadians will be operating a business from home.

- An environmental revolution which will cause the global economy to rethink the way it treats Mother Earth. Canada has one of the worst environmental records and has no choice but to face the consequences. The "blue box program" is only a hint of things to come.

- Ageing of the Canadian population. The first baby boomers will be age 65 in the year 2012, and by the year 2031 it is projected that seniors will make up 23.9 per cent of our population, a significant increase from 9.7 per cent of our 1981 population.* This greying of the Canadian population will create a need for new products and services as well as a need to tap the youth population of other countries.

- The gradual death of large Canadian cities as Canadians choose to work and live outside metropolitan areas. This trend will accelerate as the need to reduce stress and escape violence leads people to relocate to a safer, quieter environment.

---

* Statistics Canada census data. Also, J. Perreault, *Population Projections for Canada, Provinces and Territories, 1989–2011* (Ottawa: Statistics Canada, 1990).

- Fast and furious technological changes. Product life cycles will be reduced from years to days.
- Increased cultural needs, created as the world population shifts to seize business and employment opportunities.
- The trend towards sustainable development — development with a social conscience towards the future impact on our planet.

11 *Future Opportunities*

Where are the opportunities for Canada in the future and how do we hope to be a player? In his recent book, *Where the Jobs Are: Career Survival for Canadians in the New Global Economy*, Colin Campbell translates trends into suggested business opportunities for either employment or a new business.* Growth is expected in the areas of environment-conscious products and techniques, health care, genetic engineering, biotechnology, artificial intelligence, space industries, new materials (plastics with fibres, ceramics, metals), food and agriculture, and energy. A variety of economists make the following recommendations:

- We must develop Canadian-owned companies that can pursue global strategies from Canadian headquarters.
- We must increase spending and incentives on research and development of new products.
- We must manufacture products from our raw materials before we export.
- We must improve education in the area of verbal and written communication skills.
- Education must promote independent thinking through the development of cognitive skills to encourage an entrepreneurial mentality instead of the traditional employee mentality.
- In the new knowledge-based economy, Canada must improve its science, technical, and engineering training programs. This must include increased access for women.
- Although it is likely that English will remain the language of business,

---

* Colin Campbell, *Where the Jobs Are: Career Survival for Canadians in the New Global Economy* (Toronto: MacFarlane, Walter & Ross, 1994).

we must renew our focus on other languages and cultures and make the effort to welcome business people and travellers from other countries, especially from Asia and Latin America.

Although economists' recommendations vary, the theme is the same. We must think globally and we must compete globally in a changing world. The key word is *change*: we have no choice but to assess and adapt quickly, acquiring and using new skills that were never taught in school but are demanded by the marketplace.

11 *Making It Happen*

The past three decades were a period when positioning and timing in the marketplace were fundamentally irrelevant. In the consistently booming economy, a businessperson had to be totally inept to fail. If you were an idea person with access to the financing to start a business, you were virtually guaranteed success. A business plan was not a necessary tool three decades ago. While most people opted for the security of large corporations, government jobs, or unions, businesspeople and lenders sat and talked about the idea of a new venture. Yesterday's businesses sold gadgets and features. Entrepreneurs and their businesses were driven solely by money. Money was the purpose, the turn-on and the result. Money and profit were considered dirty words by the majority, and stable was the description of the marketplace.

The world economy in the 1990s and on demands precision when you are considering how to position yourself or your product in the marketplace, and timing is not only critical, it is everything. There is no place for mediocrity: you have to be great at what you do, and your product has to be the best, the most affordable, with the most benefits. Today, business is about benefits, not gadgets and features. Today's business is not driven by money, although profit is not a dirty word by any means. Money is seen as a by-product of having fun. Everyone's stress levels have risen to the limit during this current restructuring period, and the focus is now on balancing one's life and having fun. Survival is based on loving what you do and doing what you love.

The first step toward success is doing a business plan. In formulating this plan you must find an idea that emotionally drives you with enough strength to carry you single-handedly over a very long and rough road.

That road begins with the conception of the idea and travels toward an elusive end. Some like to think the journey's end is the day the business planning stage is complete. Others think it is the day when the business opens its doors for the first time, or the day when it first begins to show a profit, or even the day when the business has two or three profitable years in a row. In fact there is no journey's end. Success is in the journey.

Constant change and chaos will remain a part of this world for some time, perhaps forever. That means that a successful business this year may be a failure next year unless you change quickly enough. The journey's end will always remain elusive.

The bottom line is that the emotional drive is the only thing that will carry you. Financial success is important, but be careful not to make it the primary goal; the quest for dollars is not in itself a strong enough motivator. The true motivator is the love of the journey, and so the planning never ends because the journey never ends.

▋▋ Strategy, Focus, and Goals

A prerequisite for success is a compelling vision. This is the driving force for a successful business. The best example is the space industry. Americans in the 1960s had a vision of putting a man on the moon by the end of the decade. That vision mobilized and focused everyone to a common direction. Had they merely said they wanted to be the world leader in space exploration, they would not have been organized or focused. Strategic vision provides the force to organize and focus the entire organization. No one has to ask "where are we going" when the strategic vision is known to all. The vision is a picture of where you want to go and where you see your business in the future. The vision must be written. Successful businesses write a five-year plan, identifying goals and methods of achieving them, with input from all their staff and consultants. A new business is asking for failure unless the entrepreneur begins with a strategic vision and then backs it up with a written business plan. The business plan is a road map which considers all obstacles and allows the entrepreneur to move in the direction of the vision. Success boils down to a driven vision and a well-researched business plan. In today's economy, that is how you make it happen.

To help get you started, an outline of the business plan is provided in the following section.

BUSINESS PLAN OUTLINE

EXECUTIVE SUMMARY

A. THE PRODUCT OR SERVICE

This section describes the unique features and benefits of your product or service.

This section might include the following information:

- A brief business history of your company (if you already have a business)
- A description of your product or service in terms of
  - benefits (i.e., what market needs your product or service is satisfying)
  - features or characteristics
  - price (include rationale for pricing)
  - what makes it unique
- A statement about how you will get your product or service to the market (e.g., retail store-front, direct sales, mail order)

B. THE MARKET AND THE TARGET CUSTOMER

This section explains the market need for your product or service and describes the target customer that will buy it.

You might want to organize your information in two subsections:

1) *Industry Overview and Market Niche*

This subsection would include:

- A description of the industry and the industry segment in terms of
  - current size (in dollars)
  - stage of the industry life cycle (e.g., embryo, growth)
  - current trends related to your service or product
- A description of the market niche within the industry segment

2) *The Target Customer*

Include the following information in this subsection:

- A description of the primary target customer in terms of
  - demographic characteristics (e.g., sex, age)
  - needs

- location
- demographic trends related to your service or product
- buying habits and behaviour
- A description of the secondary target customer (in same terms as above)

C. THE COMPETITION

This section indicates how your product or service is uniquely positioned in the market in relation to the competition.

In this section, describe:

- Your potential competitors, including details on
  - their strengths and weaknesses (e.g., price, characteristics of product or service)
  - whether their business is steady, increasing, or decreasing
- How your business will take advantage of the market gap ignored by the competition

D. PROMOTION STRATEGY

This section explains how you will connect with your customer to sell your product or service.

In this section, include information on:

- Your promotional mix, including an explanation of why elements were chosen in terms of
  - how your target customer receives information about your product or service
  - your promotional objectives
- Your strategy to build a customer list and keep in touch with the customer and his/her needs

E. LOCATION

This section explains why you have selected your location and how it satisfies the needs of customers and your business.

Describe how your location satisfies the needs of customers and the business. Your description should include the following key considerations:

- How close or accessible your location is to the target market
- The distribution channels you intend to use to reach your customer (if you do not have a store-front location)
- How the location satisfies the exterior and interior requirements of the business (if possible, include floor plan or photos in the appendix)
- How close the competition is to your location
- The possibility for expansion
- Whether the building is leased or owned; indicate whether the lease has been reviewed by a lawyer (include proof of ownership or copy of lease in the appendix)
- Whether the location is in conformity with municipal by-laws

F. MANAGEMENT

The purpose of this section is to indicate that you have the management skills to run a business.

You might want to present the information in four subsections:

1) *Goals*

In this subsection, include:

- A statement of your overall business goal (mission statement)
- Short-term (1-year) and medium-term (3-year)
  - marketing objectives (e.g., sales)
  - financial objectives (e.g., profit)

  (If you are already in business, rather than just starting up, also indicate your long-term [5-year] objectives)

NOTE: Include your vision statement and personal goals in the appendix.

2) *Organization*

In this subsection, include:

- An organization chart and a short narrative rationale for your organizational structure (if your business is to include several employees or partners)
- A description of legal structure (e.g., corporation, partnership [limited or full], proprietorship)

3) *Leadership Strategies*

In this subsection, describe:

- Your strategy for motivating your team to achieve business goals (e.g., involving team in establishing and reviewing business goals and objectives; implementing a system of employee empowerment; implementing a recognition or incentive system)
- Your strategy for building working relationships with key consultants and professionals

4) *Control System*

In this subsection, describe the control strategies that will be used to monitor your business to ensure that goals and objectives are met (e.g., periodic reviews of goals and objectives; computerized accounting record systems for receivables and payables; inventory control and reporting systems)

G. PERSONNEL

This section describes your team and how the team can contribute to your business success.

- List the members of your team, including a description of
  - the functions they will perform
  - their strengths (e.g., skills, experience, qualifications)

NOTE: Include their résumés in the appendix.

- If positions are not filled, describe the positions and the qualifications required
- List other key consultants/professionals

H. FINANCIAL INFORMATION

This section describes your financial requirements and indicates how and why your business will be financially successful.

This section consists of five subsections:

1) *Application and Sources of Funds*

Include two tables that indicate (1) application of funds and (2) sources of funds. Include also a short statement that summarizes:

- Financial requirements of the business, including funds required for
  - start-up (including a short description of the type and value of insurance)
  - equipment
  - leasehold improvements
  - cash reserve funds

NOTE:　You may want to include in the appendix detailed quotes for equipment and leasehold improvements.

- Sources of funds, classified in terms of equity (owner's investment), loans (investment from others), and credit

2) Opening Balance Sheet

Include an opening balance sheet as well as a short statement that summarizes your

- assets
- liabilities
- equity

Include also the following three ratios and a statement on how they compare with industry ratios to indicate the financial health of your business (before its doors open):

- Liquidity
  - current ratio (working capital ratio)
  - quick ratio (acid test)
- Solvency
  - debt-to-equity ratio

3) Cash Flow

Include a monthly cash flow for the first year and annual cash flows for the next two years. Also include an indication of your break-even level of sales (vis-à-vis your cash flow) and a statement that indicates you have enough cash to operate your business.

4) Projected Income Statement

Include a projected income statement for the first three years. Include also a narrative summary containing the following information:

- Your profit for the first three years

- Your major assumptions
- Your profit-to-sales ratio for the first three years and how it compares with industry averages
- Your profit-to-owner's-investment ratio
- Your break-even level of sales (vis-à-vis your income statement; this may or may not be the same as your cash break-even point)

5) *Balance Sheet*

Include a projected balance sheet for "period ending" (e.g., year one, year two, year three). Include also the following three ratios and a statement on how they compare with industry ratios to indicate the financial health of your business (on this projected date):

- Liquidity
  – current ratio
  – quick ratio
- Solvency
  – debt-to-equity ratio

Your narrative summary should also contain information on any changes in asset value and equity value from the opening balance sheet and explain the rationale for those changes.

APPENDIX

You may wish to include the following support materials in the appendix:

- Customer surveys
- Personal information (personal goals and vision statement)
- Secondary research that supports your plan
- Lease/ownership documents
- Photos and floor plans of business location
- Résumés of team members
- Quotes for detailed equipment and leasehold improvements

SOURCE: Ronald A. Knowles, produced for the TVO series *Writing a Small Business Plan*, 1994.

1 1 *Enter the Entrepreneur*

Small businesses are started by entrepreneurs. Webster's dictionary
defines an entrepreneur as "one who undertakes a business enterprise." In 1991, *Encyclopaedia Britannica* stated: "If the allocation of
resources changes during the course of growth and development, it
does so under the leadership of an entrepreneurial class. The quality of
entrepreneurship is seen by many economists as an important explanation of differences in the rate of technical progress between countries.
The influence of entrepreneurship has received little attention so far."
Canadian statistics indicate that large corporations in 1991 represented
only one-tenth of one per cent of the total businesses in Canada. Small
businesses accounted for 99.5 per cent of the 2,068,253 businesses in
Canada. The ratio did not change drastically over the 10-year period
from 1981 (fig. 1.1). What has changed is the attention that is being paid
to this information. The federal government, specifically Industry Canada and the Department of Finance, released a publication in February
1994 called *Growing Small Businesses*. Figures 1.1 and 1.2 are both
extracted from this publication. The first chapter, entitled "Focus on
Small Businesses," begins: "The federal government recognizes the
vital role that small business plays in the Canadian economy. Small
businesses create jobs, they generate wealth, and they provide satisfying careers for a growing number of entrepreneurs." This publication
is devoted to exploring ways of creating a favourable environment in
order to foster the growth of small business. In addition to finally
paying attention to the glaring statistics, the federal government has
realized that hope must be restored in the hearts of Canadians.

Adults and teens no longer have faith in the large corporations or
governments who, although forced by a declining economy, ruthlessly
laid off workers, downsized middle management, and created an aura
of complete chaos and uncertainty for the remaining workers. The
federal government has confirmed that throughout the early 1990s
almost 90 per cent of the jobs created came from companies with less
than one hundred employees (fig. 1.2). This trend is predicted to continue. According to Statistics Canada, in 1993, 86,000 jobs were created
by self-employed people, 70,000 by the private sector, and 10,000 by
family businesses. In contrast, government departments lost 23,000

jobs. And in February 1995 we learned this trend will continue. These figures serve to show the importance of small businesses to the job market and to the Canadian economy as a whole. Welcome to the new entrepreneurial society. Governments and people world-wide are hanging their hopes for the future on entrepreneurs. Even large corporations are giving their employees entrepreneurial training for infrastructure development. IBM, Dupont, and Ford are just a few examples of large companies who have developed small business thinking under the umbrella of the corporate structure. Finally we are teaching entrepreneurship in our Canadian high schools and offering courses at colleges and universities.

Today each of us has to take responsibility for creating our own job, whether it be within an existing company or within a newly started business venture. Leadership is not a comfortable position for many people, but with the help of personal development courses/books and the support of family/friends each of us can take the leadership role in controlling our own lives and creating stability amidst this changing chaotic world. We are entrenched in a decade where people are learning the hard way that "if it is to be, it is up to me."

Figure 1.1. NUMBER OF BUSINESSES IN CANADA

	1981		1991		Change
	Number	%	*Number*	%	%
SELF-EMPLOYED	678,000	49.3	1,146,000	55.4	69.0
EMPLOYER BUSINESSES					
< 5 (employees)	522,358	38.0	678,447	32.8	29.9
5–19	125,928	9.2	174,966	8.5	38.9
20–49	30,024	2.2	43,588	2.1	45.2
50–99	10,049	0.7	13,897	0.7	38.3
100–499	7,753	0.6	9,334	0.4	20.4
500 +	2,030	0.1	2,020	0.1	-0.5
SUBTOTAL	698,142	50.7	922,252	44.6	32.1
ALL BUSINESSES*	1,376,142	100.00	2,068,253	100.0	50.3

Figure 1.2. EMPLOYMENT CREATION BY FIRM SIZE, 1991

FIRM SIZE *(employees)*

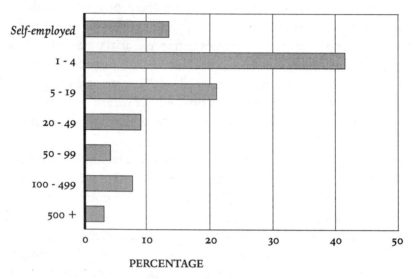

PERCENTAGE

SOURCE: John Manley and Paul Martin, *Growing Small Businesses*, February 1994, based on statistics from Industry Canada / Statistics Canada.

Despite the fact that hundreds of studies have been carried out to determine who and what an entrepreneur is, the simple fact is we really do not know. Therefore, there is no way to clone an entrepreneur. What we can do, however, is describe the characteristics and behavioural traits of successful entrepreneurs and then ask you if you see yourself. This is why we have included an Entrepreneurial Questionnaire in this section. We also know that many of these behavioural traits can be learned. So if you do not fit the pattern of a typical entrepreneur, have faith. Research has told us that anyone can learn to be an entrepreneur. The qualities and character of an entrepreneur — the skills and attitudes — can be taught at an early age in the home and during the early school years. Entrepreneurship can also be taught to adults. We have found that it is never too late to learn these much needed skills.

Entrepreneurship is a state of being whose time has come and whose time will never end. In order to understand small business issues, we must first understand the entrepreneur who begins and fuels the growth of small business.

ENTREPRENEURIAL QUESTIONNAIRE

Take a few minutes and complete the following questionnaire. There are no right or wrong answers, so please try to be as honest as you can. Answer each question with a yes (✓) or no (✓).

SECTION I

	MOSTLY OR YES (✓)	RARELY OR NO (✓)
1. Do you prefer to go shopping for a major (expensive) purchase alone?	_____	_____
2. Do you tend to speak up for an unpopular cause if you believe in it?	_____	_____
3. Do you usually wait for people to invite you to go places?	_____	_____
4. Do you believe that one of the most important things in life is to be liked by most people you know?	_____	_____
5. Do you usually behave in a way you think other people who are important to you want and expect you to behave?	_____	_____
6. Do you feel you can determine your desire to earn a decent living?	_____	_____
7. Do you like the feeling of being in charge of other people?	_____	_____

SECTION II

8. Do you often feel, "That's just the way things are and there's nothing I can do about it"?	_____	_____
9. When things go right and are terrific for you, do you think, "It's mostly luck"?	_____	_____
10. Do you know that if you decide to do something you'll do it and nothing can stop you?	_____	_____
11. Your friends and family tell you that it's foolish to want a certain career you are very interested in. Are you likely to listen to them and choose to do something else?	_____	_____

	MOSTLY OR YES (✓)	RARELY OR NO (✓)
12. If you want something do you ask for it rather than wait?	_____	_____
13. Do you normally wake up "excited" in the morning?	_____	_____
14. Do you see yourself running your own business?	_____	_____

SECTION III

15. Do you like trying new food, new places, and new experiences?	_____	_____
16. Can you walk up to a stranger and strike up a conversation?	_____	_____
17. If you are frightened of something, will you try to conquer the fear?	_____	_____
18. Do you need to know the answer before you ask the question?	_____	_____
19. Have you ever gone on a date with someone you did not really know?	_____	_____
20. When you are given a project do you try to do exactly what is expected of you?	_____	_____
21. Do you believe that business owners take huge risks?	_____	_____

SECTION IV

22. Have your family or parents ever encouraged you to go to college to learn how to start your own business?	_____	_____
23. Do you like to be involved in starting things like clubs, plays, church groups, and so on?	_____	_____
24. When you think about your future, do you ever see yourself working for a large corporation?	_____	_____
25. Do you believe that it is important to have security in a job?	_____	_____

	MOSTLY OR YES (✓)	RARELY OR NO (✓)
26. Have you ever, on your own initiative, obtained a job for which you got paid?	____	____
27. Has a person you know and respect ever told you what it is like to own a business?	____	____
28. Have any of your friends ever started a business, even if it was just very small?	____	____

SECTION V

Have you ever taken a course or been introduced to the basic principles of:

	MOSTLY OR YES	RARELY OR NO
29. Marketing	____	____
30. Accounting	____	____
31. Management Operations	____	____
32. Personnel Management	____	____
33. Business Finance	____	____
34. Communication	____	____

SECTION VI

Have you ever put into practice *or* been exposed to the following business skills?

	MOSTLY OR YES	RARELY OR NO
35. Marketing	____	____
36. Accounting	____	____
37. Management Operations	____	____
38. Personnel Management	____	____
39. Business Finance	____	____
40. Communication	____	____

THANK YOU!

▌▌ Answers

Potential entrepreneurs would tend to give the following answers:

SECTION I

1. Yes
2. Yes
3. No
4. No
5. No
6. Yes
7. No

Relationships

Entrepreneurs do not generally rely on others for approval, support, and companionship. Their relationships tend to be task or goal driven as opposed to activity driven or socially motivated. This is not to say, however, that they are "loners." They want to accomplish tasks with people. They have little need to control people.

SECTION II

8. No
9. No
10. Yes
11. No
12. Yes
13. Yes
14. Yes

Beliefs

Entrepreneurs are positive. They are driven by the belief that they can accomplish a task. They wake up "excited" in the morning because they believe they can control and change their lives. They want to run their own business to control their destiny and accomplish goals.

SECTION III

15. Yes
16. Yes

17. Yes
18. No
19. Yes
20. No
21. No

Risk Taking/Personality Traits

Entrepreneurs are innately curious and do take calculated risks. They need the excitement of the unknown and tire quickly when situations become repetitive. They need to be reminded to focus and complete the task even though it may appear boring to them.

SECTION IV

22. Yes
23. Yes
24. No
25. No
26. Yes
27. Yes
28. Yes

Career Aspirations

Successful entrepreneurs, as change agents, need role models. They need to know that what they feel is also felt by others and that they can be happy owning a business. People are influenced by their family, friends, and environment. If small business and entrepreneurship is not already "in their lives," many people do not fulfil their entrepreneurial potential.

SECTION V

29. Yes
30. Yes
31. Yes
32. Yes
33. Yes
34. Yes

Business Skills

In addition to the skills of change, entrepreneurs require basic business and management skills. Entrepreneurship is the process of translating needs into opportunities. Business is the process of translating opportunities into social or financial benefits. The bottom line: a small business entrepreneur requires business skills to translate opportunities.

SECTION VI

35. Yes
36. Yes
37. Yes
38. Yes
39. Yes
40. Yes

Business Exposure/Experience

Entrepreneurs are more likely to have been exposed to basic management/business skills.

❙❙ *Overall Evaluation of Competencies/Skills*

This questionnaire tests the following competencies/skills:

I. PERSONALITY SKILLS	QUESTIONS
• Leadership	2, 5, 7, 13, 14, 17, 20, 23, 26
• Motivated by Task Achievement	1, 4, 8, 9, 10, 26, 27, 28
• Ability to Communicate Freely	2, 12, 16, 18, 23
• Self-Confidence	2, 6, 8, 10, 11, 14, 16, 17, 25
• Independence	1, 3, 5, 6, 11, 14, 22, 25, 26, 27, 28
• Creative Thinking/Risk Taking	8, 9, 15, 16, 17, 19, 21, 22, 24, 25, 27, 28

II. BUSINESS SKILLS	QUESTIONS
• Marketing	29
• Accounting	30
• Management Operations	31
• Personnel Management	32

SOURCE: Ronald A. Knowles, "Canadian Small Business: An Entrepreneur's Plan," Appendix C.

▌▌ Characteristics of an Entrepreneur

Entrepreneurs, fondly named Type "E," are as varied as dinner menus. However, there is a common thread: each has a selection of skills and attitudes from the following groups. The combination of characteristics will vary from person to person, and these differences are indicative of each entrepreneur's individuality.

LEARNED SKILLS AND ATTITUDES

PERSONALITY INDEX

- Self-motivated
- Self-confident
- High self-esteem
- Dogged determination
- Never stops, never quits, no matter what
- Knows he/she is different
- Knows he/she does not fit the normal mould
- High level of energy and drive
- Sets short-term and long-term goals and is committed to meeting objectives
- Not overly anxious in uncertain situations

- Sets own standard for performance on tasks
- Likes to get feedback on performance
- Measures progress
- Gathers as much information as possible before making a decision
- Prefers games of skill rather than games of chance
- Has a positive mental attitude
- Is flexible
- Adjusts quickly to change
- Objective
- Innovative
- Possesses sound knowledge in chosen business field
- Does not believe in perfect solutions, only the best solution for the situation
- Does not get overly anxious about the consequences of his/her decisions
- Not afraid of failure and views failure as a learning experience
- Treats others with respect and dignity
- Bored by routine and repetitive tasks
- Prefers solving challenging problems
- Seeks help from others in order to accomplish objectives and goals
- Believes in actions, not luck or fate, to accomplish goals
- Takes initiative
- Takes personal responsibility for own actions and decisions
- Takes calculated risks
- Trusts own intuition
- Able to make decisions
- Self-reliant
- Patient with customers, staff, suppliers
- Has leadership qualities
- Resourceful
- Keen sense of trends and change
- Optimistic
- Enthusiastic
- Proud
- Independent

- Enjoys success most when it is a result of personal efforts
- Task oriented
- Organized
- Superior time management skills
- People oriented
- Able to sell products and ideas when she/he has personal belief
- Possesses courage of own convictions
- Recognizes that personal age is immaterial when starting a new business
- Eagerly seeks out adult continuing education courses even if she/he is one of the many entrepreneurs who never completed their formal education

MOTIVATION INDEX

- Visualizes and dreams
- Needs freedom
- Has a deep need for personal achievement
- Needs more challenge constantly
- Succeeds and sets tougher goals
- Needs control over own destiny
- Needs variety
- Works hard, but does not forsake family and friends
- Needs to have fun
- Able to persevere through tough times
- Competes with self
- Able to stay ahead of the competition
- Creative
- Thrives on planning and implementation process
- Results oriented
- Motivated to use skills and ideas to benefit economy or society
- Thrives on opportunities to be creative
- Prospers on ability to identify needs in the marketplace (niches), to translate those needs into opportunities, and to translate opportunities into social or financial benefits
- Welcomes the challenge to innovate

- Lives by a firm sense of business ethics
- Enjoys working with a team
- Feels comfortable making a profit from own work and work of employees
- Values honest dealing, dependability, and reliability over making a fast dollar at the customer's expense
- Willing to change own standard of living to accommodate the financial needs of business venture
- Enthusiastically measures progress and success
- Possesses leadership skills
- Seeks the accumulation of wealth as one tool of measuring progress

LIFE EXPERIENCE AND LIFE CYCLE INDEX

- Has a varied work experience
- Has a close relative who is or was a business owner
- Has friends who own and operate a business
- Worked in small firm and had close contact with owner
- Owned or was part-owner in a business venture
- Worked in small division of large business but had close contact with division chief
- As a child sold lemonade, had a paper route, or organized similar money-making projects
- Has access to financial resources
- Prudent manager of money
- Lived in three or more cities
- Been fired or quit because of disagreements with boss
- Has work experience in variety of functional areas
- Had bosses reject own innovative ideas for change
- Spouse or family is supportive of new venture
- Respected by subordinates, who work hard even if they do not necessarily like him/her personally
- Finds it easy to get along with people
- Never believes in luck, but rather recognizes success as result of hard work
- Sees problems as challenges and takes action

- Conscious of good health
- Willing to devote long hours to new venture
- Aware of impact of new venture on family and friends
- Aware that other personal goals and desires may have to wait while focus is on new venture
- Willing to live with uncertainty and insecurity caused by self-employment
- Willing to risk savings or investments or home to start new venture
- Sees new venture as vehicle to attain life goals
- Has changed jobs frequently due to frustration
- Clearly understands personal motivation for owning a business

WHAT DRIVES ENTREPRENEURS?

After thousands of studies, there are very few conclusions about entrepreneurs. They rarely fall into the typical Type A or Type B personality, so we have named them uniquely Type "E." We do know that they have some key characteristics as outlined in the introduction. After interviewing such legends as Ed Mirvish (the owner of Honest Ed's, Toronto's Royal Alexandra Theatre, etc.) and Milo Shantz (a man with a vision who redeveloped the town of St. Jacobs, north of Kitchener/ Waterloo, Ontario, into a family experience and shopper's haven, with 100 village artisans and vendors at the farmer's market and flea market, while maintaining the small town's original rural charm), we have found a common thread of traits that drive entrepreneurs. No matter how an entrepreneur travels the path to self-employment, they all feel that they have finally come home, driven by:

- the need for freedom
- the "pull" catalyst
- the "push" catalyst
- emotion
- vision
- the challenge of new ideas

⒈⒈ *The Need for Freedom*

This phenomenon is underestimated and rarely understood by entrepreneurs. The need for freedom is a feeling, and until entrepreneurial types take the necessary steps to acknowledge and act on that feeling, the loss of freedom stifles them and they wonder why. The general public have absolutely no idea what drives this Type E beast but would guess it is the need for a large house, an expensive sports car, or some other materialistic measure of success. Money is definitely not the driving force, although the need for money and profit cannot be ignored, because money allows you to have freedom. Wilson L. Harrell, the former publisher of *Inc.* magazine, says it quite simply in a 1994 article: "Freedom is the need to get your head above the crowd. Freedom to be your own person. Freedom to have an idea, turn it into a business and turn the business into an empire, if you can. Freedom to serve your customers. If it all works, you earn the freedom to tell bankers, 'Get lost!' Freedom is about doing what you want, where you want, and with whom you want, not because you have to, but because you want to. Freedom allows you the flexibility to control your hours and provide yourself and your family with the time required to adhere to your important values. On the other hand, freedom is also about making mistakes — trying again, and failing in order to pick yourself up and start all over again. Freedom allows you to be the best you can be, every day, forever. The need for freedom is present in all entrepreneurs regardless of whether it was a pull or a push catalyst that got them started."

❚❚ *The "Pull" Catalyst*

Some people are drawn into self-employment by a magnetic force. These people have an inner drive to do it their way and a burning desire for freedom, often feeling the "pull" by 10 years of age. Many begin their work career by following traditional employment with success. However, some begin to feel that the glove does not fit quite right. The glove of employment constricts their creativity and their freedom to be the best they can be. Others feel the glove does not allow them the flexibility and freedom to set their own priorities around the personal needs of their family and a balanced life.

Still others soon come to realize that the glove does not belong to them. There is nothing wrong with the job, but they simply do not fit anywhere in the organization as long as they are there in an employee capacity. Throughout a traditional employment career, entrepreneurs seek constant change and challenge. It is impossible for them to visualize themselves doing the same job for the rest of their lives. Even a view of moving up the ladder if they stay long enough does not satisfy them. They finally accept that they do not fit the role, and they begin their move to self-employment. The move progresses at varied speeds. Finally they discover the world where they fit — a world where their needs and abilities are satisfied and rewarded.

Some entrepreneurs have never worked for someone else. These people never felt a desire to try the glove on for size. Some finished their formal education, while others did not complete secondary school. Either way, these people were pulled into entrepreneurship at an early age. A lack of education does not prevent most from seeking continuing education courses in business management or their interest field. Some troubled teens who constantly fight the system become very successful entrepreneurs. Business becomes their medium for rebelling. Family-owned businesses often pull a child into the nest of comfort, while other children travel in any direction that will ensure they stay away from the business.

❚❚ *The "Push" Catalyst*

There are many factors that may individually or in combination create the push an entrepreneur needs to seek change and self-employment.

A few of these factors are:

- Loss of a job
- A move to a new country
- Lack of promotion
- Demotion
- Unwanted transfer to another city
- Insecurity triggered by downsizing of staff through layoffs
- Frustration with management and mediocrity
- Lack of appreciation and recognition on the job
- Change in family structure or responsibilities
- Scarcity of jobs in an era of high unemployment

The "pull" catalyst must also be present, otherwise the chances for success are slimmer. Remember, the need for money cannot be the driving force. Change is feared by most people. Financial commitments and a degree of comfort with the known environment cause some people to resist a venture into the unknown. That resistance disappears when a powerful force or many small forces accumulate. The forces trigger emotion.

▌▌ *Emotion*

Do not be afraid to be emotional. Emotion is a driving force, and being a driving force is what leadership is all about. All decisions in our life are based on emotion, and humans find the logic to reinforce their decisions. Regardless of whether it was the pull catalyst or the push catalyst that caused a person to become an entrepreneur, the drive to begin was based on emotion and supported by masses of logic. The same emotional drive pushes an entrepreneur to continue, to weather the blustery storms, to seek new ideas, and to challenge change. Entrepreneurs accept their emotions and, supported by their logic, envision a plan for the future driven by passion.

▌▌ *Vision*

All entrepreneurs are visionaries. They see a complete mental picture of where they and their ideas are going. They envision the future with clarity. This imagery is sometimes difficult for them to translate into words, but when they overcome this translation block and can articulate their vision for others, they are able to seek opinions and utilize the expertise of staff and outside professionals. Non-entrepreneurs need a concrete model and/or a fully scripted business plan to share the vision. And entrepreneurs themselves will benefit from having the plan in writing: a clearly delineated plan of action helps them maintain focus and foresee potential obstacles. One stepping stone entrepreneurs use naturally to translate their visions to a written plan has been labelled *mind mapping* (fig. 1.1). This exercise allows ideas, visions, and plans to be linked in writing and is the first step towards a written business plan.

Figure 1.1. MIND MAPPING:
VISION AND MARKETING STRATEGY

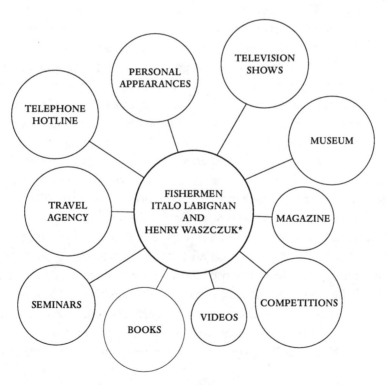

* Italo Labignan and Henry Waszczuk are two entrepreneurs who have reinvented game fishing. Their marketing strategy is discussed in the story "Fishing Buddies Tackle Big Time."

The entrepreneur envisions how a need in the marketplace will be filled, how an idea will be implemented, and what will be required in the market 10 years from now. This ability to focus on both present and future needs makes communicating the business idea even more of a challenge. However, it is also this visionary ability that enables the entrepreneur to meet new challenges.

∎ ∎ *The Challenge of New Ideas*

With over 80 per cent of the population dreaming of being their own boss and every person having at least one "good idea," there is not, nor will there ever be, a shortage of ideas. Consider that many of those 80 per cent have two or three "great ideas" and you begin to understand the depth of the idea well.*

Some entrepreneur help centres and courses teach that ideas are only a small part of the business success equation. It takes a tremendous amount of work to translate an idea to a vision and then to a written plan which can be realized by the successful opening and operation of a viable, profitable business. Some go so far as to say that ideas are a dime a dozen. You must understand that the process of formulating ideas is important to the birth of a venture, but that the idea itself is only the very beginning, and the road to success is much like rearing a child from infancy through to adulthood. The birth alone does not guarantee a successful adult. Success comes through planning, commitment, time, nurturing, financing, and being positioned to seize opportunities. The Canadian Industrial Innovation Centre (funded by the federal government and Waterloo University) is one non-profit company that evaluates and offers a critical assessment of inventions. The industry expert panel routinely puts up the stop sign to more than 75 per cent of the ideas presented to them, for one reason or another.

Linda Beatty, owner of a Cruise Holidays franchise in Toronto, was quoted in the York University alumni magazine (1994): "Someone once told me that in your own business you can choose to be a land mine or a heat-seeking missile. If you are a land mine, you wait until someone

---

* Based on an unpublished August 1993 survey by Geo Partners Inc., Toronto, conducted in six major North American cities.

comes to you; if you are a heat-seeking missile, you go out and find business. I guess I am a heat-seeking missile."

Once an entrepreneur has achieved operational success in a venture, the drive to seek new challenges re-emerges. The challenge may be to expand the existing venture, or it may take a completely different direction. It is the need for constant challenge that perpetuates new ideas. It is the challenge and satisfaction of putting a deal together that drives the entrepreneur onward.

11 *Your Right to Have a Mentor*

It is your right to find a mentor! Remember, every business owner is a stakeholder in your success. Insist that the college or university program you are enrolled in incorporate a link to business in its curriculum. You will not have difficulty locating a business owner who wants to help. They are simply waiting for the opportunity to share their knowledge and experience. Every business owner has made mistakes, and there is a need inside every entrepreneur to prevent others from making the same mistakes they did. Find the five most successful businesses that resemble the one you want to start and tell the owners why you respect them and their business. Arrange to meet each over coffee at his or her convenience. Ask questions and be prepared to listen and take notes. Offer to work free to get on-the-job skills training. Remember, you are nurturing what may be a lifelong friendship. And after you start your business, bless the day when a student calls you — that will be the day you begin to give the payback. What goes around, comes around.

In January 1994, we interviewed on our radio show Ed Mirvish, the 80-year-old self-made multi-millionaire who dropped out of school at age 15 to help his widowed mother in the family grocery store and now owns Honest Ed's discount retail store (named a tourist attraction in Toronto), arty Mirvish Village, the Royal Alexandra Theatre, Ed's Restaurants Warehouse, the Princess of Wales Theatre (all in Toronto), and the Old Vic Theatre in London, England. He publicly admitted that he has made mistakes and has had failures, but the most impressive statement was that he always makes time for people who call him because they want to start a business. How many people have had the nerve and confidence to pick up the telephone to call him? How many have let this life-changing opportunity slip by? He has written an excellent book for all to read, but every small business student has the opportunity to have a one-on-one consultation with this genius of a gentleman.

One of our favourite stories is of a student whose family owned a trailer park and a large parcel of land, including substantial lake frontage, outside of Ottawa. In 1990 the family was exploring the possibilities of expansion, and the possibilities included adding camping cabins, a motel, a restaurant, a lodge, water activities, boat rentals, and so on. They voted that their youngest child, then about 20 years old, enroll in the Small Business Development program at Algonquin College. This student — let's call him Derek — sent out 100 letters to family-owned businesses across Ontario. Being a member of several tourism associations, Derek was able to choose 100 businesses that had some if not all of the expansion amenities that his family was considering. In his letter, Derek explained what his family currently had in their business, what was available, and what they were considering for expansion. He asked for the help and advice of all 100 businesses that he appealed to. Derek sent his letters out in May, the beginning of the busiest season for the businesses he contacted. Whenever we tell this story, we always love to ask the question, "How many of those businesses do you think replied to Derek?"

The answers vary from zero to fifty per cent every time we ask. The fact is, 100 per cent of those businesses took the time in the busiest season of the year to reply to Derek, and they replied promptly. Every reply had valuable information for Derek and his family. The reaction of everyone that hears this story is best described by one word, *shock*. How many entrepreneurs do you think Derek and his family will help over their lifetime? What goes around, comes around.

In February 1994 we interviewed Milo Shantz, who is a visionary and the driving force behind the redevelopment of the small town of St. Jacobs, north of Kitchener/Waterloo, Ontario. This town was in economic trouble in the early 1970s, but because this caring visionary helped small businesses get started, it is now a thriving tourist attraction with 100 artisans situated in the village and 400 vendors in the farmer's market and the flea market. All of this has been accomplished without destroying the beauty of the town, river, and countryside. By forming partnerships or turning controlling interest over to employees, many people share in the ongoing success of a town that has thrived and grown throughout the recession of the early 1990s. Many home-based businesses have begun and expanded as a result of the healthy retail and artisan trades. This man has been a mentor and facilitator for most of these businesses. A genuine gentleman, he is what leadership and entrepreneurship are all about.

SMALL BUSINESS NOTES

Take That, Ralph

ONE MYTH comes from Ralph Waldo Emerson's frequently quoted statement that if you build a better mousetrap, the world will beat a path to your door. Emerson probably would not have made a successful entrepreneur. Thousands of potential entrepreneurs have been side-tracked, even ruined, by taking Emerson's advice to heart.

Unfortunately, just the opposite is true. Regardless of the superiority of your product or service, customers do not beat a path to your door. Producing the best product or service does not guarantee market share — it simply means you have an edge over your competition.

Many aspiring entrepreneurs make the mistake of looking for a completely new idea and never find one. Instead, they should be focusing on bettering or enhancing existing ideas. Inventors invent new products, but entrepreneurs seek new opportunities anchored by customers' needs, a competitive edge and good timing.

SOURCE: Courtney Price, *Scripps-Howard News Service,* as appearing in *The Globe and Mail,* 9 May 1994, p. B2.

📖 No Place Like Home in the New World of Work

JEAN-PIERRE BEAUDRY, 51, was laid off after 23 years with Shell Canada Ltd. Neither bitter nor regretful, he's looking forward to his new life as a sales and motivation consultant, working from a home office in Toronto.

Mike Babcock, 56, was vice-president of mining at Cameco Corp. in Saskatoon when the company laid off 70 people in June, 1992. Although busy as a mining consultant, he misses his old job and hopes to find employment that is more permanent.

This is the new world of work for many Canadians. Job security until age 60 or 65 has disappeared, to be replaced by home offices and self-employment.

Books for Business, a specialty store in downtown Toronto, has two shelves full of self-help books on starting your own consulting business. Many are bestsellers.

While some people find it exhilarating to go on their own, others can't stand the isolation and pine for a steady pay cheque.

Terry Buddin, 47, spent two decades in investment management before being laid off a few years ago. Unsuccessful in finding another full-time job, he now does contract work and has learned to like it.

"You can choose the work you want to do," says Mr. Buddin, a financial services consultant with a home office in Mississauga. With each contract, he guarantees to achieve a certain level of results or no fee is charged.

"There is more incentive to work and less worry about the political games. With a full-time job, you worry about the company's financial health and you can be let go at a moment's notice. But with self-employment, you feel more in control of your destiny."

Losing a job leaves a big hole in people's lives, says Earle Bain, a Halifax psychologist who works with companies that are eliminating jobs.

"You have to deal with the grief first, then the cash flow issues."

In his view, most people are not cut out to run their own businesses. Successful self-employment requires a set of skills — being able to attend to detail while not losing sight of the big picture — that few possess.

In psychological terms: "You have to be both left-brained and right-brained."

Mr. Bain left a full-time job with Peat Marwick Stevenson & Kellogg two years ago at age 50. The firm had gone through several mergers, half of the partners had left and the work no longer was fun.

"I had a big learning curve in the first two years, but it's now behind me," he says. "I don't think I'd ever want to work for a big company again."

Getting kicked out of the nest, he says, forces people on "a journey of self-discovery" to find out who they are, what they value and what skills and talents they have.

For Mr. Beaudry, the change was exciting. "I had a great 23 years at Shell, but the writing was on the wall for some time and as I got closer to 50, I had been thinking of starting my own business."

The family still has one steady income, since his wife also works for Shell. But changes were needed to cope with reduced cash flow.

After buying a house 18 months ago, Mr. Beaudry had been paying off a $70,000 mortgage as fast as possible. Now, he plans to stretch the loan over 20 years, up from seven, to reduce his monthly payments.

Adjusting to a smaller, irregular income can be difficult, even for those with a paid-off house and grown children.

Mr. Babcock of Saskatoon had a good year as a mining consultant, working on five contracts, including three in the former Soviet Union. "But to say my take-home pay is as good as it was at Cameco would be an absolute lie."

He continues to look for full-time work but there are many applicants for each job and being over 50 doesn't help.

"Even though I have 30 years of experience and was near the top of my field, I've been bluntly told there are a lot of people applying for the job who are 10 years younger than I am."

Heather Chisvin, 49, a self-employed advertising writer in Toronto, finds business is brutally competitive — much more so than in the late 1980s, when she also worked on her own.

"In 1988, the phone never stopped ringing and I was turning work down," she says. "Today, I still have some clients coming to me, but not enough."

After running ads in Marketing magazine, Ms. Chisvin is finding new business. But there are many writers looking for work, forcing prices down. Her income is lower and she's had to severely cut back spending.

"I'm on a serious budget for the first time in my life and I'm making ends meet — but just."

Neil De Koker, 50, also has gone through a cut in income. In 1989, he was a partner in a successful Toronto corporate communication firm employing 35 people. Business fell off sharply during the recession and he sold out in 1991.

He is now president of the Automotive Parts Association of Canada, drawing on his work experience of 23 years at General Motors of Canada Ltd. and four years at Magna International Inc. But a trade association salary does not go as far as a stake in a growing business.

"It's a quite dramatic cut," he says. "I went from driving a Cadillac to something with four wheels that goes. My wife and I don't go to restaurants and shows as often and we focus on vacations at the cottage, not vacations in Europe."

Mr. De Koker is not complaining, saying he loves the job. Running his own communications firm as it went downhill was far more stressful.

But he's had to give up some frills, such as topping up contributions to a registered retirement savings plan. "My focus is on day-to-day living, not on the future. It's probably not very smart, but that's what you do."

In tough times, saving for retirement is a lower priority for many people. Ron Knowles, a partner in Western Management Consultants in Toronto, says it's hard to put away money for the future when your income is stagnant.

Most employees are working longer hours for the same or slightly less compensation than two years ago, he finds. As they see colleagues get the axe, they feel insecure about their jobs, resulting in declining morale.

Mr. Knowles, 52, a consultant in human resources and organizational change, faces the same dilemma himself.

"I am working much longer hours, 20 to 25 per cent more in a typical month. But there is a lot of pressure on fees and the partnership incomes sure haven't been growing.

It's causing me to see retirement as further away than I would like it to be. I've been working steadily for 30 years and I really wanted to be freed before 60 or 65. I've lost the feeling of choice."

Brian Morrison, also a partner at Western Management Consultants, is relocating to Vancouver from Toronto this month, hoping the move will restore some balance to his life.

"I'm in the executive-search business, which tends to go as the economy goes," he says. "When times are tough, companies are recruiting fewer executives. I've had to work harder to maintain the same level of income."

Now 48, Mr. Morrison wants to find more time for leisure and to use technology to work from home as much as possible. His wife, a community health worker, plans to shift to part-time from full-time work.

"Vancouver suits the kind of life my wife and I want to lead, if our work allows us to lead it. I hope our dream of more balance in the next 10 years isn't only an illusion."

Many Canadians feel they are working harder than ever just to stay in the same place — and some say the constant slogging is wearing them down.

Penny Downer, owner of Hemisphere Freight and Brokerage Services Inc., a Toronto customs broker, says the company's volume is up but profit is eroding.

"We haven't been able to raise our prices or charge for a lot of extras," she says. "In this day and age, customers don't like extra charges."

Ms. Downer works with importers who are bringing products into Canada. Lately, she's been taking courses to find out how the North American free-trade agreement will affect her customers.

To economize, she is thinking of amalgamating her two offices next year. And she recently spent $20,000 on software, hoping it will replace hiring another person. She has 10 employees now.

Ms. Downer, 45, a single mother with three children age 7 to 14, says she is extremely well organized and hopes to continue working for another 15 to 20 years. "If you like what you do, it isn't really work."

Krystyna Cunjak definitely is feeling the pressure. Six months ago, she took over a downtown Toronto restaurant that she had backed financially for several years.

Ms. Cunjak owns Raclette, a 72-seat restaurant and wine bar in the funky Queen Street West area. To increase traffic, she slashed prices on food and liquor.

Sales are higher now and the restaurant is busier, but she doesn't know whether this will last through the traditionally slow months of January and February.

"People still like to go out, but they're more calculating about how much they spend," she says.

"A smaller number are willing to have three or four courses, with aperitifs and cocktails. I'm working 12 to 14 hours a day at times and not getting any salary or profit. This is taking longer than we all anticipated, considering the energy my staff and I have put in."

For Ms. Cunjak, however, there is one consolation. Owning a restaurant, she says, is better than her former business — commercial real estate and renovation.

SOURCE: Ellen Roseman, *The Globe and Mail*, 4 January 1994, pp. B1, B2. Reprinted with permission from *The Globe and Mail*.

📖 Fishing Buddies Tackle Big Time

ALMOST NO ONE can pronounce their names but Henry Waszczuk and Italo Labignan are superstars of sportfishing.

They are to fishing what Wayne Gretzky is to hockey.

They are, like the Great One, among the best in their sport. And they promote it tirelessly — through television shows, magazines, videos, seminars, competitions, telephone hot lines and personal appearances.

In less than a decade, the two men have built a vertically-integrated business called the Canadian Sportfishing Communications Network, which has spawned a weekly television show on The Sports Network (TSN), a glossy Canadian Sportfishing magazine published five times a year, paperback and hardcover books, a travel agency, a national fish registry and museum and a series of seminars that are expected to draw about 100,000 participants next year.

Henry and Italo — they are known throughout the fishing world by their first names — have reinvented game fishing much as Montrealers Ben and Joe Weider recreated the sport of bodybuilding.

Last April, advertising guru Syd Kessler, who built Toronto-based Supercorp Entertainment into a $200-million entertainment conglom-

erate for John Labatt Ltd., received an unexpected gift from a client —
a free fishing lesson from the two superstars.

One look at the demographics of fishing — a third of Canadians over
the age of 12 are registered anglers — and Mr. Kessler was hooked.

Fishing buddies Mr. Waszczuk and Mr. Labignan needed more muscle — in finance and marketing — to expand their business and Mr.
Kessler agreed to become their 50-per-cent partner. He invested — he
won't say how much — and then began planning to make the Canadian
Sportfishing Network the major player in outdoor television program-
ming.

"I was astounded to learn that this $8-billion-a-year industry attracts
everybody — men and women, young and old, blue-collar and white-
collar, urban and non-urban," Mr. Kessler says. "And they all have to
buy the right stuff to catch the right fish. This television series is a
natural buy for every advertiser from sunglasses to chocolate bars, from
beer to batteries."

With 680,000 weekly viewers, *Canadian Sportfishing* is Canada's
most-watched fishing show. Beyond TSN, it is seen in syndication across
North America and in Europe, where it's broadcast in Dutch, Italian
and German.

The program is a showcase for fishing equipment, clothing and
accessories, recreational vehicles, boats and motors, wilderness lodges,
sunscreen and insect repellent. And every issue of Canadian Sportfishing magazine, which boasts an audited circulation of 85,000, touts the
television show and the products and services of the Canadian Sportfishing Communications Network.

Mr. Waszczuk and Mr. Labignan formed their partnership following
a chance encounter in 1985 at the Toronto Boat Show, where they were
representing the same fish-finder manufacturer.

Mr. Waszczuk, nearing the end of a 10-year career as a centre for the
Hamilton Tiger Cats football team, was an avid fisherman who ran a
charter boat service as a sideline.

Mr. Labignan, a professional taxidermist with a background in fish
and wildlife technology, also had a passion for fishing. "I was fishing my
brains out whenever I could," he says.

By the time the Boat Show was over, the two men had an agreement
to promote the sport together.

"It was just a regular handshake and we went to town," Mr. Waszczuk says in an interview. They began visiting major shopping malls to talk fishing with anyone who would listen.

"We took fishing very seriously," he says. "We became very visible to thousands of people. Until that time, we had Americans coming to Canada and telling Canadians how to fish. There's nothing wrong with that but there's an attitude there."

Canadian Sportfishing Communications Network is now nibbling at the market share of its U.S. competitors, the largest being In Fisherman and the Bass Anglers Sportsman Society. The Sport Fishing Institute of Washington estimates that game fishing was a $27-billion (U.S.) industry in 1985, the latest year for which figures are available. It also pegged the number of anglers at 60 million.

Mr. Waszczuk and Mr. Labignan publish a book every year. Last year's table-top edition sold 33,000 copies, 70 per cent of them in the United States. Another book, *In Quest of Big Fish*, for Key Porter Books, is due out next year.

Their seminar business is also growing. The two men will conduct 10 so-called Secret Strategy sessions this year, teaching 1,000 participants at each sitting — at $20 a head — how to catch big fish.

In all, Mr. Waszczuk and Mr. Labignan will attend 50 to 70 events this year, most of them between January and April, says Jim Westman, the organization's special events manager. "We didn't expect it would grow this quickly," he adds.

Their travel business is growing at a similar pace. A toll-free telephone number has been running on fishing shows in the United States, and the Canadian Sportfishing Communications Network travel arm has been flooded with calls. It expects to book hundreds of trips in 1994, including corporate packages as well as expeditions to exotic locations such as Venezuela.

But the Canadian Sportfishing Communications Network is more than a money machine. It has a moral code. Mr. Waszczuk and Mr. Labignan advocate releasing any fish caught except those to be eaten. And they suggest handling fish with a filet glove to minimize damage to the coating and scales.

"Get in the habit of catch-and-release and encourage your companions to do so as well," Mr. Waszczuk says in one of his magazine editorials. "That way, we can all rest assured that Canada's great fishing heritage will continue for generations to come."

SOURCE: Harvey Enchin, *The Globe and Mail*, 13 December 1993, pp. B1, B2. Reprinted with permission from *The Globe and Mail*.

📖 Small Players Sell Big Ideas

IT'S AN UNLIKELY ARRANGEMENT: a giant advertising agency encourages two bright, young ad men to set up their own shop to develop ads for one of the agency's most prized clients.

But that's precisely what DDB Needham Worldwide Ltd. did last spring, signing a two-year contract with Bruce & Myers Creative Directions to produce Volkswagen ads for DDB — before Duncan Bruce and Brad Myers had even opened for business.

The unusual relationship is just one of several non-traditional routes being taken by recession-battered ad agencies — and their clients — to tap into alternative sources of talent while keeping costs down.

It comes as many agencies, none more so than the mammoth global ones, try to shed layers of management so that clients can deal with fewer people and spend less money — and less time — developing the advertising.

Among other moves, DDB has put together teams from various marketing disciplines such as promotions and public relations, to work on specific client accounts.

For its Volkswagen business, DDB took the unconventional route of hiring Mr. Bruce, 30, and Mr. Myers, 35, who had been thinking about setting up their own firm for a while.

DDB had been seeking new talent after its crack creative team on Volkswagen left for another agency.

The senior DDB team had grown restless working exclusively on the Volkswagen account, Mr. Carder says.

"Any really good senior team would love to work on Volkswagen, but don't only want to work on Volkswagen," he says.

For Mr. Bruce and Mr. Myers, it's been a dream come true.

"I think you'll see more places like us," Mr. Myers says of his firm, whose contract with DDB is expected to be long-term.

The two partners like to point out their unconventional style, even refraining from officially calling their firm an ad agency.

"We're a creative source, a place to buy thinking," says Mr. Myers, motioning to their green-painted, open style offices with a pool table, on the 13th floor of a downtown Toronto office tower.

"We're not going to become an agency. We don't ever want to have that much overhead. We have no layers. There's just us."

The two friends have diverging tastes and personal interests: Mr. Bruce is single, has worn an earring since he was 17, favours Doc Martens boots, listens to new wave and rap music and takes adventurous windsurfing vacations.

Mr. Myers is married with two small children, prefers jazz to new wave and is off with the family to Disney World next week. His taste in footwear runs to sneakers.

What they have in common is a desire to break free and build their own business, outside the traditional agency structure.

They had discussed setting up shop together when Mr. Myers received a call from a headhunter about directing the Volkswagen assignment for DDB.

Mr. Myers declined. But the message that came back was: "Let's meet. DDB is interested in something new."

The big agency was even more enthusiastic when it learned that Mr. Myers was to team up with Mr. Bruce, a former DDB employee who had created award-winning Volkswagen commercials.

These included the so-called Blind Date ad for Volkswagen's Passat, in which a woman walks past her date and his Volkswagen — she is looking for an old Volkswagen Beetle instead of a sleek new VW model.

"From that moment, it was just like a snowball rolling," recalls Mr. Myers, who made his name creating ads for Campbell soup at his previous employer, another multinational agency. "They were delighted to grab us both in one fell swoop."

During the summer, in a whirlwind of work highlighted by all-night sessions and pool games to ease tension, the partners cooked up Volkswagen's latest ad campaign for the new Jetta with the theme line: "Definitely not middle of the road."

Volkswagen Canada says it is pleased with the new ad team.

"It's a gain to create much more focus and probably new energy," says Antony Denham, general manager of marketing at Volkswagen, which spends more than $11.6-million a year on advertising.

DDB continues to do ads for Volkswagen's Audi and Porsche models, although this represents only about 10 per cent of vw's ad spending. DDB also does other marketing, such as promotions, for Volkswagen.

In what DDB calls a coincidence, its parent in the United States — where Volkswagen's business has been even more sluggish than in Canada — the big agency has spun off a separate unit, headed by former DDB adman Andy Berlin, to breathe new life into the car company's advertising.

There's nothing new about tiny breakaway agencies conceived by creative stars from larger agencies. Indeed, the fathers of Mr. Bruce and Mr. Myers — veteran ad men Dennis Bruce and Marty Myers — were hot properties at an established ad agency in Toronto 11 years ago when they bolted and put together their own small agency. It is now a mid-sized shop called Miller Myers Bruce DallaCosta Inc.

What is unusual is that today's breakaway agencies are often starting with large, coveted accounts, the senior Mr. Bruce says. He points to the IBM Corp. personal computer assignment in the United States and the T. Eaton Co. account in Canada, which last month were each switched to upstart agencies.

"Today, anything goes," he says. "Advertisers are looking for alternatives. Ad agencies must provide those alternatives or risk losing the business.

He advised his son not to repeat his own mistakes: taking on work the agency couldn't manage just because clients were knocking at the door, and saddling himself with high office and staff costs.

It is advice the giants are beginning to heed as well.

Mr. Carder, chairman of DDB, types his own correspondence at a computer in his office — the agency recently eliminated secretaries.

He says he is looking for a more entrepreneurial spirit of the type he finds in Bruce & Myers, as well as Robins Sharpe Associates Ltd., one of two smaller ad agencies DDB acquired last August.

"We're open to doing things differently."

SOURCE: Marina Strauss, *The Globe and Mail*, 8 November 1993, pp. B1, B8. Reprinted with permission from *The Globe and Mail*.

📖 A Driver Deal Maker in a Wireless World

WITH ONE PHONE in his car and another in his pocket, communications deal maker John Simmonds is always in touch. He can juggle two conversations at once or link both in a conference call.

Today, he's picking up voice-mail messages from an acquisitions adviser scouting for takeover targets, a stockbroker helping him trade foreign currency, a horse trainer he works with and two of his teenage children.

Mr. Simmonds, 43, is a compulsive collector of companies, who thrives on working long nights and weekends plotting to buy competitors. He's also the middle of seven children in a business family — and is determined to outdo his siblings.

"I was the kid who was never going to be a success in business. I was a non-conformist," he says.

This mix of brashness and insecurity drives his ambition. His three-year-old radio systems company, Simmonds Communications Ltd., is on a buying spree, gobbling up faltering electronics firms. In August, he fulfilled a childhood dream, acquiring a 50.1-per-cent control block of the family business — A.C. Simmonds & Sons Ltd. — for $1-million.

"I want to have a Canadian telecommunications business that can compete globally with the large multinationals," he says, describing his ultimate dream.

Many family businesses, racked by succession squabbling, never make it to the third generation. A.C. Simmonds is an exception. John's grandfather started out 75 years ago as a distributor of wireless radio parts. The company, based in Pickering, a half-hour east of Toronto, now distributes a range of audio and electronic products.

But it was almost torn apart in the mid-1970s, when the founder's two sons, Claude (John's father) and a younger brother, David, shared control. The business wasn't big enough for both, so they parted ways. David started a company that distributes cellular phones.

All of Claude Simmonds' four sons joined the company; three daughters chose other careers. But unlike his brothers, John skipped university and went straight to work at 17.

"John doesn't have the education, so he may feel he has more to prove," says brother Bruce, 40, a chartered accountant.

John's father gave him jobs no one else wanted — in purchasing, credit and personnel. "I spent a summer tearing carbons off paper," he says. Today, he realizes Claude, now 76, did him a favour by exposing him to all aspects of the business.

He vows his own children will follow the same path. He was married at 21 and had four children by 26. Separated since 1985, he's a single parent with sole custody of his two girls and two boys.

The need to prove himself left a mark on John Simmonds. "He's driven by building, by trying to achieve and overachieve. He wants desperately to be the predominant brother," says Mark Borkowski, president of Mercantile Mergers & Acquisitions Corp. of Toronto, who has worked with the Simmonds family.

Some entrepreneurs are operators, who like signing cheques and tracking down shipments, Mr. Borkowski says. Mr. Simmonds likes buying and expanding, while handing day-to-day details to professional managers.

Mr. Simmonds cut his teeth on deal making in the 1980s. Working for the family business, he helped to acquire and build Glenayre Electronics Ltd., a Vancouver mobile communications company. In 1989, Glenayre was taken over by a competitor, TCG International Inc. of Burnaby, B.C.

Flush with a $250,000 buyout from the new owner, John got bored doing nothing. Luckily, he'd negotiated a settlement that allowed him to compete with his former company. He started his own shop in October, 1990, with $660,000 raised from business associates.

Today, Simmonds Communications, listed on the Toronto Stock Exchange, has a market capitalization of $40-million. It distributes two-way radio products and designs large-scale systems for police, utilities and government.

Bidding against giants such as Motorola and L.M. Ericsson, Simmonds has won contracts worth $17-million from B.C. Hydro, Nova Scotia Power and Revenue Canada Customs and Excise.

"We're systems integrators," Mr. Simmonds explains. "Taking black boxes and configuring them is where the real profit lies."

For example, his firm added a personal alarm to a two-way radio system for 300 Canada-U.S. border stations. Customs officials were having a problem with smugglers, who would drive through and push their car doors into security guards to daze them. The alarm signals which station is in trouble.

But despite his success outside the family fold, Mr. Simmonds had trouble gaining control of A.C. Simmonds. He tried in 1991, but the deal fell through. Two years later, he finally succeeded in buying it from family members.

Working with his brothers is the toughest challenge he's faced, John says. But he believes the company would not have survived if he hadn't stepped in.

The transfer of control has meant some give-and-take. Older brother David, 47, who had been running the company, "was focused on maintaining the business, not growing," John says. "You have to keep growing."

John installed his youngest brother Paul, 39, as chief operating officer and David became vice-president of sales and marketing.

To pay for current and future acquisitions, Simmonds Communications raised $7.5-million this summer by issuing special warrants at $1.25 each. The issue was bought in two days by institutional investors.

But the prospectus underlines a risk with entrepreneurial firms. The company's expansion strategy, it says, depends significantly on chairman, president and CEO John Simmonds. If he goes, there may be no one to take his place.

"John is the visionary behind the company, the one with the grand plan," says Brian Faughnan, corporate finance analyst at Canaccord Capital Corp., the issue's underwriter. "He sees opportunities in the marketplace for mergers, joint ventures and technology transfers as his competitors go through tough times."

Right now, John is targeting two companies in the United States and two in Canada. "The businesses we've acquired, including the family business, have tired management. They were going to die. We're bringing capital and management to the table."

But above all, he's in it for the fun. "It's a game and I love it."

SOURCE: Ellen Roseman, *The Globe and Mail*, 11 October 1993, p. B4. Reprinted with permission from *The Globe and Mail*.

📖 Generation Faces Grim Job Outlook

JENNIFER ADCOCK'S BIRTHDAY is today — Labour Day — and the irony doesn't escape her.

At 25, her job — not to mention her entire life — is light years from what she had imagined it would be.

There is no car, no spacious apartment, no expensive vacations, no career. She lives in a one-room basement apartment in Halifax, the entrance to which is through a narrow alley. Work — a downtown bistro where she waitresses double shifts — is a 25 minute walk away, as is the library where she tries to squeeze in research for her masters thesis whenever she has a spare moment.

"When my mom was my age she was a teacher, she had a child, she was married. I can't imagine ever getting married, ever owning my own home, ever owning a car or ever having children.

"I'm just not going to have that," says Ms. Adcock, who for the past three years has put all her spare cash into RRSPs because she also can't imagine ever having a pension.

Besides an honours degree in political science, Ms. Adcock has two years' experience working for the Nova Scotia government. Her career should be on pretty firm ground. But when corporations and government departments cut costs, the recent graduate is among the earliest casualties. The only option, Ms. Adcock decided, was to keep her mind busy with a second degree while waitressing full-time. She is not alone.

The recession continues to hurt all age groups, but the twenty-something generation has additional obstacles to overcome. In a poor economic climate, employers are reluctant to take chances on the inexperienced. Unions protect workers on the basis of seniority. And changes in the Canadian economy have all but eliminated many of the jobs for which graduates have been prepared.

These realities affect young people in all fields — those with professional and technical training as well as those with liberal arts and science degrees. And even when they find jobs, these are often unskilled or far from where they had intended to spend their working lives.

For a generation with a higher percentage of university graduates than any that came before, underemployment is as serious a problem as outright joblessness.

"I think we're all a little lost. People just don't know what to do next," says Claire Querée, 28. In 1990, after failing to land a job with the Vancouver law firm where she completed her training, she came to Toronto to look for work. After sending out more than 200 résumés, and spending a year living on unemployment insurance, Ms. Querée found a job with the Department of Immigration. Recently, she was told that budget cuts may cost her this job, too.

"There was a group of us when we were articling who were going to open a bar called The Pro Shop because you had to be a professional to work there and have a minimum of two degrees," she says.

"We'd hang your degree somewhere in the bar — mine was going to go in the washroom — and when you introduced yourself to the customers you'd state what your degree was in. I'd say, "I'm Claire, I have degrees in history and law, and I can discuss contract law if you'd like.' "

Statistically, the youth unemployment problem is actually less severe than it was in the 1981-82 recession, when a large segment of the baby-boom population was in their 20s, says David Foot, a professor of economics with the University of Toronto, and an expert in demographics.

The difference this time is that students don't seem to have any hope for a job recovery, says Bill Ungar, a professor of architecture at the University of Waterloo.

Although statistics are not available for student employment after graduation, Waterloo does record the number of architecture students placed during four-month work-terms. During this year's summer terms, only 33 per cent were placed in an architectural firm, compared with 85 per cent in the summer of 1987. And if students aren't getting four-month contracts, they're certainly not getting full-time jobs, Mr. Ungar says.

What unemployment statistics don't show is the number of people who are underemployed.

"I've had five graduate students complete their masters degree in the last year," says Frank Vecchio, a professor of civil engineering at the University of Toronto. "Not one of these people has been able to find a job. One guy is working part-time as an usher at SkyDome and another one is . . . packing cookies."

Even law, traditionally seen as one of the safer bets for a top graduate, is suffering. An informal survey by the Law Society of Upper Canada, showed that 42 per cent of students completing their bar admissions course had not found jobs. In 1989, that figure was 25 per cent.

David Maslak, 28, has a masters of law degree from Duke University in North Carolina and a year of work experience at a prestigious downtown Toronto law office. In the past eight months, he has sent out 80 résumés. The result has been only two interviews — both with firms that were not ready to hire. He is living with his parents to save money.

"It's not so much that you're worried about the time that has gone by, it's the uncertainty about looking down the road and not knowing how long it will go on," Mr. Maslak says.

Faced with dismal job prospects, many graduates are opting for more practical training. John Parrett, executive director of the Ontario College Application Service, estimates applications this year will be as much as 55 per cent above last year's.

This is especially interesting when one considers that the success rate of Ontario colleges — the percentage of graduates employed in their field six months after graduation — plummeted to just over half in 1991, compared with nearly three-quarters two years earlier.

Elaine Girard, 27, says all her college diplomas got her were $18,000 in student loans. After completing a two-year general accounting program at St. Clair College in Windsor, Ont., to please her parents, she took a year-long audio engineering course to please herself. She graduated in 1989 and immediately began scouring first Ontario, and then Canada, and then North America, for work.

When nothing panned out, she fell back on her accounting background, only to be told her computer knowledge was outdated. After another year of audio training, she ended up working full-time at a bookstore and part-time evenings for a crafts retailer.

"Yes, this is a job, but that's my career," says Ms. Girard. "That's how I distinguish the two. It's something that I can't let go."

An increasingly popular approach is to round off a university degree with some college education. Ten per cent of this year's college applicants already have some university experience, says Mr. Parrett, adding that some colleges are developing specific programs for university graduates.

But while it sounds like a shrewd move, the reality is that even a combination of practical and theoretical education is no guarantee of success. Ryerson Polytechnic University, for example, offers a two-year, practical journalism course for those who already have degrees from other universities.

Older generations don't understand how serious the problem is, says Ms. Adcock, and that makes it harder to deal with. "Older people have absolutely no idea what it's like out there. I'm sure they look at people my age and think we're a pack of whiners."

Sadly, she is probably right, says the U of T's Dr. Foot, adding that a demographic reason lies behind the lack of understanding.

The 60-year-old businessmen currently running Canada's top corporations were born during the depths of the Depression. At that time, Canadian birth rates were very low, and as a result, those born in that period had very little competition when they entered the work force.

"They didn't necessarily get to the top because they were good. They got there because they were in short supply," Dr. Foot says. "They didn't have a problem so why should you? They worked hard. They don't understand that even if you work hard you're still going to have a problem."

Bob Conyers, director of the McGill University's Career and Placement Service in Montreal, says most of the students he sees have already altered their expectations and do not expect to rise quickly through the ranks — one of the reasons corporations should be hiring them.

He says students walking into a company already have lower expectations. "They don't have to be taught them, there's no learning curve to get rid of all the old value structure — they walk in ready."

Using a job search approach Mr. Conyers says is unique to McGill, the placement centre has increased its success rate by an estimated 40 per cent in the last year.

Under the McGill system, counsellors help the students define their needs and skills. Then they are shown how to begin a "focused" job search that includes finding companies for which they would like to work and tailoring their résumés and other correspondence to those firms.

Where most placement centres point students to job boards, McGill teaches them to look in places where jobs are not officially available.

Students are told to sell their skills aggressively — to convince a blasé business executive they can offer something nobody else can — in the hope of creating a job where none has existed. At the same time, McGill is actively selling the advantages of its graduates and attempting to boost on-campus recruitment.

Claudine Lapointe, 23, is living proof of the value of the McGill method. With a commerce degree specializing in international business and marketing, fluency in three languages, and three summers of work experience, she began looking for a job the fall before she graduated.

After drawing up a list of companies for which she would like to work, she sent out 80 résumés, which she followed with phone calls and thank you cards. Most companies did not have openings, but she met with their representatives anyway, to find out more about each firm and to make contacts. After 35 interviews she landed a job with a Montreal marketing company.

"Don't ever do it the straight way," she advises, leaning forward across her desk. "Find some little thing to distinguish your résumé from everyone else's."

Pierre Parkinson, 25, used the McGill method to narrow in on the province — British Columbia — and the industry — telecommunications — in which he wanted to work. Apart from the usual letters, résumés and phone calls, he volunteered for a day at a Montreal firm that had a Vancouver office, and flew to Vancouver at his own expense to talk to a prospective employer and attend a trade show where he could make more industry contacts. By the time he graduated he had a job waiting at a small Vancouver telecommunications firm.

"You've got to be tougher, smarter, quicker, and you have to be leaner," Mr. Conyers says. "The people that know how to do that are the ones who are going to succeed tomorrow."

Young people know that, Ms. Adcock says. In fact, as part of being "leaner" she has decided she will never marry or have children because she believes mobility is essential to long-term employment. The problem is persuading employers to take a chance, and overcoming an institutional bias which favours seniority over young blood.

"I don't have material aspirations. I don't want to have the Mercedes, or the BMW. I don't want the summer cottage in Muskoka and the big home and the kids. I just want something to keep me going."

In the meantime, she says, it is hard not to become bitter.

"When I look at those stay-in-school commercials that are on right now, with the girl who gets up, and all the doors are slamming in her face. I almost want to say: 'Honey, it doesn't matter if you stay in school or you don't stay in school.'"

"I know it's a terrible thing to say."

SOURCE: Danielle Bochove, *The Globe and Mail*, 6 September 1993, pp. B1, B3. Reprinted with permission from *The Globe and Mail*.

📖 Venturing Out on Their Own

CATHY BUTLER and Steve Stein launched their business for a simple reason.

"We had nothing to lose at that point — literally," the 25-year-old Ms. Butler says. "We didn't own anything."

Ms. Butler and Mr. Stein, who run a tree-planting business in British Columbia, are part of a growing number of twentysomethings who, frustrated by a shortage of satisfying jobs, are creating their own.

Ms. Butler and Mr. Stein launched Whistler-based Natural Borders Reforestation in 1990 after several years as tree planters and planting-team managers. "One day we realized that we could do this on our own," Ms. Butler says.

But small business is proving to be no cinch. "There are many young people with no jobs attempting to start their own businesses — and it's difficult," says William Phelan, business counselling manager at Counselling Assistance to Small Enterprises, part of the Federal Business Development Bank. "They don't have a lot of capital, which can be extremely hard to get."

The new generation shares the precarious state of all expectant entrepreneurs. An estimated 21 per cent of businesses with less than five employees fail each year, says Ted Mallett, a senior economist with the Canadian Federation of Independent Business.

But young people wrestle with particular barriers. Age can be an issue in trying to land suppliers. Banks are often reluctant to loosen

WHAT DRIVES ENTREPRENEURS? 69

credit strings for untried operators. Potential customers get skittish when they realize the age of the owner.

"Sometimes you're looked down on, especially in dealing with manufacturers," says Peter Neal, 26, who runs a specialty food company with brother Chris, 28. "We're not 40-year-olds pulling into the parking lot in a Jaguar. We're young guys pulling into the parking lot with some dreams."

Neal Brothers Inc. had its beginnings in a leased bakery in Aurora, Ont., where the two cut loaves of bread into croutons using electric knives. Peter was a university student, Chris had just graduated.

"We didn't need a lot of capital at first, since we made all the croutons ourselves. Our packaging began as sandwich bags that we tied with ribbons," Chris says.

But orders increased rapidly — at one point, the brothers were working 22 hours a day. The pair decided to invest in a bread-cutting machine.

They turned to Youth Venture Capital, an Ontario government program that lends up to $7,500, interest-free for the first year. The applicant must personally invest 20 per cent of the loan value in the business.

Almost all provincial governments offer business startup loans, some geared specifically to youth. The federal government offers startup and development loans through numerous agencies, including the Federal Business Development Bank.

Christina Spiropolos used provincial funding to open her business early in July. Spurred by a need for a summer job and an aversion to "working for $5.50 flipping burgers," the 19-year-old university student started By the Seat of Your Pants, selling used jeans and clothing in Halifax.

She will keep the store open when she returns to classes this month — a decision that partly reflects confidence gained through hard experience. She has learned to be wary of a certain kind of supplier. "They hear a young female voice on the telephone and they are more likely to try to swindle you for extra bucks."

As businesses expand, funding becomes even more difficult, says Jonathan Bowman, 24-year-old owner of a paint contracting company in Oakville, Ont. With revenue of $500,000 projected this year, the five-year-old company employs 45 painters and five project managers.

Mr. Bowman needed his father to co-sign a bank loan when he wanted more equipment. "If small business is to be the engine of economic recovery, tight credit policy and a lack of access to capital is stalling that recovery," he says.

Expansion wasn't as difficult for the Neal brothers. Faced with a flood of orders, they shied away from rapid growth. "We didn't want to be manufacturing on that scale — it didn't make sense. We decided to branch into different products and do it on a smaller scale," Peter Neal says.

The company launched a line of nacho chips, then salsa, both tailor-made for the brothers by suppliers. In July, the pair launched a potato chip product.

Peter Neal says their decision to back away from larger-scale manufacturing actually made the bank more accommodating. When the brothers approached the bank with their plan to expand into potato chips, they were given a warm reception.

The food company's sales will top $750,000 for the year ending Oct. 31, he says, up from $70,000 in 1989, its first year.

The brothers say they benefit from targeting a specific market: upscale, deli-style stores. That's a common theme among young entrepreneurs: a niche is essential to success. Mr. Bowman paints mostly condominiums; Ms. Spiropolos has found a lucrative market for her second-hand jeans in a university town.

But pinning down suppliers is another story. "Some were really not receptive because of our age," Peter Neal says. "One told us not to waste our time with them. They would never be our suppliers."

Michael Jackson, 25, who started his own beachwear clothing company in London, Ont., five years ago, avoided this problem by being highly selective in suppliers. "They had to be open to my ideas. They had to have a young outlook.

"I noticed that some are aware of the age difference. But the bottom line is, as long as you pay on time, they don't care how old you are."

He formed the idea for Grubwear Inc. while he was in high school in Calgary. He started by making bermuda shorts for his friends. "My mom taught me to sew."

Now, Mr. Jackson has a line of baseball hats, T-shirts and winter outerwear. Last fall, he launched a snowboard business with $3,000 borrowed from his grandmother. He has a Japanese order for 325 boards and he hopes to sell 700 this season.

Low overhead is critical for the under-30 crowd. Mr. Jackson's apartment has doubled as a warehouse and office; Mr. Bowman's living room is his headquarters. Ms. Spiropolos gathers free scraps from a fabric store for her jean-patching service and uses her own sewing machine. Ms. Butler and Mr. Stein run their reforestation business out of their Whistler home.

As the tree-planting industry is becoming more competitive, Ms. Butler says, the company that can do it more cheaply is getting the contracts. A key market — the pulp and paper industry — has been battered, and the big tree-planting companies, bulky and rife with high overhead, have felt the crunch.

"But we were just starting when the pulp companies started cutting back. So we started off scrimping and saving, keeping our overhead low and only growing as much as we could."

Ms. Butler says she now enjoys an ideal situation: her company has weathered the recession and she has emerged free from the shackles of a corporate job. "It's nice to know that I can call my own shots, and that now I don't have to hunt around for a job."

SOURCE: Natasha Bacigalupo, *The Globe and Mail*, 6 September 1993, pp. B1, B3. Reprinted with permission from *The Globe and Mail*.

11 *Questions*

1. What is driving each of the entrepreneurs profiled? Write the vision statement for each. Which of these people were or will be challenged to expand their existing venture, in your opinion? Which do you feel will be challenged to start a completely new venture?

2. Using the list of characteristics of an entrepreneur found in the Personality and Motivation Index in the introduction of this book, list the characteristics of each entrepreneur profiled.

3. Decide whether each characteristic listed in the introduction is a skill or an attitude. Decide whether each trait is innate or whether it can be learned. Do you believe all entrepreneurs are born or can entrepreneurship be learned?

4. Interview five very successful entrepreneurs in your community. Write a character profile of each person and determine what drives that person. This is the beginning of your search for a mentor.

5. Complete the Entrepreneurial Questionnaire in the introduction of this book.

6. List your strengths and weaknesses honestly on separate pages. List solutions to compensate for or overcome your weaknesses.

7. List your life experiences. What have you learned from these experiences?

8. What do you know and feel about rich people? How do you describe the business practices of the rich? What are your attitudes towards rich people? (You must come to terms with your attitudes before you will subconsciously allow yourself and your business to succeed. Success may put you into this group of rich people; however, if you think negatively of the rich, your subconscious will direct you to sabotage your business.)

9. What are your attitudes towards money? What was the first thing you were told as a child when you found a penny lying on the ground and you picked it up, then likely put it into your mouth?

10. What is your vision? Begin to write your vision statement. Do a mind map of your business idea to assist you.

2

START-UP
PAINS

James was an electrical engineer who had spent the last 15 years as a senior manager for one of Canada's major hydroelectric companies. A few months ago, he was laid off in one of those typical downsizing operations. All his life, he had never been without work. But this time the job search seemed different. He had sent out over 100 résumés in the last two months but he hadn't even received a nibble. Fortunately, the company had given him a decent "golden handshake," and he and his wife Brenda had a few dollars to rely on until he could find another job — but they were both getting frightened. They did not know how long they could hold out before they would have to put a second mortgage on their house.

After a great deal of soul searching and networking and numerous family discussions, both James and Brenda came to the conclusion that this time they would have to control their own destiny. The job market was no longer safe and secure. They would have to start their own business — but they were not sure where to begin.

You do not normally find a business in the "business opportunities" section of your local newspaper. So, how do you find a business — one that you will be happy doing and one that you can earn a living at? A summary formula for success is provided in figure 2.1.

Figure 2.1. GUIDELINES FOR STARTING
A SUCCESSFUL BUSINESS

1. Make a list of the things you love to work at.
2. Make a list of all the market opportunities or needs you can find.
3. Find a market need (step #2) that is confluent with your strengths and interests (step #1).
4. Make a plan to satisfy this market need and translate the results into a benefit to you and the customer.
5. Work with people you trust and respect — and money will follow.

To help you reduce the uncertainties of finding and starting your own business, we will briefly take you through the step-by-step process that Brenda and James followed. Then we will turn our attention to start-up issues faced by successful Canadian entrepreneurs.

▌▌ Step 1. Gather information

James and Brenda spent two weeks gathering information, and their main advice is to have fun and treat the process as an adventure. If you are not having fun, you will not have the enthusiasm to "keep digging."

You are looking for both information and people — but the people are the most important. If you find the right person, you may be able to get all information you need in a few hours. Keep a separate list of sources of information and sources of people.

Collect all the information you can about where to get help on how to start a business. Speak to as many business owners as you can. Ask them where to get help. Check with your local college. Be persistent. Believe us, somewhere at this college there will be a small business expert, and one of your first jobs is to find him or her. Be sure to check also with your provincial government. Most provinces have self-help centres or agencies that can help. Ask a lot of questions, and be sure to write things down. Your last major source of information is your local library. The number of books written lately on how to start your own business will boggle your mind.

Give yourself enough time to collect the information. It may take a week. It may take a year. It will depend on the nature of the information. Do not stop collecting until you feel comfortable with the information you have found.

▌▌ Step 2. Get the necessary business training

James and Brenda got their training *before* they started their business. They decided to begin their training program with a "Look before You Leap" seminar at a local college. "In retrospect," says Brenda, "this was the best thing we could have done. After the two days, we knew what we had to do and where to get most of the information." They also decided to take a three-month "fast track" course on how to start and run a business. "Without this course, there is no doubt we would have gone bankrupt — more than once," says James.

How long does it take to become an engineer? How long does it take to become a medical doctor? These professions take years of education and training. How long does it take to become a small business person? Some people jump into business overnight with no training or experience. They may survive for a while, but without the proper training, they will eventually pay the price of ignorance.

▌▌ Step 3. Make a list of the things you love to do

"We have learned that you have to love what you do and do what you love," say James and Brenda. "It took us a long time to decide what business we wanted to start. But we felt good about our business because we both had a clear picture of the kind of business we wanted to build." "For example," says Brenda, "I had a goal to help the 'third generation' become more comfortable with the computer. I learned in my training program how easy it was to operate a computer, and now

I want to help others in my generation (50+) to use the computer. My love was to teach and train. James, on the other hand, had a love to 'fix' things. We also realized why James had not been happy in his last job. He had a need to fix things and they wanted him to manage a large research unit. We realize now that his job loss was the best thing that could have happened to us. That job would have killed him."

As you will also learn from our case studies, business is not driven by money. It is driven by emotion. It is driven by that internal desire to "make it happen." So, ask yourself, "What is it I love to work at?" Make a list and add to it each day.

▮▮ Step 4. Make a list of market needs and opportunities

"How many rich inventors do you know?" quips James. "Inventors may be happy, but are they making a living? They are doing what they love, but if there is no market love for what they are doing, then chances are they will not be financially secure. In our small business class, we had to bring in a market opportunity every day. At first, Brenda and I thought that this was a little silly. But the point was, it made us constantly look for opportunity. Not only did this help us determine our business, by making us focus on market needs, but we now use this process each day in our business. Every week, now, we meet and decide on what new opportunities to pursue. It is a different way of thinking. When I was in big business, I looked for problems. Now we look for market opportunities."

▮▮ Step 5. Find a match between what you love to do and what the market loves

In steps 3 and 4 above, you listed the things that you love to do and the market opportunities or needs. The kind of business you should start must satisfy these two conditions. James and Brenda made their list. Brenda loved to help people learn. That is why she loved teaching. James loved to fix things and that is why he loved engineering. Through primary and secondary research, they discovered a market opportunity to fix and service computers and a need to train the third generation (those over the age of 50) to use computers. Their business idea . . . fixing computers and providing friendly computer training. There was confluence between what they wanted to do and what the market wanted.

▐▐ Step 6. Find a mentor

James and Brenda found their business mentor at the local college. They were able to bounce ideas back and forth and get valuable feedback from a woman who had 25 years of experience in the school of hard knocks. "We couldn't have done it without her," says Brenda. "She gave us strength, direction, and confidence. She agreed to be our mentor on the condition that we become a mentor for a new business owner once we became successful. That made us feel good. For her it was not a question of *if* we were going to be successful, it was a question of *when*. She believed in us — unconditionally."

A business mentor is someone who

- you respect and admire,
- believes in you as a person,
- is excited about your business vision,
- will truly listen and can empathize,
- is open and honest and has the courage to tell you the truth
- wants to share time with you.

Much of what is learned in business comes from experience since business is an art. To be successful, we need to know how successful entrepreneurs think. We need help and direction, and many times we will not be able to get what we need from a book. That is why we need a mentor. Figure 2.2 provides some guidelines for choosing your mentor.

Figure 2.2. TIPS ON FINDING A MENTOR

YOUR MENTOR MUST	MENTORS ARE
have extensive business success	winners
have at least one admitted failure	humble
truly care about you as a person	caring
truly believe that you can move mountains	believing
be able to guide and direct without preaching	guiders
be able to encourage the answer from within you	encouragers

have the strength and knowledge to be honest with you	honest
be able to empathize, not sympathize	empathizers
want to spend time listening to you	listeners
be excited about your ideas	excited

▋▋ Step 7. Do a business plan

It took Brenda and James over six months to complete their plan, and they had to take it to three banks before they found the money they needed. Today, they run a successful computer repair and service business. Their advice to those who want to start their own business: "Have a plan and use it."

Once you know what you want to do, and you think there is a market need for your idea, it is time to do your business plan. The purpose of a plan is to set goals and determine ways to achieve them. In your plan you must clearly demonstrate that there is a customer need for your product or service. You must show how you are going to satisfy this customer need. Lastly, you must demonstrate that you can translate this need-satisfying process into a benefit to you the owner as well as the customer.

In the introduction, we provided you with an outline for a business plan. We now encourage you to go back and review the components of the plan so you know the types of information you will need when you come to the planning stage.

▋▏ *What Form Is Best?*

One of the most common questions asked by people wanting to start a business is, "Should I incorporate?" There is no single best form of business venture. It depends on the stage of development, funds available, and the goal of the entrepreneur. This is an issue which will be dealt with in the management section of your business plan. However, to get you started thinking, figure 2.3 provides a summary of the advantages and disadvantages of the three most common forms of business ownership: sole proprietorship, partnership, and corporation or limited company.

Figure 2.3. FORMS OF OWNERSHIP:
ADVANTAGES AND DISADVANTAGES

FORM	ADVANTAGES	DISADVANTAGES
Sole Proprietorship	low costs to start and easy to register	difficult to raise capital investment
	free of regulations	limited liability
	owner directs and controls everything	may be difficult to sell as a going concern
	possible tax advantages	
Partnership	low costs to start and easy to register	unlimited liability and legal exposure for all the partners
	additional partners bring more capital and expertise	many entrepreneurs often find it difficult to work with partners
	few regulations	
	possible tax advantages	
Corporation	limited liability	expensive to create
	broad investment base available	requires ongoing paperwork
	continuous existence with easy ownership transferability	highly restricted and regulated
	easiest form to raise capital	comprehensive record-keeping required
	specialized tax treatment	taxed at the corporate level and at the personal level when profits are distributed

SOURCE: Ontario Ministry of Economic Development. Reprinted with permission from Publications Ontario.

SMALL BUSINESS NOTES

📖 Trends of the Time

FOUR MAJOR TRENDS that are affecting small business today:

1. **Technology:** "Technology is having an equalizing effect, allowing small companies to conduct business in ways that previously only large institutions with large capital investments could. A small business today can behave like a mega-billion-dollar business in many ways."

2. **Strategic alliances:** "Large companies are beginning to hire other businesses to do things they used to do in-house. This is creating opportunities for small businesses to get involved with each other and with larger companies."

3. **Personalized service:** "This is one of the most important trends taking place in the marketplace. Entrepreneurs will find much of their edge will come from personalizing their service or product."

4. **Personal well-being:** "People are becoming increasingly concerned with their health, personal safety and financial security. Small businesses whose products or services are in line with one of these areas have a good potential for growth.

   "Entertainment, education, health care (mental, physical and cosmetic), spiritual enhancement or religion, ethnic-related concepts, self-discovery, personal services, financial security and personal safety and security," are predicted to be up-and-coming enterprises.

SOURCE: Quote from an interview with Edith Weiner, *Entrepreneur*, as appearing in *The Globe and Mail*, 27 June 1994, p. B8. Reprinted with permission from Entrepreneur Magazine, June 1994.

📖 Where the Action Is

ENTREPRENEUR MAGAZINE assembled a list of what it considers the "hottest businesses for 1994." Here's a sampling of enterprises that might well be hot tickets on your block:

- Staffing services, especially technical, professional and medical personnel.
- Comic-book stores, to cash in on the more than 500 titles published every month in a $900-million (U.S.) industry.
- Children's apparel, whether in retail stores, consignment shops or mail-order catalogues.
- Employee training, in such areas as computer technology, customer service, leadership and sales-force motivation.
- Environmental waste prevention/recycling.
- Garden stores.

SOURCE: *Entrepreneur*, as appearing in *The Globe and Mail*, 20 June 1994, p. B8. Reprinted with permission from Entrepreneur Magazine, June 1994.

📖 Making Noise

MANY STARTUP COMPANIES give potential customers the impression they are bigger than they really are. Northwood Press, a small Wisconsin book publisher, used to simulate a real office environment by playing a tape of typing noise when anyone called.

SOURCE: *Inc.* magazine, as appearing in *The Globe and Mail*, 29 November 1993, p. B8.

📖 Born to Be Riled

CALGARY MOTORCYCLE DEALER Brian Taylor dreamed of being the Canadian distributor for an exotic brand of Italian motorbike. He never imagined it would take more than a year and cost him nearly $500,000.

Mr. Taylor finally won the rights to import the $19,000, fire-engine red Moto Guzzi machines last November, but only after travelling across Canada six times and to Italy once — and struggling with the arcane complexity of Canadian motorcycle standards.

"Anybody who is here for a quick buck has to be crazy," said Mr. Taylor, who is on a recent cross-country tour to sign up dealers. "It's been a real headache."

His ordeal is typical of many entrepreneurs who take the big step to becoming importers. They are big fans of the product — usually, they've been owners themselves — but lack experience in the hard facts of licencing and importing complex merchandise, such as motorcycles.

"This industry is plagued with people who are enthusiastic, but don't have the business skills to stay alive," said John Wittner, technical adviser for Moto Guzzi, which is based in the Italian mountain village of Mandello del Lario. "They drive us crazy."

Mr. Taylor, 39, is, above all, enthusiastic. His love of fast motorcycles goes back to his days as an engineering student at the University of Alberta. He dropped out and set up shop as a motorcycle mechanic in Cochrane, Alta., midway between Calgary and the Rockies.

Mr. Taylor kept his costs down in a low-overhead operation that allowed him to combine hobby and career. He eventually moved to Calgary as a dealer for Ducati, a popular line of sporting Italian motorcycles.

The Ducati association provided a crash course in dealing with foreign suppliers. "I had a great relationship with them," he says. Still, it was hard coping with the Italian company's quirky working hours, haphazard dealer support and frustrating bureaucracy.

By the early 1990s, Mr. Taylor tired of being just a dealer, and thought about moving into distribution. He got the idea of complementing his Ducatis with Moto Guzzis, another venerable line of high-priced machines, made by Italy's GBM SpA.

Moto Guzzi's North American importer had retired a decade earlier, leaving a pent-up hunger among aficionados. The machines became collector's items, tucked away in the back of garages, where owners lovingly polish them on Sunday mornings.

On the advice of his wife, Patti, an accountant with a Calgary company, Mr. Taylor bought four new Moto Guzzis from a recently established U.S. importer. He trucked them around to trade shows and dealerships, chatting to potential customers and gauging interest.

Reaction was positive, and he soon located dealers in Western Canada and Quebec to handle the bikes. But some dealers, particularly in recession-struck Ontario, shied away from the price tags of $13,000 to $19,000.

This seat-of-the-pants research was helpful, but Mr. Taylor needed hard numbers to satisfy bankers. He studied sales figures for comparable motorcycles. For example, Canadians bought 12,485 street bikes in the 12 months to August, 1993, but only about 50 were Ducatis. Yet Moto Guzzi sold 750 top-of-the-line Daytona models in the United States last year, more than twice the original projection.

Running through the numbers, Mr. Taylor figured he could sell about 35 bikes across Canada in 1994. That was a long way from his early predictions, but he wanted to be conservative.

"If I meet my projections, my bankers will be happy," he says. "If I sell 100, they'll lend me more money."

Mr. Taylor's toughest challenge was steering the machines through the federal Department of Transport. He once thought importing was a matter of placing an order and paying a tariff. Now he discovered that Canada's motor vehicle specifications differ from those of Italy and the United States.

Right away, he had trouble bringing in the four demo bikes from the United States. Customs inspectors refused entry at the border, and only relented when he promised not to licence or sell the products in Canada. He was left with $60,000 worth of idle machines — and hefty financing costs.

Converting the four bikes to Ottawa's standards would take 10 months and cost $5,000 a model. Says one federal inspector: "It's virtually impossible for an amateur to import a motor vehicle from Europe."

In his efforts to meet Canadian regulations, Mr. Taylor had to follow 20 pages of detailed instructions, write numerous letters to Ottawa, and arrange for federal inspectors to visit his dealership three times over the next 10 months.

Meanwhile, back in Italy, Moto Guzzi was getting anxious. Instead of diverting U.S.-spec machines into Canada as planned, it would have to produce a special line for the tiny, seasonal Canadian market.

"We'll make a special line of our bikes for Canada if he sells 100 a year," Mr. Wittner warned in an interview last fall at Moto Guzzi's factory. "But it's not worth the bother if he sells only two or three."

For the demo models, Mr. Taylor installed new $300 speedometers — the original U.S. bikes were calibrated in miles not kilometres. He needed new windshields, reflectors on the side of the bikes, and special wiring so the headlights stay on while the machine is running.

Some conversions would be too difficult without factory help. Labels for vehicle identification numbers, safety warnings and instructions must be bilingual in Canada — and installed by the manufacturer. "It's a hassle, but we can print up some special labels, I guess," says Mr. Wittner.

Perhaps the most arduous task was testing the brakes. Canada insists on torture testing from a variety of speeds, along with careful measurements of brake temperatures and wear rates. That was far beyond Mr. Taylor's capability, so he persuaded Moto Guzzi to do it.

The entire process was so expensive that Mr. Taylor lowered his sights — he would offer only five models, instead of the complete line of 25 bikes.

Last October, his company, Moto Italia of Canada Inc., finally won Ottawa's blessing to import and licence Moto Guzzi products. The next step was signing contracts with the Italian company.

In some ways, this was the most difficult step. He travelled to Moto Guzzi's village to convince management that he was the best person to handle their products.

Mr. Wittner wanted to know whether Mr. Taylor had a sound business plan and adequate financing, plus the drive, endurance and acumen to handle the responsibility.

Mr. Taylor had questions of his own: "I wanted to see how serious they were about the North American market before I committed myself."

In the end, both seemed satisfied with the answers, and the Canadian market belonged to Mr. Taylor.

But the headaches aren't over. He is back touring the country this week, signing up dealers. He'll be in high gear by next March, when the first shipments of Canadian-specification bikes land from Italy. Then, he'll see if his gamble pays off.

This time, Moto Guzzi is sharing the suspense. "We've put a lot of work into this bike," Mr. Wittner says. "We're confident it will take off."

SOURCE: Oliver Bertin, *The Globe and Mail*, 10 January 1994, p. B6. Reprinted with permission from *The Globe and Mail*.

📖 School of Hard Knocks

LINDA WHITE jumped out of bed this morning to get a running start on her 12-hour workday.

"I work for myself now," explains Ms. White, 38, casting an attentive eye over the display cases at Bauble-Lou's, her new fashion accessory outlet in a suburban Regina shopping mall.

The store's opening early this month capped a tumultuous time for Ms. White. Within 18 months, she (a) quit her job with a financial institution; (b) spent a frustrating time on unemployment insurance; (c) landed on her feet as a fledgling entrepreneur.

She credits her recharged batteries to months of preparation in a new school for entrepreneurs at the Regina Business and Technology Centre. This is among a handful of private institutions across Canada that, with government help, serve as incubators to hatch new business minds.

The Regina centre, housed in a building near the city's airport, guides students — mostly pulled from unemployment insurance rolls — through five months of planning, drumming up financing, networking, eyeing the marketplace and scouting suppliers and competitors.

The school is one answer to the 1990s economic dilemma — what to do about the rising wave of unemployed but talent-laden individuals. Major corporations have laid off more people than they've hired in the past five years; small business accounts for the majority of hirings.

The centre doesn't promise to turn out perfect clones of aggressive, self-starting business people. "There's no formula for a successful entrepreneur," says Randy Beattie, manager of Prairie Financial Management, the private company that supplies the centre's training program.

"But you can see if individuals have qualities and capabilities similar to other entrepreneurs who are successful. You can help people be where they want to be."

In Ms. White's case, she knew where she didn't want to be. In July, 1992, she left the trust company where she's been employed for eight years, recently as a loans and estate officer. The reason: a personality conflict with her boss.

What she hadn't counted on was a tight Regina job market. Forced to draw unemployment insurance, she was eventually steered to the Self-Employment Assistance program. That's a federal training program administered by experts from the private sector, like Mr. Beattie's firm. Over the past four years, it has helped 4,000 unemployed Canadians form their own businesses.

Earlier this year, Ms. White was among the first 26 people to join the program in Regina. Mr. Beattie selected the 26 — including former managers, PhDs and auto mechanics — from 187 applicants. Ottawa foots the tuition for UI students — $6,000 apiece. Anyone else pays his own way.

Mr. Beattie says he looks for those rare people with the drive, the dream and the courage to risk their necks and money. Starting a new business is extremely risky: various studies suggest about 80 per cent fail within five years.

A large part of the training is psychological — making the switch from being order-takers to order-givers. "Half of what we do is talk to them about transition," says Mr. Beattie, whose training firm uses an instruction model developed by two U.S. industrial psychologists.

Mr. Beattie, a former corporate recruiter, relies heavily on networks and role models in the local business community. Bankers come to talk about financing. Applicants get public speaking training. They are encouraged to talk with spouses and families about preparing for a new life.

Ms. White says she made two key changes during the transition: she crafted a solid business plan, and she changed her mindset from that of employee to entrepreneur.

"I'm a pretty positive person," she says. "But in business you have to be flexible and resilient. I really enjoy problem solving. And I found when I was working for a corporation, I just wasn't being challenged to do that."

The course also provides opportunity to network with other aspiring owner-managers. Ms. White's bookkeeping and inventory control programs were developed by another graduate.

Instructors treat students as if they're already running their businesses. The centre provides office space and support while they're enrolled. It follows up after graduation to make sure the business plan is being implemented.

"The emphasis is on the individual. We do a lot of monitoring," Mr. Beattie says.

But from his company's experience, some people can't cut it in the entrepreneurial world. "Sometimes, the match to the business idea isn't good enough. They're out of here. Some people just aren't ready for it."

Mr. Beattie says only one of the 26 people in Ms. White's class — which ended in September — slipped back into a regular job. Three others were offered jobs, but refused. They did, however, agree to do the work on a contract basis. "When we saw that, we knew they'd turned the corner."

He sees three types of candidates for the program. First, there are UI referrals such as Ms. White. The second type are walk-ins so eager for a new challenge that they're willing to cut a $6,000 cheque. Then there are corporate referrals, the victims of downsizing.

It is too early to measure results of the Regina program, but it has given hope to people who once saw unemployment as their long-term future.

Maria Clemett, 46, has launched Sew What?, her own sewing and clothing supply company. "Going into business has changed my life," says Ms. Clemett, who gave up a job when her husband was transferred from Burlington, Ont., to Regina last year.

"I'd been on UIC twice and I'd been to every job-finding club I could find. There were just no jobs. The options were to keep pounding the pavement or do something for myself."

SOURCE: David Roberts, *The Globe and Mail*, 22 November 1993, p. B3. Reprinted with permission from *The Globe and Mail*.

📖 Startup Memories

A BUSINESS knows the score. Startups are all about round-the-clock work, skeptical friends, shaky suppliers and a frantic scramble for funds.

The people profiled below went through those teething pains. (Some have more teething to go.) Their experiences vary widely, but most have a horror story or two about financing.

Beneath the bravado, there is a sense of wonder and surprise that they have survived this far. Here are their tales:

PETER MCAUSLAN knows about self-sacrifice. To raise money for his new microbrewery, he sold his West Montreal home in the 1980s and moved to a cheaper place 45 kilometres away.

Mr. McAuslan, a former college administrator, and his wife and business partner, Ellen Bounsall, would wake up every morning at 4:45 to be at work by six. During a stretch of 96-hour workweeks, the two slept on a hideaway bed in the staff lounge in the brewery.

"We'd go to sleep with the hissing sounds of the brewery and I'd think 'That's the independence of your own business, right?' "

His experience with banks was also bumpy. When he first sought seed money in 1987, it looked easy. "We had a one-hour meeting with a bank and we got the money. I remember thinking, 'That's it?' "

But over the next three years, the bank became reluctant to fund expansion. It decided microbreweries were no longer a good investment, Mr. McAuslan says.

"They wanted to get rid of us as a client — it was as clear as that. One minute they're there for us, the next minute, they're not."

Mr. McAuslan was forced to fund equipment purchases through the brewery's cash flow — "a frightening experience."

But persistance paid off. Brasserie McAuslan Inc. opened its doors in 1989, producing its St. Ambroise Pale Ale. In 1991, it added a stout and two new ales. Projected revenue for the fiscal year ending Oct. 31 is $3.5-million, and Mr. McAuslan, 47, says he makes money.

He credits some of this to unorthodox marketing. He used to drag a 20-litre keg from tavern to tavern, giving patrons tastes of McAuslan beer. Illegal, but effective. "If the customers liked the beer and I wasn't thrown out, which I sometimes was, it was a great reason to give the owner as to why he should carry my beer.

"There's nothing like direct sales."

GILLIAN SMART knew she was in trouble when she returned from a long holiday and found her warehouse bulging with products that should have been distributed.

It was a harsh blow for a new company that was marketing central vacuum systems. Ms. Smart learned that her supplier — the products' manufacturer — had informed dealer clients that he was now the distributor.

"We called our dealers and they were amazed to hear we were in Canada, since they had been told we were gone for good."

That incident in 1976 was "a disaster" in more ways than one. Ms. Smart didn't believe in debt. She was financing inventory from sales. No sales, no company. She quickly rounded up enough dealers to sell off the old inventory.

But her aversion to debt didn't waver. Her company, Beam of Canada Inc. of Oakville, Ont., was a nation-wide distributor before Ms. Smart took her first loan. That was only when it began manufacturing its own products in 1984.

"I'm in horror of debt. Yes, an influx of money can create a large growth spurt for the company, but I always ask: 'Is the infrastructure of the company ready to support that quick growth?' "

Ms. Smart, 46, has always been resourceful. She and her husband at the time came from South Africa in 1971 with almost no money. They launched a residential construction and painting company in Regina.

Fed up with seasonal business, Ms. Smart answered an ad looking for product distributors. The manufacturer couldn't sell her on portable toilets, so he showed her his central vacuum system. She loved it.

Beam, a pioneer in central vacuum products, has grown to more than $20-million in annual sales, and holds half the Canadian market.

"I was always entrepreneurial — I think it has a lot to do with where I come from. In South Africa, the problems create an attitude in everyone. Whatever you want to do, you have to do it yourself."

STRAIGHT out of engineering school, 23-year-old Arnold Furlong became the first employee of Brooke Ocean Technology Ltd. in Dartmouth, N.S. Ten years later, he and a partner own the place.

Brooke Ocean was born as a research and development company working on technology for marine and ocean industries. It designed equipment that could withstand harsh marine conditions.

When the owner decided to retire in 1990, Mr. Furlong and Geoff Lebans — his co-worker and former classmate — stepped forward.

The company had a lucrative contract in hand. But Mr. Furlong discovered how hesitant banks are with technology companies. "Here we were, two young engineers with a contract. Needless to say, it was a tough sell."

After four months trying to get credit, the pair worked out a "cooperative purchase" with the owner. He agreed to extend the sale over a flexible period.

"Luckily, we were his only option to sell the company quickly. We knew the details of the business, and had done the day-to-day operations."

Eighteen months later, the two finally persuaded a bank to back them. Until then, they had financed the company through their savings accounts and cash flow.

The owners have expanded the four-employee company into consulting and equipment servicing. Their latest project: a semi-submersible, robotic system for ocean floor mapping.

"Now we market the technology and try to solve real-world problems, rather than just innovate," Mr. Furlong says.

RESTAURANT OWNER LeRoy Fuller credits much of his early success to a chance encounter.

A small-town Montana native, Mr. Fuller decided in 1956 to open an A&W franchise. U.S. cities were already full of the fast-food outlets, so he headed north to Alberta.

But he had trouble financing the property — until, in Edmonton, he ran into a real estate investor who offered a lease-back arrangement. "I had no idea what a lease-back was. I was just a farm boy with the idea that I wanted to open an A&W in Canada."

It was a 10-year, fixed-cost lease of $500 a month. At the end of the term, Mr. Fuller could renew the contract or buy the property for $50,000.

The deal set off his career. The burger outlet — the first A&W in Canada — did so well, he had no trouble buying the property. That led to 17 A&Ws in the Edmonton area. He joined with other A&W dealers in forming a larger company. But he stepped away from the business in 1983, when it was sold to Keg Restaurants Ltd. of Burnaby, B.C.

He didn't stop being entrepreneurial. His latest venture, Earl's Restaurants Ltd., operates 39 restaurants in British Columbia and Alberta.

It's a long way from Montana. "It seems like I started out at least 100 years ago," says Mr. Fuller, 64.

SPORTING GOODS retailer John Forzani is almost apologetic. He has no horror stories of bankers slamming doors in his face.

Part of the reason is timing. The former Calgary Stampeder football player — along with two brothers and a friend — opened a small Calgary store in 1974 at the beginning of the fitness craze. "The business took off from there," he says.

Mr. Forzani, 46, says the idea came from the fact that specialty athletic footwear was impossible to find in Calgary. Even the Stampeders had to order cleats from U.S. suppliers.

Forzani Group Ltd. now operates 90 stores in Western Canada under five names, including Forzani's Locker Room and Jersey City. It expects sales of $73-million in the year ending Jan. 30, 1994.

The owners funded the first store by throwing in $2,500 apiece. "It wasn't supercomplicated. We only had about $10,000 in inventory at cost."

A year later, they got a $15,000 loan and a $10,000 operating line from a bank. "We didn't have any trouble, especially since our company made money from its first day."

SOURCE: Natasha Bacigalupo, *The Globe and Mail*, 18 October 1993, p. B6. Reprinted with permission from *The Globe and Mail*.

❘❘ *Questions*

1. What is driving or motivating each of the successful entrepreneurs? Is it money or vision?
2. What were the start-up problems faced by each company? Could these problems have been avoided? How?
3. Using the guidelines provided in this chapter, select a business which you would like to start.
4. Start an entrepreneurial adventure notebook. All you will need is a three-ring binder. In the first section of your book, begin listing — each day — the opportunities you see in the marketplace.
5. Begin researching secondary (written or published) sources of information. Visit your local college, government office, and public library. Start an information section in your entrepreneurial work-book. Keep track of all the major sources of secondary information.
6. Using the guidelines in this chapter, start looking for a mentor. Keep a list of potential candidates in your entrepreneurial workbook.

3

FINANCING
AND BANKING

▌▌ *Finding Money*

Before you begin looking for money, you must first focus on what your vision is for your business and determine what is driving you into business. Frankly, if it is only money that is driving you, go and get a job (even part-time) to satisfy your need for money, until you can grow a business part-time to meet your need for money.

The next step is to determine how much money your business needs to start and sustain itself until the sales are high enough for it to be a self-supporting entity. Determine what your start-up costs will be and do a cash flow projection (see exercise 3.7) for the first year to determine whether you have enough projected income to cover your costs. If you do not have enough money, your cash flow projection will tell you that. The best place to go bankrupt is on paper (the initial cash flow projection), because it won't cost you your house, your job, or your savings.

The third step is determining how much money you have yourself. Then you will know how much money you must obtain from outside sources. Bankers and investors want to see you take a risk also. They want to know that you have risked virtually everything you have before asking them to take a risk. Some people believe it is better to start a business small and keep some of your assets, like the family home, sacred if possible. Others believe that the greater your dollar investment is, the greater your commitment is. Some people advise that if you do not have two credit cards, apply for them before you start a business. Our caution to you is that credit cards carry the highest interest rate of all of your options, and if credit is misused you can find yourself in a terrible position. If you have credit cards and feel you can make wise choices and full payments each month, then increasing the limit on these cards may not pose as much of a danger. If you have a full-time job and a clear credit history with the credit bureau, you may be able to secure a personal line of credit. A word of caution: do not lie to your bank, but be advised that using a line of credit to start a business is not amongst their favourite reasons for lending. There have been success stories that stemmed from the use of credit cards to finance a business start-up, but for every success story there are a host of horror stories. Be a responsible credit user by not letting the cost of borrowing send your business into bankruptcy. Completing the two forms in exercise 3.1 and 3.2 — Managing Your Personal Budget and Finances, and Statement of Personal Current Financial Sources — will help you assess how much money you have to personally invest in your business.

The key to obtaining money for your business is the viability of your business plan, complete with supporting research documents and cash flow projections. Another word for all of this is *prospectus*. Take your business plan to several banks even if you do not require outside money. If your business plan is approved for a loan, you will have gained more confidence that your vision is solid and has a chance to succeed. It is a good idea to call the closest credit bureau to get your new company name registered with them and to check your own credit file to be sure the information on file is correct. You will likely have to attend in person to do both, but ask what information you should bring with you. Whether you need money from outside sources or not, you *must* do a *financial plan* as part of your business plan in order to determine whether your idea and vision are workable.

Start-up money and growth money, called *capital*, could be obtained from the following sources:

- Relatives and friends
- Banks
- Government-guaranteed loans
- Government programs
- Partnerships
- Silent partner loans
- Private investors (limit of 10)
- Community-owned investment companies
- Suppliers
- Worker co-operatives
- Asset leases
- Public offering

All of these options (see also figure 3.1), mean that you will give up something in terms of management control, decision making, time to report, or moneys to repay the lender or risk taker. The moneys will be in the form of return on investment to investors, loss of return on your own investment money, or interest payments. To get money you will forsake something. You have to live with the investor and often give up shares in your company and provide a decision-making position on your board of directors, if not a management position in the day-to-day operations. Sourcing capital from outside is a short-term gain for what can be a long-term pain. Financing your business yourself may mean short-term pain but will ensure a long-term gain.

Now, let us take a realistic look at each of these options.

Figure 3.1. TOP 10 SOURCES OF START-UP CAPITAL

Companies with annual sales of $1.5-million

I.	Personal savings	73%
2.	Bank* loan with personal guarantees	56%

3.   Loans by family or friends 30%
4.   Infusion of money by partner 20%
5.   Bank* loan without personal guarantees 10%
6.   Venture capital 5%
7.   Issuing equity shares 5%
8.   Federal Business Development Bank 5%
9.   Government grant 4%
10. Government loan 4%

Companies with annual sales over $25-million

1.   Personal savings 33%
2.   Bank* loan with personal guarantees 31%
3.   Issuing equity shares 28%
4.   Infusion of money by partner 23%
5.   Bank* loan without personal guarantees 23%
6.   Loans by family members and friends 14%
7.   Venture capital 11%
8.   Government grant 7%
9.   Government loan 5%
10. Federal Business Development Bank 2%

* Includes other financial institutions

SOURCE: The Canadian Chamber of Commerce, as appearing in *The Globe and Mail*, 4 July 1994, p. B6.

▌▌ Relatives and Friends

Choose your moral and financial support carefully. It will be necessary to report the progress of your business to these relatives and friends. Do they trust you enough to ride the rough times? Do they know enough about business to understand the process of a new business? Complete an agreement setting out the repayment schedule and specifying what interest payments, if any, will be made. Stipulate clearly whether these lenders are being sold shares in your company or not. Just as good fences can make good neighbours in suburbia, good written agreements can keep good friends and relatives content.

▮▮ Banks

Douglas Gray and Brian Nattrass, Vancouver lawyers, point out that banks should be at the bottom of the list when you are looking for funds. The high cost of borrowing can drain the cash flow of a young business. They also say entrepreneurs lose a good deal of control when dealing with banks. The big institutions can call in their loans or freeze your line of credit with little warning, just because of a change in their lending practices.*

Many people have the false belief that a banker is there to help them. Understand that a banker is in business to make money for the bank. A banker's role is to make as much interest on loans as possible. A simple example is the fact that banks, unless you successfully argue with them, will *sell* you the longest house mortgage possible so that the bank can earn the most interest possible. A $100,000 mortgage at 10 per cent costs $268,347 to repay over 25 years at $894.49 per month. You borrowed $100,000 and it cost you the difference in interest, or $168,347. The same mortgage over 15 years requires payments of $1,063 per month (only $168 more per month) and costs $191,340 to repay. Again you borrowed $100,000 and it cost you the difference in interest, or $91,340. A mortgage over 10 years costs even less than a 15-year mortgage. Over the past few years, banks were forced by the competition of trust companies to accept weekly and bi-weekly payments instead of just monthly payments on mortgages, and to reduce the principal amount owed immediately. This step is a significant saving to the consumer. You can purchase a small book that contains tables showing monthly payments on personal loans and one for mortgages ($3 each) in order to calculate for yourself the cost of borrowing. Be informed so that you can argue successfully with a banker to obtain what is best for you and/or your business.

What banks want to see for a new business:

- Personal budget
- Personal balance sheet
- Business opening balance sheet

---

* From Jerry Zeidenberg, "Why Your Bank Is Last Place to Look," in *The Globe and Mail*, 10 January 1994, p. B6.

- Source and application of funds
- Cash flow statement
- Projected income statement
- Ending balance sheet

Choosing and using your banker:

- Have your business plan, including the financials, complete.
- Select a branch that offers small business banking.
- Choose a banker that you are comfortable with.
- Keep your bank manager informed.
- Avoid surprises.
- Identify and meet key branch staff.
- Keep your personal and business accounts completely separate.
- Document everything to do with the finances of your business.

Banks want hard assets as security, especially if they know you are investing the money into a business. The bank also wants to see a good credit rating, honesty, commitment, vision, a full financial plan, and control mechanisms in place to protect your business assets. They want you to show them that you can do what you say you can do. Banks will usually take a lien on whatever assets you have to secure repayment of a loan. If you have a full-time job, you may be able to acquire a personal unsecured loan of less than $10,000.

Assets such as your car, your house, and your investments will be considered for security lien by the bank. If you default on the payments, the bank can take legal action to take over ownership of your assets. They will then sell the assets to recover as much as possible of the money they loaned you.

Without government-guaranteed loans, banks would not be involved with business start-ups. They do, however, compete for your business when you are successful and you do not need them. Look forward to this day!

What banks want to see for an existing business:

- Personal budget
- Personal balance sheet
- Aged accounts receivable
- Aged accounts payable

- Inventory list
- Comparative income statements
- Comparative balance sheets

∎ Government-Guaranteed Loans

Under most government programs for business, a bank processes your loan application in a normal fashion with the attached form for government guarantee. If your loan application, supported by your business plan, is accepted, then the government program will guarantee to the bank that if you fail to make the payments, the government will pay the bank and proceed with legal action against you to recover the moneys. The guarantee is really a guarantee to the banks. This type of loan became necessary when banks stopped lending to new and growth businesses unless there was no risk.

The federal government has a program called the Small Business Loan (SBL), which is also referred to by government as the Business Improvement Loan (BIL). The SBL program requires the security of hard assets, such as equipment, furniture, and leasehold improvements. The lending is a maximum of 80 per cent of movable asset costs and a maximum of 90 per cent of immovable asset costs (such as leasehold improvements or real estate). During the 1970s and 1980s, there was a minimum requirement that made it impossible to access this program unless your business was well established and profitable. Many entrepreneurs were told to come back when they got bigger. In 1993, the loan limit was increased to $250,000 from $100,000, and equipment purchased within the last 180 days prior to loan application became eligible for refinancing. There is a two per cent up-front administration fee payable to the chartered bank to process your application, and there is now a ceiling of approximately 25 per cent on the requirement for personal guarantees. In rare instances, it is possible to obtain financing of 100 per cent of the asset cost.

During the 1990s, statistics have shown the federal government that job creation has and will continue to come from small and medium businesses.* This reality has forced the federal government to start a

---

* John Manley and Paul Martin, *Growing Small Businesses*, February 1994.

new loan program more accessible to small business and to make the original SBL more accessible. In 1991, the Venture Loan program was started. Little collateral is required as this program acts as an investment in the future earning potential of a company, and the repayment schedule is structured to meet the ability of your company to repay based on your cash flow projections and actual profitability. The government does not own shares in the company.

Some provinces have also started guaranteed loan programs. The chartered banks do all of the lending; however, if the proper criteria are met, the bank is guaranteed payment if you default on the loan. If you default, the provincial government will commence legal action against you to secure full payment.

▮▮ Government Programs

The Federal Business Development Bank (FBDB) once had a handy book called *Assistance to Business in Canada* that included all federal and provincial government programs and loans available and a computer that was up to date with the same programs. This information can still be secured from your local FBDB office by telephoning. You may also call the government departments that apply to your new business (for example, call the Ministry of Tourism if your new business is a tourist-driven business, or Agriculture Canada if your business is farming). You must be persistent to obtain all of the information.

▮▮ Partnerships

Sometimes this type of investor is fondly called an *angel*. This investor is more informal and may be a retired business owner or a successful executive who always dreamed of being a business owner. They usually command ownership of shares (equity) and/or an active company operating role.

▮▮ Silent Partner Loans

These investors do not want an active role in the operation of the business for a variety of reasons. They do however want a high return on their investment in return for what they perceive as a high risk. Your business plan must sell them on the possibility of a high rate of return. Some silent partners do not have any experience in the type of business they invest in and others do. The key to attracting any investor is the feasibility of the business and the confidence they feel in the entrepreneur(s) starting the business.

▌▌ Private Investors

These investors, often called *venture capitalists*, may be unknown to you at the beginning. You may find them through a lawyer, an accountant, a banker, or a simple newspaper ad in the classified section. You may find one investor or a venture capital company capable of handling money in excess of $250,000. This type of financing can easily take up to six months to secure. Most private investors will want to own company shares, have a participatory role within a company's management structure, and be involved for long periods up to eight or ten years. The interest rate or return on investment that you must pay venture capitalists is higher than bank lending rates. You may only make offerings to a limited number of investors and secure a limited number of investors (usually 10) to maintain the status of a private offering.

▌▌ Community-Owned Investment Companies

Across Canada, community-owned investment companies have been established in the major cities. Some provinces have received Revenue Canada approval to issue Registered Retirement Savings Plan (RRSP) receipts, and other provinces are awaiting this approval. Community investment companies accept local investment moneys with the mandate of investing in local small business. Communities are demanding more corporate responsibility to the community. During the recession of the early 1980s and 1990s, many towns and cities have been significantly affected as corporations shut down plants, only to reopen them two or three years later as a result of shutting down in some other town or city. This roller-coaster ride for communities can be stopped by the communities taking a more active, assertive role in local businesses. An entire community is affected by a large lay-off of workers. If people leave, school enrolment decreases, grocery stores close, property taxes increase to maintain services for the remaining residents, and the list goes on. Everyone is a stakeholder in local business.

▌▌ Suppliers

Suppliers at one time provided credit to everyone. However, the last two recessions have caused most to tighten their credit extending rules. If you spend the time sourcing your suppliers and providing them with a credit application, it may be possible to purchase on credit. If you are refused, it is worth your time to meet with the owner and provide a copy of your business plan. If the owner sees potential in your business, he or she may be willing to take a risk. Using credit to purchase goods and selling them for cash is a technique that will allow you to begin and to grow, as long as you make regular payments to your supplier. Always have two suppliers sourced as back-up for whatever you must purchase. Being dependent on single sourcing is a dangerous situation and one that has spelled disaster for many firms. You must communicate regularly with your supplier to keep them up to date and to avoid being cut off. If you pay your bills regularly at the end of every month, you will establish a good credit rating and a special rapport with your suppliers. When you cannot make the payment on time, call them — do not avoid them. They are like a partner in your business success, without the ownership or legal status.

▌▌ Worker Co-operatives

You must consider whether it is better to own 100 per cent of nothing or 10 per cent of something. Worker co-operatives are gaining in popularity because so many people have lost what they thought was a secure lifelong job. In a worker co-op, every investor gains a job in the new business venture. Security becomes something each person has control over, and the community is assured that the new business will not move away, but instead continue to provide employment and investment back into the community. The workers spend most of their earnings right in the community, paying for merchandise, services, rent, property tax, and so forth. As worker/owners, people are motivated and committed to bringing in business, and the community is motivated to support the business. It takes a diligent team to work through the strengths and weaknesses of each member and to establish roles and guidelines that ensure a successful operation. It can be done. It is being done.

■ Asset Leases

Leasing of equipment, furniture, and vehicles has become very popular due to the low down payment (first and last months lease payment) and the fact that cash is left free to use for the operation of a business. Negotiate a purchase price for the asset and then negotiate the terms of payment, interest rate, and buy-out price (if any) at the end of the lease term. You can negotiate all of this with the supplier of the asset or sometimes a bank. The pain/gain rule applies here as well. Low down payment is a short-term gain, but the total paid over the term of the lease can be a long-term pain. To purchase assets outright can be a short-term pain in terms of loss of available cash, but the total value of the asset over the same number of years of use can be a long-term gain.

■ Public Offering

To attract more than 10 investors, ultimately called shareholders, is an expensive endeavour. This avenue requires that a chartered accountant prepare the financial portion of the business plan (prospectus) and that all documents be registered with the Security Exchange Commission. This step is best taken when your company is well established. These shareholders will stay for varying lengths of time and must be provided with audited financial statements regularly. Companies like Mitel Corporation and Corel Corporation began very small, became successful, and then went to public funding to expand. It can be done; however, you give up ownership to secure this funding.

❙❙ *Improving Your Chances of Getting Financing*

Gerald Slan, national director of entrepreneurial services for Ernst and Young, offers some advice on how to enhance your chances of getting financing:

- *Improve management skills.* Poor business planning and management skills are the main obstacles to financing. Learn to manage innovation and to apply new technologies and management practices. You are doomed if you always do things the old way because it's the way that you've always done them.

- *Expand business networks.* Get out and meet people. Leverage every opportunity that presents itself. The more relationships you develop, the better your chances of success.

    Don't be afraid to seek outside help. Many small and medium-sized businesses have benefited from the input of a board of advisers. Such boards can serve as a reality check, helping solve your thorniest problems.

- *Examine alternative financing techniques.* If you need seed capital, look for investors who know your industry and believe in its opportunities. Look for backers who believe in your strategies and management style. They will likely want a piece of equity in exchange for capital. But if the fit is right, the sacrifice will be worth it in the long run.

- *Embrace change.* Innovation and change are vital to your long-term success. After all, your competitors are going all out to capture the biggest share of the market they can. Unless you are prepared to roll with the punches, your company will be left behind.

SOURCE: Excerpt from Gerald Slan, "Some Advice for Raising Capital," *The Globe and Mail*, 2 May 1994, p. B1.

11 *Protecting Your Assets*

You may think you are in business after you have been approved for a loan from your creditor(s). A word of caution: Consult a professional business adviser before you take the plunge. Here are a few ideas that can help ensure that your assets will be protected from seizure by creditors should your business get into financial troubles:

- Never sign a *personal guarantee* for a loan without thoroughly reviewing the terms of the document and having a clear understanding of your obligations and liabilities under the loan agreement.

- Whether you own or lease the premises in which your business operates, you can control the real estate in a *separate corporation* whose shares are held by family members or family trusts that are not involved in the business.

- Make sure that you obtain adequate *insurance* to deal with claims against corporate directors or partners should these occur.

- If you or your family contributes financially to the business, keep the capital you invest to a minimum and, instead of putting in equity, lend the funds to the business under *security agreements*. This ensures that if your company fails, you will be treated as secured creditors rather than shareholders, who are paid last.

- Your principal residence and significant *personal assets* may be acquired by, or transferred to, a spouse who is not involved in the business. These assets should be owned solely by the spouse, not owned jointly with you.
- Make use of a *spousal* RRSP which gives you a tax deduction and your spouse the pension asset. Or, purchase the RRSP through an insurance company and designate an irrevocable beneficiary.
- Use a *discretionary trust* to own assets or the shares of an investment corporation. The trustees can be given complete control to distribute income or capital to any beneficiary and exclude any beneficiary who may be insolvent.
- Change the *beneficiary* of a will or insurance policy from yourself to your spouse or family trust. Designate someone other than a partner or a shareholder in your company to be the beneficiary of a disability insurance policy.

All of these measures together can help ensure that if your business fails, your spouse and children will enjoy a degree of protection in the event of bankruptcy proceedings.

SOURCE: Excerpt from Stuart Mitchell, "How to Keep Creditors from Seizing Your Assets," *The Globe and Mail*, 18 July 1994, p. B6.

❙❙ *Exercise 3.1*

MANAGING YOUR PERSONAL
BUDGET AND FINANCES

MONTHLY EXPENSE ITEMS	FAT BUDGET	BARE BONES BUDGET
Food	. . . . . .	. . . . . .
Clothing	. . . . . .	. . . . . .
Shelter: Mortgage / Rent	. . . . . .	. . . . . .
Utilities	. . . . . .	. . . . . .
Maintenance / Cleaning	. . . . . .	. . . . . .

Car: Payments	. . . . . .	. . . . . .
Gas/Oil	. . . . . .	. . . . . .
Maintenance/Repairs	. . . . . .	. . . . . .
Dependents' expenses	. . . . . .	. . . . . .
Credit card bills	. . . . . .	. . . . . .
Other	. . . . . .	. . . . . .

Annual Expenses (convert to monthly)

Taxes	. . . . . .	. . . . . .
Auto registration/dues	. . . . . .	. . . . . .
Holidays, gifts, vacations	. . . . . .	. . . . . .
Other	. . . . . .	. . . . . .
	————	————
TOTAL MONTHLY EXPENSES	————	————

Monthly Income

Your income (if it will continue)	. . . . . .	. . . . . .
Your spouse's income	. . . . . .	. . . . . .
Interest on savings	. . . . . .	. . . . . .
Stock/bond dividends	. . . . . .	. . . . . .
Retirement	. . . . . .	. . . . . .
Trust fund	. . . . . .	. . . . . .
Insurance payments	. . . . . .	. . . . . .
Other	. . . . . .	. . . . . .
	————	————
TOTAL MONTHLY INCOME	————	————
MONTHLY SAVINGS	————	————

▌▌ *Exercise 3.2*

STATEMENT OF PERSONAL
CURRENT FINANCIAL SOURCES

SOURCE		AMOUNT OWING	CREDIT LIMIT
Bank Credit Cards:	VISA	. . . . . .	. . . . . .
	MasterCard	. . . . . .	. . . . . .

		Col A	Col B
	Diner's Club	. . . . . .	. . . . . .
	Discover	. . . . . .	. . . . . .
	American Express	. . . . . .	. . . . . .
	Other	. . . . . .	. . . . . .
Oil Companies:	Shell	. . . . . .	. . . . . .
	Esso	. . . . . .	. . . . . .
	Petro-Canada	. . . . . .	. . . . . .
	Other	. . . . . .	. . . . . .
Department Stores:	Bay	. . . . . .	. . . . . .
	Sears	. . . . . .	. . . . . .
	Eaton's	. . . . . .	. . . . . .
	Other	. . . . . .	. . . . . .
Personal Line of Credit:			
	Bank	. . . . . .	. . . . . .
	Trust Company	. . . . . .	. . . . . .
	Credit Union	. . . . . .	. . . . . .
	Other	. . . . . .	. . . . . .
Any other unsecured credit		. . . . . .	. . . . . .

TOTALS   _____   _____

Difference is available credit   . . . . . .
Equity in home/cottage/etc.   . . . . . .
TOTAL AVAILABLE CREDIT AND EQUITY   _____

This is how much you have to invest in your business. Now you know how much you have to find from outside sources!

▌▌ *Exercise 3.3*

SOURCES AND APPLICATION
OF FUNDS STATEMENT

Sources

EQUITY:

Your Investment   . . . . . .

Relatives and Friends   . . . . . .

Partners	. . . . . .	
Investors	. . . . . .	
LOANS:		
Relatives and Friends	. . . . . .	
Bank(s)	. . . . . .	
Mortgage	. . . . . .	
TOTAL EQUITY AND LOANS	_____	(A)

Application of Funds

Start-Up Costs	. . . . . .	
Leasehold Improvements	. . . . . .	
Estimated Equipment Costs	. . . . . .	
Cash Reserve	. . . . . .	
TOTAL APPLICATION OF FUNDS	_____	(B)

A = B

▌▌ *Exercise 3.4*

OPENING BALANCE SHEET

Name of Business	_____
Date of Statement	_____

ASSETS

Current Assets

Cash	. . . . . .	
Bank Accounts	. . . . . .	
Inventory (at cost)	. . . . . .	
Prepaid Expenses	. . . . . .	
Other Current Assets	. . . . . .	
TOTAL CURRENT ASSETS	_____	(A)

Fixed Assets

Land	. . . . . .
Buildings	. . . . . .
Equipment	. . . . . .

Furniture & Fixtures	. . . . . .	
Automobiles	. . . . . .	
Leasehold Improvements	. . . . . .	
Other Assets	. . . . . .	
TOTAL FIXED ASSETS	_____	(B)
TOTAL ASSETS (A + B)	_____	(C)

LIABILITIES

Current Liabilities (debt due within next 12 months)

Bank Loans	. . . . . .	
Other Loans	. . . . . .	
Accounts Payable	. . . . . .	
Current Portion of Long-Term Debt	. . . . . .	
Other Current Liabilities	. . . . . .	
TOTAL CURRENT LIABILITIES	_____	(D)

Long-Term Liabilities

Mortgages Payable	. . . . . .	
Loans Payable	. . . . . .	
Less: Current Portion	. . . . . .	
Shareholders' Loans Payable	. . . . . .	
Other Loans	. . . . . .	
TOTAL LONG-TERM LIABILITIES	_____	(E)
TOTAL LIABILITIES (D + E)	_____	(F)
NET WORTH *(Investment – Equity)*	_____	(G)
TOTAL LIABILITIES AND NET WORTH (F + G)	_____	(C)
WORKING CAPITAL (A – D)	_____	

▌▐ *Exercise 3.5*

ENDING BALANCE SHEET YEAR 1

Name of Business   _____

Date of Statement   _____

ASSETS

Current Assets

Cash Bank Account	. . . . . .
Stocks and Bonds (at cost)	. . . . . .
Life Insurance (cash value)	. . . . . .
Accounts Receivable	. . . . . .
Less: Doubtful Accounts	. . . . . .
Inventory (lower of cost or market value)	. . . . . .
Prepaid Expenses	. . . . . .
Other Current Assets	. . . . . .

TOTAL CURRENT ASSETS _____ (A)

Fixed Assets

Land	. . . . . .
Buildings	. . . . . .
Equipment	. . . . . .
Furniture and Fixtures	. . . . . .
Automobiles	. . . . . .
Leasehold Improvements	. . . . . .
Other Assets	. . . . . .

TOTAL FIXED ASSETS _____ (B)

TOTAL ASSETS (A + B) _____ (C)

LIABILITIES

Current Liabilities (debt due within next 12 months)

Bank Loans	. . . . . .
Other Loans	. . . . . .
Sales and Payroll Taxes Payable	. . . . . .
Accounts Payable	. . . . . .
Current Portion of Long-Term Debt	. . . . . .
Other Current Liabilities	. . . . . .

TOTAL CURRENT LIABILITIES _____ (D)

Long-Term Liabilities

Mortgages Payable	. . . . . .
Loans Payable	. . . . . .

Less: Current Portion   . . . . . .
Shareholders' Loans Payable   . . . . . .
Other Loans   . . . . . .

TOTAL LONG-TERM LIABILITIES   _____ (E)

TOTAL LIABILITIES (D + E)   _____ (F)

NET WORTH *(Investment + Retained Earnings)*   _____ (G)
TOTAL LIABILITIES AND NET WORTH (F + G)   _____ (C)
WORKING CAPITAL (A − D)   _____

I I *Exercise 3.6*

PROJECTED INCOME STATEMENT

	FIRST QUARTER $	SECOND QUARTER $	THIRD QUARTER $	FOURTH QUARTER $	TOTAL YEAR I $	TOTAL YEAR 2 $
SALES						
Less: *Cost of goods/ services sold*						
GROSS PROFIT						
Less: *Selling expenses*						
Office expenses						
General expenses						
Interest expenses						
OPERATING PROFIT						
Less: *Taxes payable (corporation)*						
or *Owner(s)' drawings (partnership or proprietorship)*						

NET INCOME/ NET CASH (available for loan repayment, etc.)						

SOURCE: Ontario Ministry of Economic Development. Reprinted with permission of Publications Ontario.

❙❙ Exercise 3.7

CASH FLOW FORECAST FOR YEAR ENDED ____

Month	APR	MAY	JUN	JUL	AUG	SEP	OCT	NOV	DEC	JAN	FEB	MAR	total
Est. sales													
CASH RECEIPTS Cash sales													
Collections													
Other													
Loan													
TOTAL													
CASH DISBURSE-MENTS Equipment													
Occupancy													
Labour													
Material													
Owner salary/adv.													
Licence/Ins.													
Selling													
Office													
Other													
Loan/Int.													
TOTAL													

	APR	MAY	JUN	JUL	AUG	SEP	OCT	NOV	DEC	JAN	FEB	MAR	total
Month net surplus/ (deficit)													
Cumulative surplus/ (deficit)													

SOURCE: Forum for International Trade Training Inc. (FITT), *Global Entrepreneurship*, 1993, module 11, p. 17.

SMALL BUSINESS NOTES

How Not to Get a Bank Loan

HERE are six common mistakes that result in loan rejections:

1. Not making a specific request for the amount, term or purpose of the loan.
2. Being unable to present financial information on the business prepared by reputable, independent accountant.
3. No seed capital. Banks are generally not seed capitalists; they lend money to facilitate activities of businesses with track records.
4. Not making a personal guarantee. People should be prepared to stand behind their businesses.
5. Refusing to assume the cost of an appraisal and environmental study when commercial real estate is used as collateral.
6. Not developing a relationship with a bank. A bank expects an applicant to maintain deposits with, and buy other services (credit cards, RRSPS, for example) from it.

SOURCE: Excerpt from a newsletter by chartered accountants Bessner Gallay Schapira Kreisman, as appearing in *The Globe and Mail*, 15 November 1993, p. B4.

📖 There's a Cost

"NO ENTREPRENEUR should forget that anyone who puts serious money into a new venture will want a number of board seats and a significant say in how the new company is run.

"But all too many entrepreneurs, eager to secure the cash they need to fund their dreams, forget that they will have to live with their investors for a long time."

SOURCE: Joseph Garber, quoted in *Forbes*, as appearing in *The Globe and Mail*, 25 October 1993, p. B6.

📖 Sound Familiar?

TOO MANY British entrepreneurs are taking cash out of their businesses too quickly, warns *The Economist*. "That puts them at the mercy of banks for finance. The best and most reliable source of cash will always be internal."

SOURCE: *The Globe and Mail*, 25 October 1993, p. B6.

📖 Bean Counters Should Do More Than Just Count

ENTREPRENEURS often overlook a rich source of guidance for their emerging companies — their own accountants.

Consider Ross, the owner/manager of an expanding manufacturing company. His business was profitable, but lately it was running short of cash. Was it because it was growing too fast, and would this pattern continue?

Desperate for advice, Ross (a real person, although not his real name) thought of his accountant. He had paid his annual accounting fees up front to have his financial statements and tax returns prepared. Perhaps, his search for an answer could start with an analysis of these statements.

He arranged a meeting to review his financial numbers and get some advice on his cash management. This is where Ross got a surprise that sent his blood pressure soaring.

Despite a prearranged meeting time, his accountant was in a hurry to get to another appointment. He said he would look into Ross's cash shortage, which he attributed to the poor economy. As he rushed out, he reminded Ross that he would have to come up with extra cash to pay his business taxes.

For Ross, this was the breaking point. That night he met with Steve, his long-time business associate, to share his frustrations. Steve reminded him that his own business had become successful when he learned how to add value for his customers.

Accountants — in fact, any professional who is hired — must do the same thing. An entrepreneur cannot afford to pay any professional unless that person adds value to the business — and the return on those services can be measured.

Steve handed Ross a list of services through which an accountant can improve a client's business:

- Use the client's service or product if at all possible — and give an honest feedback on the quality and service delivered.

- Refer business to the client.

- Actively link clients that can expand their businesses through formal and informal associations.

- Sponsor training and information seminars dealing with topics that help the business grow. A training session on managing cash would be a good place to start. These sessions will also allow networking with other business owners, which is both a learning experience and a source of new business leads.

- Send regular newsletters to clients containing educational information on changes in tax laws, investment opportunities, marketing ideas and management techniques. The accountant can profile industries, and clients can write about their particular strengths, such as teamwork, hiring or servicing customers.

- Answer client questions, or refer them to books and courses.

- Provide a full range of accounting and taxation services including preparation of cash-flow projections, financial statements, personal tax returns, business corporate tax returns, statement of sources and application of cash, financial planning and retirement planning.

After his conversation with Steve, Ross knew what he wanted — an accountant who would service his needs for cash management and bring him new business. Today he works with a new-style home-based bean counter who actually visits his factory once a month.

Ross's bookkeeper does much of the basic work under the accountant's supervision. The accountant's job is to save money, control cash flow and lead him to new customers. And this relationship is working.

SOURCE: Debbie White and Ron Knowles, *The Globe and Mail*, 25 July 1994, p. B4.

📖 Help with Loans

SMALL LOANS are money-losers for financial institutions, which typically spend more on paperwork than they earn back in interest. As a result, many home-based businesses have difficulty in arranging bank financing.

To reduce the cost of credit delivery, Vancouver's VanCity credit union has launched the peer-assisted lending program, or PAL.

A loans committee is set up consisting of four separate businesses, each of which requires credit. The committee is trained to assume responsibility for reviewing and approving the loan requests of its members, while the financial institution simply disburses funds and collects payments. PAL loans start at $500 and go up to $5,000.

The non-profit program is sponsored by Calmeadow Foundation, with support from the Vancouver Foundation and VanCity Community Foundation.

SOURCE: *The Globe and Mail*, 25 October 1993, p. B6.

📖 As You Pass Go, Put Up $100,000

WHEN DANIEL GIRARD was 16, he drew a baseball board game on a pizza box with crayons. His friends loved it, so he kept fine-tuning the game as he went through university and began working for Radio Canada in Regina.

Today, a commercial version of his pizza-box game, called Diceball, is sold for $30 at 100 Hudson's Bay Co. stores and 50 Toys "R" Us stores across Canada and is featured in a U.S. games catalogue.

"Americans ask how a French Canadian invented the best baseball game on the market today," he says. "I say it's because I played 4,000 games of Diceball before putting it on the market."

The game draws on the statistical magic of baseball, using dice and a board that resembles a playing field. But Mr. Girard, now 30 and a Montreal TV producer, hasn't made a penny on Diceball — nor has his partner, Louis Desjardins, 34, a commercial printer.

They don't plan to quit their day jobs. Their company, Intellijeux Inc., raised $200,000 from family and friends to produce the game and hasn't come close to breaking even.

Six-figure outlays aren't unusual in the game business, which has become a popular area for entrepreneurs. Experts say $100,000 is the minimum required just to play in the big leagues. That means getting a new product onto crowded shelves of department stores and toy emporiums during the crucial pre-Christmas sales binge.

Luckily, many inventors find it easy to raise money from investors. Everyone dreams of backing the next Trivial Pursuit, the fabulously successful board game created by Canadians that sold 60 million units worldwide. (A 10th anniversary edition of Trivial Pursuit is in stores this Christmas.)

Forced indoors by harsh weather, Canadians have developed a talent for board games. The best-selling adult games of the past decade — Trivial Pursuit, Scruples, Balderdash and Pictionary — were all invented by Canadians.

Still, it's hard to come up a winner in the brutally competitive toy market, where only one or two of 100 inventors even recoup their costs. As for the odds of making a million, "Lotto 6/49 is better," says Kenny Albert, vice-president of marketing at Canada Games Co. Ltd., a major toy and game maker and distributor in Bramalea, Ont.

Canada Games sees 2,800 new products a year and licences just a handful. "It's hard to find good ideas, but it's fun looking," says Mr. Albert, one of three brothers in the business along with father Harvey Albert.

Canada Games saw the potential in Balderdash, a game in which you take real but unusual words and conjure up definitions to fool other players. Balderdash has sold three million units since 1985 — and a TV game show is in development — but the inventors' next game, Jabberwocky, was a flop.

A newer Canada Games product, Hedbanz, has sold 150,000 units in Canada, Australia, New Zealand, Mexico and Argentina, and has spun off a kids' version. It's an updated version of 20 questions, in which you guess your identity (a person, place or thing), displayed to other players in a card strapped to your forehead.

The secret of Hedbanz' success? "It's not a serious game, it requires absolutely no intelligence and you can understand the rules within 30 seconds," says Toronto inventor Doug McFadden, 40, who has worked in the game business for many years.

Mr. McFadden spent 18 months developing Hedbanz before going to Canada Games, which immediately offered him a licencing agreement. Three months later, he and his investors were collecting royalties. (The game sells for $30 to $35.)

Hooking up with an established company is a cheaper and easier way of getting a game to market, says Gary Svoboda, manager of marketing services at the Canadian Industrial Innovation Centre in Waterloo, Ont.

"If it's a good concept, you should be able to find a home for it. The people who make toys and games their business will maximize its potential. And if no one bites, maybe you shouldn't pursue it."

The centre, which helps inventors assess new products, has looked at 8,000 inventions since 1976. But its only successful board game is Spin for Sin, a provocative "adult game" invented by four women in Kitchener, Ont., to play with their husbands at dinner parties.

Spin for Sin sells about 1,000 units annually in Canada at $20 apiece and is licenced to a U.S. game company. "The adult game market is very small," says Barra Lalonde, one of the inventors. But the game cost only $40,000 to produce and made a profit in its first year.

Lacking money for advertising, the women decided to use promotional flare. Calling themselves the Sin Sisters, they posed in sexy back lingerie for a poster and garnered lots of media interviews. "With a name like that, people get curious," says Ms. Lalonde.

Advertising is a stumbling block. Retail chains won't carry a new product without some ad muscle behind it, but this can be costly. Forced to improvise, entrepreneurs stage in-store demonstrations and give out free samples.

Sampling worked well for Richard Fast, inventor of MindTrap, a collection of 500 puzzles, murder mysteries, conundrums and trick questions. (Question: "How much dirt is in a hole six feet long, two feet wide and one foot deep?" Answer: "None.")

Mr. Fast, 35, spent eight years compiling brain teasers while working as a waiter in Toronto. Big game companies turned him down — "they all said it was a dud, too cerebral" — so he wrote a business plan and raised $100,000 in two months from friends and relatives.

MindTrap came out in 1991 and sold briskly at $30, aided by a flurry of promotional cards sent to stores and media. Sales of English and French versions are expected to hit 75,000 this year at Eaton's, Toys "R" Us and other Canadian chains. The game is licenced in the United States, Europe and Australia.

With success, Mr. Fast can finally afford to advertise. He's spending $100,000 on a series of funny Christmas radio spots, but says, "I'm amazed at how much money it takes to get your product known."

Canadians are famous not only for board games. Ontario-born James Naismith invented basketball in 1891. Now, an Edmonton man wants to reinvent basketball as a street game.

Dan Horvath, 40, has designed a free-standing basketball net, called Street Hoops, for team competition. Available in five-foot and eight-foot heights (regular basketball nets are 10 feet high), he hopes it will catch on with niche markets such as young girls, senior citizens and families.

The idea came from watching his own children (he has six) play street hockey. He raised $100,000 from investors and manufactured a prototype.

"It's light enough that a child can move it, yet strong enough to support a person hanging on the rim."

He sold the first 50 units to Sport Chek, a sporting goods chain in Western Canada, but was turned down by Canadian Tire Corp. Ltd. because of the $330 retail price. He hopes volume manufacturing will bring it below $300.

Mr. Horvath, who has a Grade 8 education, spent 12 years as an open-pit miner, then turned to inventing. He designed five industrial products, with names like Hose Handler and Cable Bun, that bring in more than $1-millon a year in worldwide sales.

To finance the development of Street Hoops, he went to an unusual source — miners in northern Alberta and British Columbia.

"I know them, they know me," says Mr. Horvath, adding that men in mining communities have lots of money in the bank. "There's a real opportunity with interest rates this low.

"To get one guy throwing big money at you is hard to do. But if you ask 20 people to give you $5,000, they're willing to risk it."

SOURCE: Ellen Roseman, *The Globe and Mail*, 20 December 1993, p. B6. Reprinted with permission from *The Globe and Mail*.

Lending to the Leading Edge

THE JAPANESE OWNER of a Toronto-area electronics firm had decided to shut down the unprofitable operation. But several local managers thought they could engineer a turnaround.

They searched for someone to finance a buyout. "Banks told us, 'There's a recession on now. This isn't the right time.' They didn't understand our business," says Dov Rom, who in 1990 was manufacturing director of Murata Erie North America Ltd.'s power supply division.

The exception was Rick Lunny, vice-president and manager of commercial banking for a Toronto-Dominion Bank branch in Markham, Ont. He recognized that the division, which makes power units for computers, copiers and other equipment, had a niche market and a blue-chip customer list that included IBM and Xerox.

"The end user needed the product," he says. "IBM wasn't going to stop the assembly line for a $100 part in a $1,500 machine. So, there was a pretty good chance you would recover your receivables."

Mr. Lunny specializes in an area many bankers shy away from — financing entrepreneurs in the new knowledge-based economy. Bankers normally have a tough time lending to high-tech companies, which lack hard assets such as real estate, buildings and machinery. Their collateral is less tangible — ideas, networks and management skills.

Like all banks, TD gets its share of criticism for ignoring the needs of small business. But individual bankers like Mr. Lunny are making an effort to understand the new breed of owner-managers.

Financing technology enterprises is like "financing air," says Mr. Lunny, 38, who has managed the Markham commercial branch for four years. "You have to change your mindset, the way you've been taught to lend."

This attitude helped ease the buyout of Mr. Rom's company in April, 1991. Ascent Power Technology Inc. was born, with Gary Rokas, 42, as president, Ronald Chan, 46, as vice-president of finance and Mr. Rom, 40, as vice-president of operations. Besides the TD loan, the former owner helped by taking back preferred shares.

Mr. Lunny's sensitivity to such companies' needs is partly dictated by where he is. Markham, an industrial satellite northeast of Toronto, is home to many young technology firms. "More than 75 per cent of the hardware and software industry is based within 10 kilometres of here," he likes to say.

In assessing loan applications, he looks for companies with emerging technologies. He and his staff keep up to date with new developments by subscribing to computer magazines and going to trade shows. Each account manager has a specialty, such as software, networks, CD-ROM, printers or components.

He makes sure there is a ready market for the product or service (as with Ascent's power supply units) and a strong management team. Owners and shareholders must put their own money on the line before going to the bank.

The branch imposes strict financial controls on high-tech clients, making them report details of booked orders, cash flow, pricing and credit controls on a monthly basis. Cash flow is especially important because computer companies generally have slim margins, large volumes and rapid inventory turnover, as high as 24 times a year.

"Because of the constant change, you're more closely involved with your clients," Mr. Lunny says. "You can't wait three months to find out a company is pricing its products wrong."

The branch also monitors effective net worth (assets minus liabilities) and requires companies to maintain a minimum equity base.

Access to loans — Mr. Lunny's calling card — opens the doors to selling other bank services such as automated payrolls, credit checks, foreign exchange conversion, export letters of credit and cash management. High-tech companies make up 10 per cent of the branch's commercial loans, but half its overall revenue.

One client is Althon Inc., a Markham-based distributor of computer components such as video boards to systems developers in Canada and the United States. Launched four years ago by Hong Kong immigrants, the company is well capitalized and does not need bank financing. Its Canadian sales are $10-million a year.

Still, Mr. Lunny's staff has worked with Althon to manage its cash, reduce foreign exchange costs and give timely credit information.

"Through the bank, we know exactly how other companies are doing and whether we should supply them," says Althon director Rex Tsang. "Without their support, we couldn't come up with quick decisions — and in this business, it's just a blink before other people are supplying your customers."

Another customer is Digitcom Telecommunications Canada Inc., which markets voice mail equipment and runs a service bureau. President Jeffrey Wiener was surprised when the TD's Markham branch approached him to sell its services.

"I always thought of banks as a big bureaucracy. Why would they care for a small account like mine?" says Mr. Wiener, whose midtown office is a half-hour drive from Markham.

Only 25, he started Digitcom in 1991 and has six employees in Toronto and Montreal. He did not require any financing until recently, when he applied for a $25,000 loan to purchase equipment.

His downtown bank asked for a full financial audit, which would have cost $6,000 to $7,000, Mr. Wiener says. But Mr. Lunny's branch processed the loan quickly, approving it in principle in two days. It also offered to help him lower costs through currency hedging. Digitcom distributes Octel voice mail systems, imported from California.

But Ascent Power Technology, one of Mr. Lunny's first high-tech financings, is still one of his proudest accomplishments. It's unusual for Canadians to buy out a floundering division of a Japanese parent and make it profitable.

Ascent, with sales of $8.5-million last year, has made a profit since day one. The firm employs 100 people, including 21 development engineers.

With orders booked a year ahead, it recently took over a neighbouring building for an expanded production line.

But with such rapid growth, Ascent is pushing the limits for bank financing and needs an equity partner to replace Murata.

"Our five-year projections are great," says Mr. Rokas. "But without more money, we're going to get stuck."

Finding new equity will take the company three to six months, a time period the bank agrees is reasonable.

"We're offering to bridge the gap between conventional bank financing and what they require in an increased equity base," says Mr. Lunny. "Because of our understanding of the industry, we have a higher comfort zone."

Bank financing has fed the company's growth from inception, but now Ascent must fly on its own fuel.

SOURCE: Ellen Roseman, *The Globe and Mail*, 8 November 1993, p. B6. Reprinted with permission from *The Globe and Mail*.

A Foundry Finds Its Way

THOM SANTOS, president of a small aluminum foundry, figured his die-casting shop was a solid money-maker — until he ran the costs through his new computer model.

The computer showed that the process needed a lot of maintenance because the dies — the metal moulds that form aluminum replicas — were wearing out quickly. Setting up machinery for each product ate up time. To Mr. Santos' surprise, the activity was a loser.

Mr. Santos, president of Brampton Foundries Ltd., immediately started hunting for cost-cutting measures. But the exercise also confirmed that he had a powerful analytical tool on his hands.

The computer model is based on a new accounting approach called activity-based costing, or ABC. "ABC is a wonderful way to assess what value-added is — and isn't," says Mr. Santos, whose company is part of the Toronto-based Indal Ltd. group.

Still new to Canada, ABC helps managers figure out how much it really costs to make things and service customers. Traditional accounting spreads the great lump of overhead costs across everything the company produces. But ABC breaks down these items and attaches them to specific activities — whether the expense of setting up machinery for a new line or the cost of processing orders for an individual customer.

With this information in hand, managers can zero in on the problem. In Mr. Santos' case, it meant going to the die-casting operators for solutions.

"You can't run a machine for 10 years and not be an expert. Tell an operator what's driving the costs and he'll find a way. But nobody had told him before that there was a problem."

ABC is becoming standard practice at Indal, which has 28 subsidiaries, 8,000 employees in Canada and the United States, and annual sales of about $1-billion. (Indal is in the process of being sold to MB Caradon PLC by a unit of RTZ Corp. PLC of Britain.) Brampton Foundries, with 85 employees and roughly $10-million in annual sales, is one of 12 Indal companies that use it.

It started when John Whitworth, a cost management consultant at Indal, was casting about for techniques to sort out the group's winners and losers. He called in Paul Sharman, president of Focused Management Information Inc., an Oakville, Ont., consulting firm specializing in ABC.

Mr. Sharman says the only companies that can't learn something from ABC are those that focus on a single product with a simple production process — like an ore processor.

Indal has used it to help subsidiaries get a better handle on costs and improve bottom lines. But in some cases, the data pointed to even tougher solutions: Indal closed one whole unit in Georgia and one of three plants run by another unit in Pennsylvania.

For a company that lost $58-million in 1992, shucking off units that can't be turned around is crucial. Still, Mr. Whitworth says, that's a "solution of last resort. It's very expensive — in economic terms and social impact."

At Brampton Foundries, located northwest of Toronto, the transformation in the approach to costs has paralleled a revolution in the foundry process, which involves taking carefully designed and tooled shapes and making aluminum copies.

With one method, called sand casting, the foundry creates a mould of the shape by packing damp sand around it; then molten metal is poured into the mould. In the permanent mould method, steel replaces the sand. The die casting process also uses hard steel, but this time the hot aluminum is injected under pressure into a shaped cavity.

All this used to happen in bleak surroundings. On first visiting the plant in 1988, Indal manager Eugene Genin felt he was "walking into a Dickens novel. There were shafts of sunlight piercing the black dust. All that was missing was the child labour."

The casting process was considered an art that could be mastered only by old-style craftsmen. Sand-casting specialists would judge the moisture content of the sand by running their hands through it. Products that weren't good enough were scrapped and the aluminum melted down again for another try.

Today, most basic machinery is the same, but the company has added statistical process controls. Probes linked to computers now measure the moisture of the sand. If the machinery isn't ready to cast the aluminum to the specified shape and quality, computers don't let the process begin until it is.

Just as the "black magic" of the foundry floor has given way to science, Mr. Genin says, so have the old systems of measuring costs and setting prices.

"Every product is custom-made, so it has a unique price; you can make a lot or lose a lot. Smart people understand their costs and can compete by losing the bad jobs and getting the good jobs."

That's been the contribution of ABC. Brampton Foundries has been using the method only since last spring, but Mr. Santos says it's been a big factor in winning $1.5-million worth of new business.

In one case, a Japanese electrical equipment manufacturer decided to test the abilities of the Ontario foundry against its traditional supplier, an affiliated company in Japan. It gave Brampton a worn-out die and a couple of castings to replicate.

A few days later, Mr. Santos returned with the original castings and ones his foundry had reproduced — with tape concealing which was which. The Japanese executive examined the dies and declared, " 'You boys are getting awfully close to Japan.' "

When he pulled off the tape, the "awfully close" version turned out to be from Japan; the better one came from Brampton. Mr. Santos got the order, and the Japanese company has just given him another four dies to copy.

But getting the right product — an engineering challenge — was only part of the job. Mr. Santos had to get the right price too — one that would beat the competition, but let the foundry make a profit.

That's where ABC came in. As the foundry's engineers worked out technical details for meeting the product specifications, they had access to the computer model that told them how much it would cost the foundry to make the casting.

Better yet, they could test any number of "what if" alternatives. If there were two ways to change one phase of the foundry process and each would cost $1,000, the model could tell them the payback on each option. If different changes could be made at different stages of the process, the model would point to which they ought to make first — the ones with the biggest payback.

The new system affects customer relationships in other ways. "If you know that it costs $680 to set up the machinery, you're not going to take an order for 100 $5 parts," Mr. Whitworth says. "But traditional accounting might say there was a margin of $2.35 on each part."

That doesn't necessarily mean turning customers away. But with the right numbers, salespeople can offer discounts on bigger orders, knowing the sale will be profitable.

All this is a big leap for the foundry business, which has been around so long veterans like to call it "the world's second-oldest industry."

In Mr. Santos' view, it's also been a brutal industry that has thrived by "beating up" workers, running hot, dirty, dark plants and using tough-as-nails foremen to extract every ounce of effort. Worse, it has usually expected customers to modify their needs to suit what the foundries could deliver.

That, Mr. Santos says, is why the industry is in trouble in Canada, no matter what metal it moulds. It won't get any easier in the future.

Many of Brampton's long-time customers still have fairly simply needs that can be easily met. But Mr. Santos figures that the more demanding customers he's looking for — the one who will push him to innovate — stand a better long-term chance of survival.

If he can deliver the right quality at the right price, they won't turn to suppliers from Mexico, where low wages, low benefits and more relaxed pollution rules give old-style foundries an edge.

Mr. Santos believes ABC is pivotal in preventing this erosion. He began his career as an accountant reared in the old school, but this is the most effective tool he's wielded. "Everything I was trained in was a good general background, but it had nothing to do with what I'm doing now."

SOURCE: Bruce Little, *The Globe and Mail*, 5 October 1993, p. B6. Reprinted with permission from *The Globe and Mail*.

‖ *Questions*

1. What is driving each of the entrepreneurs in the companies profiled?
2. What drives you? What is your vision?
3. Complete the two forms in exercise 3.1 and 3.2: Managing Your Personal Budget and Finances, and Statement of Personal Current Financial Sources. You must be able to manage your personal finances before you can manage those of your business.
4. Begin to research the start-up costs for your business, including equipment, leases, inventory, advertising, and so forth.
5. What are banks looking for?
6. Where is the best place for you to get your money?
7. Make a list of all the people you and your family know and keep adding to this list. Begin talking about your business to these people and tell them you are looking for investors.
8. Do a preliminary Sources and Application of Funds Statement (exercise 3.3).
9. Do a preliminary Opening Balance Sheet (exercise 3.4).
10. Do a preliminary Projected Income Statement (exercise 3.6).
11. Do a preliminary Cash Flow Forecast (exercise 3.7).
12. Do a preliminary Ending Balance Sheet (exercise 3.5), as at the end of year one.

MARKETING
AND FINDING
A NICHE

Marketing is about three words:

NEEDS

SATISFYING

BENEFITS

You must find a need, and you must satisfy the need with a product and/or service that translates into a benefit to you and your customer. Finding a need means finding gaps in the market. Gaps are market segments where needs have not been satisfied. If you are satisfying the needs of the customer in a very different way than the competition is, then you are creating a niche and you will be successful in your business venture.

Power marketing is a tool that will help you exploit these gaps in the marketplace. Power marketing is like a huge funnel equipped with a series of idea filters. You pour everything into this funnel — your goals, personality, market problems, hopes, fears, industry data, market needs — and a viable business idea drains out at the bottom. Carrying out this process gives you the knowledge of where you are going. This knowledge gives you the power and direction to find a market niche.

Once you have identified a market gap and selected your product, you must plan and implement methods of satisfying your customers with consistent benefits. You must also add new benefits at regular intervals. This is what will make you unique in the marketplace. Let your customers know what is available for them. Keep them informed through regular communications, via such methods as a customer newsletter, on-premise announcements, articles in area newspapers, or justifiable advertising. Listen to your customers. Listening does not mean waiting for your turn to talk (verbally or in print). Listening means asking constantly, *hearing* what their needs are, and then satisfying the needs. To stay in business you must satisfy needs at a profit. Profit is not just a benefit for you, it is your survival. However, profit does not ensure continued survival. Survival can be ensured only by constantly satisfying needs and adding benefits for your customers in a growth-market segment.

An excellent example of creating and maintaining a market niche is provided by the artisans of St. Jacobs, Ontario. They each have four or five sources of income and add new benefits for their customers regularly. The artisans are unique because they provide the following range of products and services:

- Handcrafted items for retail customers
- Custom crafted items for retail customers
- Custom crafted items for industry/construction customers
- Raw materials for retail customers
- Evening craft courses for customers living within a half-hour drive (Kitchener/Waterloo)
- Weekend craft courses for customers living further away (Toronto, Detroit, Ottawa, etc.)

When we owned accounting and consulting businesses, we provided the following services to small businesses:

- Newsletter to provide information and highlight client successes/new ventures, and to promote new business for each client
- Reward and recognition to clients who referred new clients to us (we rewarded by not increasing the annual fees of the existing client)
- Seminars for clients on marketing strategy, balancing work and family life, time management, management and supervisory skills, investment strategy, new tax laws, etc.
- Individual in-house training to assist businesses with growth and change
- Individual consulting with business owners to assist with their unique situations, needs, and problems
- Hand-signed birthday cards and Christmas cards with a personal note in a humorous teasing format
- Reminder telephone calls regarding the information we needed from them to do their tax returns
- Personal meetings to teach clients about financial statements and to review their financial statements and tax returns
- Accounting and tax services

We were never concerned about our competition even though there were thousands of consultants and accountants listed in the telephone book. We created our own niche. The result was that satisfied clients referred new clients regularly.

Before getting started, you are well-advised to conduct a market survey, test-market your idea, and finally, create a marketing plan.

❙❙ *Market Survey*

There are many ways to do a market survey but the purpose remains the same. The purpose is to identify customers. When you have 5,000 customers who will use your service or purchase your product, then you are ready to start your business. You find these customers by talking to people and urging those people to talk to other people. You do not have a business until you have customers!

This stage is often bypassed because of the fear of spending money or the fear of someone copying your idea. Neither is a valid excuse. Spending money and time up front to confirm the viability of an idea is far less costly than starting a business doomed to failure and losing every penny of your assets. Protecting your rights to your idea can be done by mailing a written detailed copy of the plans, drawings, and model to your lawyer, having arranged beforehand that the envelope or package will not be opened until needed to prove to a court your ownership of the idea. Also, mail an identical package to yourself and leave it sealed when it arrives complete with postage date stamp. If your idea warrants a patent or copyright, the patent fee is money well spent. Be aware, however, that another person need only make one simple change to avoid breaching your patent rights. If there is a way around, a copy-cat will find it. Sometimes it may be better to concentrate your efforts and money on getting to the marketplace quickly, rather than pursuing the long, expensive process of securing a patent or copyright, since you must divulge all details and drawings to make it a legal protection. Thus, you are giving away all of the secrets of your idea and it becomes public information. Think of it this way: would you rather let someone taste your unique cake or would you rather give them the secret recipe?

Market surveys can be as sophisticated as election polls or as simple as talking to your neighbour. Contact accomplished retirees and senior citizens and tap into their wealth of experience. It is not sufficient to know whether people will buy a product or service. You must know whether they will buy *your* product or service and why. People do not change their buying habits easily or quickly. You must obtain assurance that your idea is unique enough or improved enough to cause change in people. Word your written or verbal survey or interview carefully. Be positive that you are not just seeking the results you want instead of the truth. Never be discouraged by a few negative results or comments. Listen and use results to perfect your idea. Preparing a marketing plan without doing a market survey is like putting a cake in the oven to bake without first putting the batter into a cake pan.

▮▮ *Test Marketing*

It may be necessary to have a drawing, a model, or a written description to present to would-be consumers and experienced business people you will brainstorm with. Your sample can be as sophisticated as an actual prototype or as simple as a model made out of clay. Some people respond better to visual presentations and others respond better to written or verbal descriptions. A combination may be necessary. Listen carefully and learn from both positive and negative comments, reactions, and suggestions. This test-market stage need not be expensive but is definitely needed.

Many products and services lend themselves easily to testing sales potential at flea markets, exhibitions, fairs, conventions, or trade shows. This step is not expensive and will give you measurable results.

┃┃ *Marketing Plan*

The first step in creating the marketing plan is an exploratory assessment. It is a very important fact-finding adventure. You are exploring the needs, problems, and niches of the marketplace to determine the possibilities. You have an idea. Ideas are fabulous, but until you gather enough facts, and apply enough logic to transform an idea into a plan — a statement of mission — you must treat your idea with as much importance as you give a stone in the middle of a gravel pit. Over 80 per cent of the population dream of being their own boss and owning a business.* Every one of those people have an idea, and some have many ideas. Ideas are a dime a dozen — an old cliché, but it is statistically true. What is valuable are the ideas that satisfy a need in the market and translate into a profit.

Do not start your business until you can answer the five basic questions: who, what, when, where, and why.

WHO:

- Who requires your product/service?
- Who will benefit from your product/service and how?
- Who is providing this product/service to the market already?
- Who are the competition leaders and what are their strengths/weaknesses?

---

* Based on an unpublished August 1993 survey by Geo Parmers Inc., Toronto, conducted in six major North American cities.

- Who is your target market? (For example, McDonald's target market is not families, it is the children, and they bring the rest of the family.)
- Who will sell your product/service?
- Who will distribute your product or information about your service?
- Who will transport/deliver your product/service?
- Who will provide you with the components necessary for your product/service?
- Who can you network with to build your business? (This is often called cross-merchandising. For example, Shoppers Drug Mart gives out discount coupons for admission to Canada's Wonderland. This action promotes both businesses.)

WHAT:

- What is the description of your product/service idea?
- What makes your idea unique or improved?
- What is the need in the marketplace?
- What price is the market willing to pay?
- What size is your potential market?
- What is the profile of your potential market?
- What is the profile of your potential customer/client (age, income, type/size of company, etc.)?
- What percentage of the target market can you realistically obtain?
- What are the trends in your potential market?
- What is the market's growth potential?
- What effect will market growth have on your share?
- What fee will you charge for your product/service to make a profit but remain competitive?
- What are your expected annual sales for the first five years?
- What are the problems or deficiencies in the current provision to the market?
- What can you do to address and overcome the problems or deficiencies?
- What portion of the market is satisfied with their current service?
- What benefit can you provide potential customers/clients?
- What add-on services or products can you provide?
- What are the projected changes in your target market over the next decade?

- What will you do to respond to these projected changes?
- What is the most time- and cost-efficient method of selling to your target market?
- What will it cost to reach your target market?
- What is the profit margin in this industry?
- What do you think is a reasonable profit margin?
- What financing or leasing arrangements will you provide to your customers?
- What after-sales service will be required and how will you provide it?
- What is your emotional devotion and commitment to your idea for this product/service?

WHERE:

- Where is your product/service needed (locally, nationally, internationally)?
- Where are your potential customers/clients?
- Where and how much are these customers spending now, annually?
- Where do your competition market their product/service now?
- Where and how will you market your product/service?
- Where will you sell your product/service?
- Where will you advertise your product/service?
- Where will you promote your product/service?
- Where will you take action to raise the public image of your firm?
- Where will you provide after-sales service?
- Where can you obtain free advertising?
- Where can you best conduct a survey and test-market your product/service?

WHEN:

- When can you begin to service your target market?
- When can you add on services to maintain your market?
- When can you increase your market?
- When will projected changes in your target market occur?
- When and how will you listen to your customers/clients to obtain feedback?
- When and how will you maintain contact with your customers/clients?

WHY:

- Why should a business or individual come to you?
- Why should customers/clients continue to come to you?
- Why should customers/clients refer additional businesses to you?

11 *Creating Associations*

Creating associations is an important element of any marketing strategy — and a key to success. Associations are created in four ways, each
for a different reason: (1) networking with other small businesses, (2)
networking with big companies, (3) franchising, and (4) co-operatives
(a new form of partnership). The first two are informal methods of
creating associations, and your success depends on your ability to network. The last two forms of associations, franchising and co-operatives, are very formal methods.

■■ Networking

Networking is defined as *talking to people with a purpose*. The *purpose* is
to form associations for mutual benefit. One excellent example of this is the
association between Canada's Wonderland and Shoppers Drug Mart.
The drugstore gives away Canada's Wonderland discount coupons to
its customers. Wonderland benefits because more people are encouraged to visit the park. Shoppers Drug Mart benefits because people
intending to visit Canada's Wonderland are likely to visit the nearest
store giving out coupons, and while they are in the store they are likely
to make a purchase. For families planning to travel, a stop at a drugstore
is usually on their priority list.

Networking is not to be confused with the massive influx of multilevel marketing (MLM) companies who prefer to be known as network
marketing firms. The distributors of MLM try to sell products to everyone they know and meet and attempt to recruit their buyers to do the
same and share the profit.

Small businesses and professionals create a networking association
with others who are in touch with their target market. Accountants
may refer clients to lawyers they respect, who in return will refer clients
to the accountant. No fee is charged for the referral — the benefit is

future referrals back. Pizza delivery outlets may offer video store discount coupons to their customers as an added benefit, and in turn the video store offers pizza discounts to their customers. This effective advertising method allows both businesses to expand their customer base at a relatively low cost because they are reaching the target market.

Some individuals and small businesses create an association with a large business or several large businesses as a direct source of income. Large corporations in the 1990s have begun to reduce costs by subcontracting work that was previously done in-house. This subcontract work can be done by a small business at a profit.

▮▮ Franchising

Much has already been written about franchises as one possible way of forming an association. Before you consider a franchise, make sure that the seller (the franchisor) has a well-documented business plan.

▮▮ Co-operatives

Little has been written about co-operatives. We think that co-ops could play a significant role in the restructuring of Canada's economy. According to the Ontario Worker Co-op Federation, Canada already has 7,000 co-operatives involving more than 12 million people in their membership and holding over $100 billion in assets. These Canadian co-operatives employ over 125,000 people and show total annual sales of over $15.3 billion. Each of these co-operatives started as a small business or a combination of small businesses. These small businesses are now definitely big businesses.

There are two types of co-operatives. The first is traditional co-ops such as credit unions, housing co-ops, co-op retail stores, and farmers' co-ops. These traditional co-ops all supply services to members; however, members are not actually employed by the co-op.

The second type is the worker co-op. This is the trend that we feel will gain more popularity in the 1990s and on into the next century as unemployment and job scarcity increase. Worker co-operatives are businesses that are owned and controlled by the members. The main purpose of a co-op is to provide employment for its members. Each member pays a membership fee, and each has one vote regardless of how many dollars they have invested in the co-op. The co-op's assets are collectively owned, and surplus earnings are allocated to the work-ers according to policies instituted by the co-op. Earnings are often distributed in proportion to hours worked by members. At least three people are needed to incorporate the co-op under the Co-op Act. There is renewed interest in the 1990s in worker co-operatives, both by gov-ernment and citizens, due to the recession and massive job lay-offs that have occurred.

ADVANTAGES OF WORKER CO-OPERATIVES

- *Stable employment.* As long as the business is able to pay wages, there is little incentive to lay workers off.
- *Community control.* The co-op is started and maintained by residents of the community, who will not act like multinational firms (who relocate plants and offices with no regard for the effect on the workers or community). The social conscience of the co-op members allows for community control.
- *Ability of owners to contribute to the federal Unemployment Insurance plan.* Sole proprietors or owners of a business are not entitled at any time to contribute to or collect from UIC. Co-op workers, however, are eligible.
- *Co-operative entrepreneurship.* Small business owners often feel isolated and overwhelmed with the responsibilities of decision making. Own-ers/employees of co-ops share the decision making and do not feel isolated. Yet they are able to maintain the role of an entrepreneur.
- *Increased productivity.* There is increased productivity when the employees are also the owners of businesses.
- *Flexible employment.* Co-op employees enjoy the same flexibility as small business owners. During busy times, this does mean the freedom to work 80 hours a week. However, there is also the freedom to choose their own hours, job share, and take leaves of absence.
- *Profits from the investment stay in the community.* Profits are paid to the owners/employees, who spend their money on other products and services within their community.
- *Favourable regulations around raising capital.* Government regulations around raising capital from investors favour co-ops. If they plan to sell shares to more than 10 investors, they must file an offering statement with the government. The cost for doing this is low and enables them

to raise capital from a large number of investors. Traditional business corporations must file a prospectus with the provincial Securities Commission if they plan to sell shares to more than 25 investors. This process is costly and forces small businesses to be confined to raising large amounts of capital from just a few investors.

Figure 4.1 compares the specific characteristics of co-operatively owned businesses and traditional companies so that you may see the advantages and disadvantages of each.

Community-owned businesses are an alternative to co-operatives, and they represent a trend that is gaining some attention. If this concept does not end up as a bureaucratic make-work project for a chosen few, it may gain wide acceptance.

Figure 4.1. SPECIFIC CHARACTERISTICS OF CO-OPERATIVELY OWNED BUSINESSES AND COMPANIES

	CO-OPERATIVE	COMPANY
NUMBER OF ASSOCIATES	At least 3	1 or more
INCORPORATION	Incorporated under the Co-op Act	Incorporated under Company Act
SHAREHOLDER'S RESPONSIBILITY	Limited liability; co-op is an entity distinct from its members	Limited liability; company is an entity distinct from its shareholders
SHAREHOLDERS	It is a condition of membership that a member be employed by the co-operative; at least 75% of the employees ar members of the co-op	Owners do not have to work in the business
DECISIONS	Members/owners make the decisions concerning wages, benefits, time off, working conditions, and other policies	Owners take all decisions; employees are not involved in orientation of the business
VOTING	One member–one vote	One share–one vote
PRIORITY	Employment security; people before capital	Profits

PROFITS	shared by the members (based on the work they contribute to the business) and/or reinvested in the business	Distributed among shareholders or reinvested in business
POWER	Rests with the members/owners	Rests with the owner
SOCIAL BENEFIT	Job creation; empowerment of workers	
MOTIVATION OF EMPLOYEES	Very high, concerned for their job; increased productivity	Loyalty problem; employees limit their involvement
SHARES	Cannot be transferred; have to be sold to the co-op	Can be transferred
BENEFITS FOR OWNERS	Are eligible for UI	Not eligible for UI
SUCCESS RATE	60% in first 5 years	20% in first 5 years

SOURCE: Ontario Worker Co-op Federation.

SMALL BUSINESS NOTES

📖 Those Daring Canadians

THRIVING SMALL COMPANIES say marketing is the second most important ingredient (after management) in their success. At first glance, Canadian entrepreneurs seem a cautious lot, but many adopt aggressive marketing strategies.

That's one finding of a survey of growing small and medium-sized enterprises by John Baldwin of Statistics Canada.

The 1,500 companies surveyed ranked four marketing strategies on a six-point scale, in which five means crucial and zero means irrelevant.

Most important to them (at 3.57) was the least aggressive strategy —
selling existing products in existing markets. Least important (at 2.7)
was the far more daring — and risky — approach of trying to sell new
products in new markets.

In the middle were two strategies that "contain at least one aspect of
novelty" — selling existing products in new markets (3.11) and selling
new products in existing markets (3.1).

Mr. Baldwin's conclusion: Successful companies don't neglect their
traditional markets, but they place a lot of importance on cracking new
ones. Indeed, they outranked companies in Denmark, Norway, and
Finland in their eagerness to find new customers for their products.

SOURCE: Bruce Little, *The Globe and Mail*, 20 June 1994, p. B6.

📖 Volume Sales

FOR 20 years, Kids Can Press Ltd. occupied small and dingy quarters
across from Honest Ed's bargain emporium on Toronto's Bloor Street.
Then last year, the company bought a building in a nicer neighbourhood and hired four people, raising its staff to 14.

"We had reached a point where we had to make a conscious decision
to pull back or move ahead," president Valerie Hussey says. "We
couldn't stay where we were."

Most entrepreneurial firms face the same dilemma, although few
take two decades to get to that point. Growth hasn't come easily for
Kids Can, a publisher of high-quality children's books by Canadian
writers.

Today, the company is flourishing with annual revenue of $4-million,
including international sales. Success has arrived because the owners
have discarded concepts that didn't work and embraced unorthodox
ideas — such as selling through the Avon catalogue.

"They have taken a company that was losing money five or six years
ago and turned it into a very profitable business," says Mary Hatch,
manager of Toronto-Dominion Bank's commercial banking centre
where Kids Can has an account.

It has been a long slog since 1973, when Kids Can began as a feminist collective producing non-sexist, urban books. The messages — it's okay for girls to play hockey, boys to sew, Mom to work and Dad to stay home — were often simplistic and heavy-handed.

New York-born Ms. Hussey, who has a background in education, joined Kids Can in 1979, just as the collective was falling apart. She asked Ricky Englander, a children's librarian, to join her.

"Both of us shared a vision of producing quality books in the marketplace. The goal of making money came much later," says Ms. Englander, who observes that this is a common pattern in female-owned businesses.

The two partners worked alone, doing all the publishing jobs and drawing a minimum wage until 1986. They also juggled family obligations. Ms. Hussey, 43, has an 11-year-old son and Ms. Englander, 50, has three children aged 19 to 23.

Under their direction, Kids Can changed course. The focus moved from didactic fiction to educational books on crafts, nature and science.

They co-published books with the Royal Ontario Museum, Ontario Science Centre and Ontario Federation of Naturalists. "It's a brilliant idea because they have a sure-fire market," says Judy Sarick, owner of Toronto's Children's Book Store.

Typical of the new slant was *Cat's Cradle, Owl's Eyes: A Book of String Games*, a 1983 bestseller by Camilla Gryski. Her book on making friendship bracelets sold 100,000 copies in 18 months — a huge hit in the Canadian market — and a sequel on "boondoggle" (plastic lace) also did well.

But Kids Can's biggest success was the 1986 publication of *Franklin in the Dark* by Paulette Bourgeois, about a turtle afraid of crawling into his shell. Distributed world-wide and translated into seven languages, the book evolved into a series that sold 1.5 million copies in Canada alone and spun off a push toy and canvas book bag.

Ms. Bourgeois, a Toronto mother of two, had never published before. Today, she has 16 children's books in print and makes a good living from royalties.

Her book caught the attention of Gerry Bridges, marketing manager of Avon Canada Inc. of Montreal. At a toy fair, he asked Kids Can if there was any interest in selling books through the 55,000-strong Avon sales force.

Known for cosmetics, Avon is expanding into videos, toys and vitamins. *Franklin in the Dark* was the first book featured in its catalogue in 1991, eventually selling 50,000 copies there.

For a book publisher used to long runs, Avon's product cycle is very short — about six weeks. It pays in advance, buying huge quantities and demanding quick supply turnarounds if an item sells better than expected.

"We beat them up badly on the price," Mr. Bridges admits, citing high distribution costs. Avon Ladies now visit women's offices as well as selling door to door and they earn lucrative commissions.

When Mr. Bridges first explained how Avon works, "Valerie fell on the floor," he says. "It's very strange for these people to do business that way."

But the arrangement succeeded beyond both parties' expectations. "We don't mind giving a small Canadian publisher an order," he says. "In fact, we wish there were more of them out there."

As Kids Can made a name as a quality publisher, it began adding more people in production, editing, promotion and sales. The owners finally started taking more than the minimum wage.

"We're still a very hands-on operation," Ms. Englander says, "but the structure is in place for us to move out of that role."

Regretfully, she and Ms. Hussey have given up the time-consuming task of sorting through the "slush pile" of unsolicited manuscripts. Many of their books came in that way.

When Kids Can decided to grow last year, it added a full-time manager of special sales. One result was a Burger King promotion, in which 80,000 copies of a toddler title, *Sadie and the Snowman*, were handed out to fast-food patrons in Ontario and Quebec.

Industry colleagues praise the entrepreneurial skills of the Kids Can team.

"They're professional, innovative and international," says Beverley Topping, president of Today's Parent Group, which uses Kids Can books as subscription premiums for its magazine. "And they work really well with their people, who tend to stay with them a long time."

Kids Can offers workers lots of benefits — an employee assistance program, weekly fitness class and fully equipped kitchen. The staff is entirely female, mainly because mostly women apply. Employees often start at low-wage entry-level jobs while being trained for better things.

The owners say their biggest challenge is staying focused on books, rather than straying into multimedia applications, book-and-toy packages and videos.

"We've always been editorially driven," Ms. Englander says. "There are a lot of other things that are really appealing, but we have to pull back and look for the really great publishing idea."

An example is *The Science Book for Girls and Other Intelligent Beings*, by Valerie Wyatt of Victoria. Although some questioned its relevance, the book sold well when published last fall and garnered critical praise.

"We want to do more of the books that sell and make us feel good," Ms. Hussey says. "We take tremendous pride in sending authors a big cheque."

SOURCE: Ellen Roseman, *The Globe and Mail*, 2 May 1994, p. B6. Reprinted with permission from *The Globe and Mail*.

📖 Tubs, Showers and Curtain Calls

GINGER EISEN scored an instant hit when she opened a tiny boutique in Toronto's Yorkville area in 1961, carrying stylish European bathroom fixtures and accessories.

By the late 1980s, as baby boomers installed brass faucets and marble tubs, an expanded Ginger's International Bath Centre employed 52 people and racked up sales of more than $7-million a year. Then the recession hit, housing sales collapsed and so did her business.

One grey morning in November, 1990, she found her store padlocked. The landlord put her into receivership after missing two monthly rent payments.

"It was the most devastating thing in the world," she says about going bankrupt. "I had suppliers I'd been dealing with for 30 years. Some of them were my best friends.

"My pride was smashed and I couldn't go anywhere. I hid for three months."

Today, 76-year-old Ms. Eisen is back in business. At an age when most entrepreneurs would be throwing in the towel, she's selling them again.

Ginger Eisen's Bathrooms in Yorkville's Hazelton Lanes focuses on a growing market, bathroom fixtures for the elderly and disabled — "the physically challenged," she calls them. Her business is not yet profitable, but she's determined to make it work, applying lessons learned from past experience.

"I had to prove you can do it twice — not to anyone else, just to myself. That's the lovely part of being 76. You do things for yourself."

With her vivid red hair and skirts slit to the thigh, Ms. Eisen's looks and energy belie her age. She is now happily remarried after her invalid husband died two years ago, and she heads up Women Entrepreneurs of Canada, a branch of an international organization based in France.

"She's tireless," says long-time supplier Mariza Pal, president of Bath Creations Inc. of Toronto. "She's my example of how you don't grow old as long as you keep working."

David Hanna, a Toronto-Dominion Bank vice-president who deals with Ms. Eisen, calls her "innovative, smart and tough. She knows her customers and what they need. By tapping a select market this time, I think she's found a niche."

To succeed in business after bankruptcy requires an ability to shoulder blame and avoid making the same mistakes again. Ms. Eisen passes those tests easily.

Mistake number one, she says, was not anticipating the 1990 recession. Ginger's was supplying bathroom fixtures to several condominium projects that were halted. "All that inventory and no one to sell it to."

Mistake number two was not listening to her accountant. He said the business was in trouble and should be wound up. She swore she could turn it around.

"I threw away half a million dollars — literally threw it on the floor," she says of her attempt to revive sales with heavy advertising and discount pricing. "It was a terrible time. No one was buying."

When the business was put into receivership, she had been negotiating to sell it to Elte Carpets, an established Toronto retailer. The sale eventually went through, but Ms. Eisen was on the hook to the bank for $2.25-million.

"The first thing I tell entrepreneurs is never to sign a personal covenant. It's a bitter lesson I learned."

Elte bought the company's assets and took on most of the suppliers and staff. Ms. Eisen agreed to stay for three years, was given an office and found she had nothing to do.

"I lasted six months as a consultant," she says. "I was twiddling my thumbs."

Elte president Ken Metrick says he has great respect for Ms. Eisen's retailing skills. "She really did create an industry in Toronto. She's got great style and passion.

"But when you're running a business and someone else takes it over, it's always a difficult situation. Many things had to be changed at once."

Elte is making money with Ginger's Bath Centre, but times are different, Mr. Metrick says. Customers are more practical and buying $600 showerheads instead of $5,000 Jacuzzi tubs: "No one has time to take baths."

Ms. Eisen has never been back to the original store since she left in 1991. It would be too painful, and she's in the new store almost all the time.

That's another lesson she learned: Keep your eye on the ball. It can be dangerous to rely too much on others, especially if they don't have a stake in the business.

"I got too busy," she admits. "I was travelling a lot and I was very involved with Women Entrepreneurs of Canada. I lost control.

"You can blame anyone you like, but in the final analysis you have to face yourself in the mirror and say, 'I didn't keep my finger on the pulse. I left too many things to too many people.' "

Ms. Eisen realizes she waited too long before hiring a strong financial manager. She stuck with her general manager of 26 years, who was a close friend.

The manager later sued Ms. Eisen, who had guaranteed to pay her last year's salary if anything happened to the company. She eventually settled for $65,000, plus legal costs.

"This time, I'll surround myself with people who have specific areas of strength and have money in the business, so they'll watch what goes on."

So far, however, Ginger Eisen's Bathrooms has only one full-time employee and five part-timers. The store is taking a while to find its market.

Ms. Eisen had come upon the idea while travelling through Europe, where she had seen many specialized products for the elderly — extra-low sinks and vanities, soft rubber tubs and grab bars for showers. She felt there was demand in Canada, but Elte nixed the idea.

Striking out on her own, she opened the Hazelton Lanes store in May, 1992. Her children, aged 49 and 51, were horrified.

"They said you can't afford to lose," she recalls. "I told them I was going in with a calculated risk and I can lose only this much."

Opening the store cost $250,000, an amount that came from a refund of prepaid tax and a TD Bank loan. She had no trouble getting credit from the bank and former suppliers, although most wanted cash on delivery at first.

Once the business finds its feet, Ms. Eisen wants to find a younger partner and spend more time with her new husband. Meanwhile, despite long hours and her decision not to take a salary for now, she finds joy in trail-blazing with a new concept.

"Most accidents happen in the bathroom," she stresses. "My idea is to have safe bathrooms for seniors that aren't institutional-looking.

"One of my customers was a blind woman, who had grab bars installed along the hall of her apartment. She was thrilled. It was the first time she could get to the bathroom all by herself."

SOURCE: Ellen Roseman, *The Globe and Mail*, 7 March 1994, p. B6. Reprinted with permission from *The Globe and Mail*.

New Life for a Die-ing Art

IN A JUST-IN-TIME WORLD, there are the quick and the dead. No company appreciates this more than Batesville Casket Co. of Batesville, Ind.

Several years ago, North America's biggest coffin maker embraced ideas of lean inventories and short runs. But the transition was rocky in the metal stamping plant, where towering presses bang out casket lids, handles and other parts.

Several times a day, as production runs changed, workers replaced the 40,000-pound dies that form the metal blanks into parts. It took up to two hours to lasso an unwieldy die, hoist it away with an overhead crane, and jiggle a new one on to the press. Batesville was losing valuable time.

Enter Grant Bibby and his little engineering company, Orchid Automation Group Inc. of Cambridge, Ont. Orchid came up with heavy-duty die carriers — a marriage of structural steel and sophisticated electronic controls — that can pull off a die switch in as little as six minutes.

"We've been able to buy more production time," says Tom Heil, Batesville's senior engineer on the $500,000 project. "Orchid had a good concept and a good price."

Wander around industrial North America and you hear a lot of that talk. Tiny Orchid is a leader in quick die change technology, a fundamental pillar of the flexible factory. It makes products for an impressive roster of big-time players — from auto maker Chrysler Corp. to diversified General Electric Co.

This expertise is winning attention outside manufacturing circles. Orchid is a 1993 finalist in the small-business category for the Canada Awards for Business Excellence, to be handed out tonight in Toronto.

All this from a five-year-old company, with just 40 employees and a share of a non-descript building in a Cambridge industrial park. Orchid's flash comes from its people: 18 employees have engineering degrees and many of the others are skilled, experienced tradesmen.

In an age when software is king, these folks go bonkers about building things. "You can touch what we make — it's a 'real' technology," enthuses Mr. Bibby, founder, president and still only 30. "Manufacturing — I love it," echoes Jan Chmielowski, 42, the vice-president for manufacturing.

Orchid's bright minds are capitalizing on the just-in-time revolution. In the old days, when a product run might last for days, manufacturers didn't worry much about downtime for stamping presses. But today, presses in some plants stop 20 times a day to switch dies. The dies can weigh from 1,000 to 200,000 pounds each.

Orchid's equipment — big metal structures that usually run on tracks — solves the downtime problem. Changeovers that took eight hours are reduced to as little as three minutes. At Batesville Casket, it means stamping presses are running three hours longer during their 16-hour production days.

The systems, controlled by computer technology, also mean more safety and less labour. One worker at a console can do the job of four.

The concept is the brainchild of Mr. Bibby, a quietly intense young man with a thin moustache and prematurely greying hair. A 1986 mechanical engineering graduate from McMaster University, he joined auto parts maker Magna International Inc. after graduation as a stamping press engineer.

After a couple of years, he saw a crying need for systems that could replace dies in a hurry. Magna wasn't prepared to get into that business, so Mr. Bibby, at 24, struck out on his own. (Magna is now a good customer.)

He enlisted six partners, but five were gone after a year. The fit wasn't right, Mr. Bibby says. As new senior managers came on board, they've taken stakes in the business.

Finances were so tight that the founders put up the walls and laid the carpet themselves in the new factory. That saved $20,000. They drew on savings accounts and borrowed against their homes. "It was Avco up to here," says Rob Johnston, 33, who has been with Mr. Bibby since the Magna days and is now manufacturing manager.

After eight months knocking on doors, Orchid landed it first die changing contract at a General Electric motor plant near Chicago. That got the ball rolling. Each satisfied customer provided a reference for the next prospect.

Orchid doesn't have the market to itself. The competition is Atlas Technologies Inc. of Fenton, Mich., a relative giant with 200 employees and annual sales of $25-million (U.S.). Atlas, which makes a range of press equipment, has been in the die change business for 15 years.

Competition between the two is spirited. Ron Demonet, Atlas's sales director, sniffs: "They [Orchid] are a competitor in smaller die change systems, but they don't have much experience on the larger automotive applications."

Mr. Bibby says that's a fair comment — so far. And customers say Orchid has grabbed market share by aggressive pricing, specialization and adaptability. Mr. Heil of Batesville Casket says Atlas didn't get to bid on his job: "Atlas charges a consulting fee prior to bidding. I felt I was smart enough to come up with the concept myself."

One way Orchid competes is by offering total solutions to a company's needs in changing, storing, retrieving, cleaning and maintaining dies. It builds multilevel storage units that can reach to the ceiling. It can, in fact, design and equip an entire just-in-time factory based on its automated systems.

Now, it's moving one step beyond its die niche into robotic systems that can transfer parts between stamping presses at 2½ times human speed.

The Orchid team follows through with attentive service. "I've never seen anyone give the support in installation and follow-up that they do," says Mark Harris, manager of a Speed Queen Co. clothes drier factory in Searcy, Ark.

"They don't feed you a line of bull," says Mr. Harris, explaining that Orchid came in on its own and updated a piece of its equipment at no cost. His factory contains $1-million (U.S.) in Orchid technology.

A walk around Orchid is a tour through new and old economies. In the design area, engineers tap away at CAD terminals. On the production floor, millwrights complete the final assembly of a new die cart. Many jobs, like welding and machining, are farmed out.

"If we can subcontract and buy something, that's what we'll do," Mr. Bibby says. "Otherwise, we'd need millions of dollars of capital equipment. This way, we sink it all into computers and people."

Finding those people is getting tougher. Mr. Bibby expects to more than double his engineering team within two years. But he likes to hire seasoned people, and they're in short supply. So Orchid has hired a head-hunter to seek out recruits already employed elsewhere.

With growth has come a stronger bottom-line orientation. The company has made money the past two years, and Mr. Bibby is aiming higher. Orchid needs to attract new equity to finance expansion, including plans for a German sales office. (It has one outside venture capital shareholder.) A new plant three times the present size is also in the works.

Mr. Bibby remains committed to manufacturing in Canada — even though 90 per cent of sales are in the United States. That weighting partly reflects the U.S. economy's size, but there's another factor: "People don't believe a company is the best when it's next door. You have to establish your record elsewhere."

Orchid has consolidated its sales and marketing in Nashville, providing a convenient window on the U.S. South's manufacturing corridor.

But everything is made in Canada. Mr. Bibby feels this country still enjoys a comparative advantage in skilled workers.

Not that Orchid has ignored its home market. A couple of kilometres away, across the industrial park from its plant, is the bumper factory of auto parts maker A.G. Simpson Co. Ltd. Among the big yellow presses, an Orchid carrier shuttles 35,000-pound dies back and forth.

Simpson engineer Bruce Fleming says it's a big improvement from hauling dies around with forklift trucks. That process is not only slow; it was banging up the new cast-iron dies.

Mr. Fleming says Atlas also bid for the job — and pricing was close. But Orchid offered proximity and alert service. "With these guys," he says, nodding at Mr. Bibby and Mr. Johnston, "you get the support. In this industry you've got to have that."

SOURCE: Gordon Pitts, *The Globe and Mail*, 30 November 1993, p. B22. Reprinted with permission from *The Globe and Mail*.

A Roll Player Wins a Slice of the Pie

HENRY WONG was one frustrated food manufacturer. He was doling out thousands of dollars to some store chains to stock his new line of pizza snacks, but with no impact on sales.

To make matters worse, the Niagara Falls businessman was locked in a trademark tug of war with U.S. food giant Pillsbury Co. over rights to the product's name, "pizza rolls."

To settle the issue, Mr. Wong got a face-to-face meeting with the president of Pillsbury Canada Ltd. Surprisingly, the two men hit it off — both had grown up in St. Catharines, a 15-minute drive from Niagara Falls.

In fact, Robert Hawthorne had hung around the Wong family's restaurant as a teenager, and "some kid" had asked him to leave a few times for being rowdy. That kid was Henry Wong. "Those memories broke the ice," Mr. Wong chuckles.

It was also a breakthrough for Mr. Wong's young company, Food Roll Sales (Niagara) Ltd. of Niagara Falls. Within months of that 1988 meeting, it had a deal to supply its products for Pillsbury's own label and to be the sole registered user of the "pizza roll" trademark in Canada.

That contract laid the basis for Mr. Wong's sales strategy. Instead of marketing under his own label — the dream of many entrepreneurs — he makes his rolls for the private labels of other processors and retailers. This sidesteps the steep listing fees that chains can charge for the privilege of taking up shelf space.

"It doesn't matter if you have a good food product. If you don't have the funds, you don't get into the food chains," says Mr. Wong, 46. "That's why we stopped dealing directly with them."

The arrangement allowed Pillsbury — which takes 50 per cent of Mr. Wong's sales — to expand its product line in the competitive pizza-snack market. For Mr. Wong, it means adhering to Pillsbury's way of manufacturing. But annual revenue for his eight-year-old company is nearly $3-million — and it is profitable.

"Henry gained a high-quality customer — we pay our bills," says Mr. Hawthorne, now chief operating officer for Pillsbury Co. in Minneapolis. "He also got out of the headaches of trying to sell the product to various retail chains — which we knew how to handle."

Mr. Wong always was an enterprising type. He came to Canada at 12 with his family from Hong Kong. Through most of the 1970s, he managed the Cozy Restaurant and Tavern owned by his father in St. Catharines.

But he had other ventures, such as running an import-export company. The company received a $65,000 loan from the Federal Business Development Bank, but the venture failed after two years. "We paid the FBDB back even though we went bankrupt," Mr. Wong says.

That track record helped when he moved into food processing. One day in 1985, he was making connections at a New Jersey airport when he overheard someone raving about pizza finger food they had tasted in a bar. "They described it as an Italian egg roll or Chinese pizza."

When he got home, Mr. Wong asked an Italian friend to bring over his mother's homemade spaghetti sauce. They cooked the sauce with vegetables in a wok, added pepperoni and mozzarella cheese, then rolled the ingredients in egg roll wrappers before deep-frying them. The pizza roll was born.

Mr. Wong spent $500 whipping up rolls to give to restaurants and bars. "Within a few weeks, they called to order. We delivered them in the back seat of a Honda Civic."

In the beginning, overhead costs were low because the rolls were produced in the basement of the restaurant. But as orders grew, he bought a food-processing plant in Niagara Falls.

Mr. Wong put up $100,000 and raised $100,000 from 10 investors under a now-defunct Ontario tax incentive program. (The investors still own 45 per cent of the firm.) The FBDB provided a $275,000 loan for plant and equipment.

Mr. Wong was not as lucky in marketing. He avoided listing fees to get his product into some Ontario food chains, but had to fork over $15,000 to three chains in the Buffalo, N.Y., area.

But Food Roll Sales had not carefully researched retail practices in the United States. Its pricing did not factor in fees for warehousing, advertising and promotional allowances. It lost about 2 cents on every roll it sold.

"We were green. We went in there blind," Mr. Wong admits.

Breaking into Quebec in 1988 was also a disaster. The company paid $35,000 in fees to three chains, only to find its products "delisted" within a year because of low sales.

"We were great at manufacturing but we weren't as good at marketing because we didn't have enough people," says Gregory Parker, vice-president of Food Roll Sales.

The Pillsbury contract relieved that pressure, but added other ones. Mr. Wong had to conform to new production standards, and invested $150,000 in equipment and renovations.

Pillsbury engineers and quality control experts came aboard for several months to teach practices for improving production, inventory control and sanitation. They told the company to buy metal detection machinery to guard against metal shavings from the mixers. They asked for weight checkers to make sure that every box has at least 320 grams of pizza rolls in the four packs.

One thing Pillsbury did not want changed: the rolls were still to be hand-made by Mr. Wong's team, which consists mainly of Asian women.

But he did give up his pizza spice formula in favour of one dictated by Pillsbury — a minor adjustment, he says. He also agreed not to pursue any new grocery chain clients nor to sell pizza rolls in boxes of fewer than 12 units except under the Pillsbury label.

Mr. Wong feels he had little choice but to join up with a "big brother." Still, he is aware of the pitfalls of putting all his egg rolls in one basket. He has other products and other customers, including Pinty's Premium Foods Inc., a St. Catharines processor catering to the food-service trade, and M&M Meat Shops, a Kitchener, Ont.-based frozen-food chain with 123 outlets.

To push sales higher, Mr. Wong has expanded his product line to include Chinese egg rolls. And he has bought a stake in a once-bankrupt company in Niagara Falls that makes other lines of frozen foods.

Now Mr. Wong wants to export again to the United States but under the Pillsbury label. Pillsbury is making presentations to food chains there and — if it gets orders — could launch the product in early 1994.

But Pillsbury already sells a product there under the name pizza rolls. No problem, says the flexible Mr. Wong. "We'll just call them Italian egg rolls."

SOURCE: Shirley Won, *The Globe and Mail*, 15 November 1993, p. B4. Reprinted with permission from the author.

📖 When Support Is a Spinoff

THE NIGHT that movie actor Don Johnson fell to his "death" during the filming of *Guilty as Sin*, Ralph Mills was on hand. All in a day's work for an IBM facilities manager.

It was a fun assignment — monitoring stunts being filmed atop an IBM building in Markham. Yet Mr. Mills knew his was only a bit role. His future at IBM seemed about as promising as that of the doomed movie character.

After 31 years at IBM Canada Ltd., Mr. Mills, 55, saw little prospect of promotion in a company whose business was computers, not managing buildings. His department was being steadily culled, leaving him with less and less to do.

But that was before Mr. Mills became a new breed of manager. Just a few months after the filming, IBM spun off the management of all its facilities — indeed, all its non-computer operations — into a joint venture called Triax Infrastructure Management Corp.

Now a key part of Triax, a re-energized Mr. Mills oversees all of IBM's non-core activities at its Markham facilities, northwest of Toronto. Besides stunt men falling off buildings, he manages mail rooms and photocopiers, security guards and landscapers. What's more, his expertise is being marketed to other companies.

"The thing that has changed for me is that I have to think as an entrepreneur," he says. "I have to be very much concerned about profit and revenue, and deal with IBM as a customer rather than an employer."

Infrastructure management is a mouthful of jargon for a simple idea: many firms today are anxiously focusing on core business, while expanding the range of activities handed over to outsiders. Triax, in business since July 1, is betting companies will outsource everything except their core activities to one contractor.

For a company like IBM, Triax's first customer and minority owner, it means tens of millions of dollars. The company has already used outsourcing and workplace redesign to cut occupancy costs by $40-million over four years; Triax says it can make more big reductions.

For starters, IBM has cut the costs of employing Mr. Mills and 29 others in its facilities management department who went over to Triax. So, is infrastructure management just another way to lower body count?

"I used to think that," Mr. Mills says. "But things have become so complex that it's difficult within a corporate culture to keep up to date with all technology in all the different businesses.

"We find that suppliers provide us better service cheaper because they're focused on their specific little piece of the industry."

The new approach is mainly a tool for big companies, says Triax president Paul Gooderham, formerly with Ainsworth Electric Co. Ltd., a large Toronto-based contractor and Triax's majority owner. A company needs to have a lot of infrastructure to make it worthwhile to hire a company like Triax.

He sees it as an evolution beyond property managers, who focus on the needs of landlords, and facilities managers, who manage properties for owners or major tenants. Infrastructure managers look at a client's total occupancy — all the issues, problems and costs involved in occupying space to run a business.

That might mean negotiating leases, handling repair and maintenance, or setting up and running the cafeteria. It could include snow plowing, shipping, secretarial services, fleet management — even day care.

For IBM, it is the outside management of almost everything that isn't directly related to making, selling or servicing computers and computer products.

Well before Triax was born, Mr. Mills had seen the handwriting on the wall. Since 1989, his facilities management staff had fallen to 30 from 130 people.

"The concentration has been on downsizing and outsourcing, so you start to get used to a culture of having your arms and legs chopped off," he says. "And you wonder how long it's going to be before everything gets totally outsourced."

When the opportunity arose to go over to Triax with his colleagues, he jumped at it.

So far, Triax, based in North York, Ont., has landed only one job — its five-year contract with IBM. And this is proving to be a trial by fire. Part of the mandate is reorganizing office space in two enormous buildings in Markham.

Some people have left IBM as it struggled through tough times, which means the company doesn't need as much space in its leased headquarters. So about 1,000 employees will move to another building.

Integrating the newcomers means moving everyone in the building. Between now and early next year, 3,000 IBM employees will change places.

Triax is managing the move, but also recreating the process of moving people inside IBM. The task involves everything from re-engineering the workplace to soothing bruised egos of employees bumped to smaller offices.

"So far it is moving with a degree of precision. We have not missed any schedules," says project manager Sid Livermore, one of the IBM people monitoring Triax's work. "There's a sense of order, a sense of a critical path, of project control."

That's different than if IBM were handling it alone, he says. "A year ago we'd have been more casual because it's all one happy family."

It's easier for family members to tell you something can't be done, he says. But an outside contractor looks for solutions. For example, the support services group, which was scattered throughout the old building, wanted to come together in the new one.

Triax found a central spot in the new building. "That's something that would have been very difficult to do a year ago," Mr. Livermore says. "It was a whole lot easier to do in this new environment."

Not nearly so easy — but potentially more lucrative in savings — is the re-engineering of all the company's work space.

Triax is standardizing work spaces, or workstations, in an effort to "manage the churn" of people, says Larry Sadinsky, director of design and consulting services. Regardless of rank, everyone in the company gets either a 48-square-foot cubicle or a 145-square-foot office.

No offices or workstations are unique; therefore, moving costs are virtually eliminated. When an employee is moved, his or her files are boxed and taken to the new location. No walls torn down, no work orders.

The trick is to lay out standardized work spaces in a humanizing manner — and take away unique office space as gently as possible.

"In every case you're dealing with an ego reaction," Mr. Sadinsky says. "The office and rug and furnishings are a measure of status."

The proper approach is to bombard employees with communication about the changes and why they are being made, stroking egos where necessary. It helps if senior executives embrace the change, as they have at IBM.

But, for all the communication, those 48-square-foot cubicles have caused a lot of grumbling, especially from people coming from cubicles nearly twice the size, or who had their own offices.

Some IBM executives find that the issue is even popping up outside the office. One senior manager had to field questions from a local politician who had heard about the cubicles.

Still, adjustments notwithstanding, infrastructure management promises to cut enough costs to give IBM some new life. And for former IBMers who've gone over to Triax, it has expanded horizons after they were dead-ended in careers that were not part of IBM's core.

"It gives you a new breath of life," Mr. Mills says. "I'm very excited about seeing some career opportunities, and being able to use my experience to assist other companies."

SOURCE: Geoffery Rowar, *The Globe and Mail*, 26 October 1993, p. B3. Reprinted with permission from *The Globe and Mail*.

❙❙ *Questions*

1. How did each of the companies profiled create a market niche, or did they?
2. Examine each of the companies. Did they create an association? If so, what form of association did they create and why did they do this?
3. What is driving each of the entrepreneurs profiled?
4. Begin to research and prepare your marketing plan. Start by answering all of the who, what, where, when, and why questions listed earlier in this chapter.
5. How will you create and maintain a market niche for your business idea? What benefits will you add on to your product and service at the beginning and in the future?
6. How will you inform your customers of new benefits? How will you listen and respond to your customers' needs?
7. What associations can you create to develop your business? Why did you choose this path?
8. How will you reward your customers when they refer a new customer to you?

5

THE CUSTOMER
REVOLUTION

The customer is:

- The most important person in your business. He/she is not dependent on you — you are dependent on him/her.

- Not an interruption in your work — he/she is the purpose for it. He/she does you a favour when he/she calls you. You are not doing him/her a favour when you serve him/her. She/he is your guest.

- Part of your business. He/she is not an outsider and not a cold statistic — he/she is a flesh-and-blood human being with feelings and emotions like your own.

- Not a name or a face or a number — he/she is an individual. He/she is not someone to argue or match wits with.

- The person who buys your services and pays your salaries. He/she deserves the most courteous and attentive treatment you can give.

- The very lifeblood of your business. He/she is a person who brings you his/her wants — it is your job to fill them.
- The last person you did business with, be it your employee, your lawyer, your doctor, or your family. The customer is everyone you come in touch with.

The key to success is a happy customer. Remember that business will continue to go where it is invited and stay where it is appreciated. Reputations will continue to be created by many acts — and lost by making just one mistake.

Welcome to the new knowledge-based generation and economy, where the customer is fragile, fickle, has no loyalty, and will change opinions and support without notice. We have become very knowledgeable consumers. With the speed and vastness of media exposure, we learn of new products and services very quickly. We also learn of the competition that inevitably follows rapidly. The customer will buy another product and seek service elsewhere if she or he is not happy.

Two rules for survival:

1. The customer is always right.
2. If you think that the customer is wrong . . . re-read rule #1.

11 *The Power of the Consumer*

Customers are communicating with each other, organizing and grouping to demand what should have been theirs all along. Customers want:

- Quality products and services
- True value for their dollar
- Competitive prices
- Service on time
- Cheerful interaction
- To be listened to
- To be made to feel special
- To be treated with respect and dignity

Consumer reaction studies in recent years have revealed a lot about what customers like and dislike, but there is one important lesson to be learned: customers talk. Being human, we pass information along to others about a good movie, a good restaurant, a reliable baby-sitter, fast service, and so on. If we are happy with a product or service, we will tell three to five people. Each of those people will tell from three to five people, and so on. The picture looks like this after six levels:

Level 1	You Tell	You Tell
Level 2	3 who each tell 3	5 who each tell 5
Level 3	9 who each tell 3	25 who each tell 5
Level 4	27 who each tell 3	125 who each tell 5
Level 5	81 who each tell 3	625 who each tell 5
Level 6	243 who each tell 3	3,125 who each tell 5
Minimum total people	364	3,906

This relay of information has been called word-of-mouth advertising or networking. No matter what name it is given, its power should never be ignored. The chart above shows the results of everyone doing the same volume of word-of-mouth advertising. We all know that some people talk more easily than others, and we all know a few people who come into contact with more people in a day than others. It is safe to assume that at least a few people will tell more than three to five others. Talkers usually associate with talkers, so the impact of this free advertising can be very powerful. After their initial media advertising, many restaurants rely on this human system of referrals, and the same is true of the service industry. However, word of mouth is treated by most companies as an intangible and not measured or rewarded.

Consumer reaction studies also tell us what we do when we are *not* happy with a product or service. Being human, we pass information along to others. We all know bad news travels faster than good news, since negative emotions provide a more intense motivation, and studies have proven that we tell between 10 and 20 people about the terrible service we were given or the problems we experienced with a certain product. This passing of information is still called word of mouth, but it is not called advertising, it is called *destruction*. The power of negative networking looks like this after six levels:

Level 1	You tell	You tell
Level 2	10 who each tell 10	20 who each tell 20
Level 3	100 who each tell 10	400 who each tell 20
Level 4	1,000 who each tell 10	8,000 who each tell 20
Level 5	10,000 who each tell 10	160,000 who each tell 20
Level 6	100,000 who each tell 10	320,000 who each tell 20
Minimum total people	111,111	3,368,421

There is a valuable lesson to be learned here. To survive, you and your new business have no choice but to listen to and satisfy your customers.

11 *Customer Service*

The old way of doing business focused on the features of a product or the mechanics of a service with an emphasis on engineering-type efficiency. The attitude in the product-push environment was, "You can have any colour of product as long as it is black (or a colour that we can mass produce cheaply)." The attitude in the service industry was, "This is what we do, no more and very often less than what we just said we would do."

We have now entered the market-pull economy. Before you begin your business, you must formulate a plan that recognizes the need for your business to be *customer driven*. Your plan must include each of the following strategies:

1. Integrate the customer's needs and desires into the development of the product or service. Market needs determine which products or services are viable. Keep in mind that the target market must be in a growth stage.
2. Formulate a strategy to measure customer satisfaction. This must be an ongoing part of your business activity, not a one-time or occasional effort. You must also recognize, reward, and praise the customers that take time out of their schedule to help you measure their level of satisfaction.

For example, very few auto service centres take the time to telephone a customer within two weeks of servicing their vehicle to ask whether they were happy with the staff and work that was performed. And only a few of those who do follow up recognize, reward, or praise the customer for their time and effort in responding.

Businesses somehow see it as the customer's duty to give them feedback. Soon customers say, "Why should I bother? I am hard pressed to find the time to attend to my own business and personal affairs, why should I spend my time and money to obtain the service and then spend my time and money to appraise the service I paid for in the first place?" Remember that people like to be recognized for their efforts, whether it is in a newsletter, a customer praise board on your premises, or by personal letter from you. Even if a customer complains, thank them for their time and high level of interest in the service or product you provide for them. Ask them questions and listen to their answers.

3. Provide a continuous forum to solicit and listen to customer ideas, recommendations, and reactions. Listening does not mean waiting for your turn to talk. Listening means understanding, empathizing, and taking action. Your business will not create a permanent relationship with a customer unless you do more than collect data or make notes. You must interact. Here, once again, you must reward, recognize, and praise their efforts and time spent.

4. Constantly add benefits to your product, not features. This will set you apart from the competition and copy-cats. It will also endear you to your customers.

5. Under-promise and over-deliver. These are simple, common sense words; however, they are not so simple to follow. Give your customer a commitment as to when you can deliver and what you can deliver, then deliver ahead of schedule with more service than you had promised. A commitment is not just words, a commitment is a "do or die" dedication.

▮▮ Rules of Customer Service

1. Experiment, and if an idea works, stick with it. If it does not work, move on quickly.

2. If an idea works, do it again and again. Do not switch.
3. Anything you do to involve your customers keeps them involved with you.
4. People want a bargain and will come out any time of day, if you entertain them.
5. Servicing your customers is the ticket to your happiness.
6. Earn and develop your customers' trust.

I I The Power of Customer Profiling

There are three kinds of target customers:

1. *Primary.* This target customer is perfect for your business, and could be a heavy user of your service or product/service.
2. *Secondary.* This one almost slips away before you can focus the camera. However, it is important to remember that your secondary target customer will lead you to the third customer — who is invisible at first.
3. *Invisible.* This customer appears after you open the doors.

Identifying your target customer is your key to survival in small business. A customer profile is the tool that draws a circle around that customer. Profiling is all about identifying the needs and behaviour of people (customers). To generate that profile, you will require a combination of demographics — the statistical analysis of age (the baby boomers will continue to affect market trends), sex, income, education, and so on — and psychographics — the analysis of life-style, buying habits, patterns of consumption, attitudes, and so forth.

Why are people buying what they buy? Today, people buy products and services that reflect the needs of their life-styles — not only their sex, age, or income. Households with a double income and no kids have very different spending patterns than households with a double income and two kids. Both households have very different wants and values, which are reflected in their life-styles. Identifying the needs and desires that affect consumer purchases is what psychographics is all about. It is a process of segmenting the population by life-style and values which recognizes that people in each segment have different reasons for making a purchase.

There are a number of proprietary psychographic models in use in North America. Two of the most prominent are the VALS (value and lifestyle) model from SRI International in the U.S. and the Goldfarb model, which is Canadian and which has also been adapted in the U.S. (see figure 5.1).

Figure 5.1. CUSTOMER PROFILE: GOLDFARB PSYCHOGRAPHICS

KEY CHARACTERISTICS FOR EACH OF THE SIX GOLDFARB PSYCHOGRAPHIC SEGMENTS	% OF CANADIAN POPULATION
Day-to-Day Watchers — **Traditional Values** Research purchases. Need to be comfortable with products before purchasing. Early followers as opposed to leaders.	23
Old-Fashioned Puritans — **Very Conservative and Traditional** Home and family oriented. Heavily insured. Tend to resist change.	12
Disinterested Self-indulgents — **Hedonistic** Risk-takers. Like to be on the leading edge of product innovation. Heavy impulse buyers. Travel.	12
Joiner Activists — **Leading Edge Thinkers** Willing to spend. Shop most for clothes. Day-to-Day. Watchers follow this segment. Heavy pleasure-trip takers. Like new technology.	25
Responsible Survivors — **Cautious, Not Risk-takers** Enjoy self-rewards. Accept direction well. Brand loyal. Heavy TV viewers.	15
Aggressive Achievers — **Confident, Success Oriented** Want to be leaders. Love status-signalling goods. Bargain hunters. Flaunt material possessions.	13

SOURCE: Goldfarb Psychographics, A New Dimension in Data Analysis, July 1988.

Note that almost 50 per cent of Canadians are either "joiner activists" or "day-to-day watchers." If your market strategy is targeted to the joiner activists, it is safe to assume that you will also obtain a large portion of the day-to-day watchers.

SMALL BUSINESS NOTES

📖 Hailing an Entrepreneurial Cabbie

WARREN BENNIS, the U.S. business academic and author, tells the story of a friend who once hired a cab at New York's Kennedy Airport. But it wasn't the usual New York cab — it was clean and lacked the bullet-proof partition dividing driver and passenger.

Also absent was the trademark rudeness of the city's cabbies. "Hi, I'm Wally," the driver said, handing over his "mission statement" printed on a small card: "I want to get you to the airport — courteously, safely and on time."

As he pulled away from the curb, he offered the day's newspapers. Soon, he mentioned the basket of fresh fruit in the back seat. Then he presented a cellular phone — local calls for a dollar a minute.

The curious customer finally asked where the driver learned this service approach. "On a talk show." How long had he been doing it? "Two, three years." How much extra money does he earn because of it? "I figure about $14,000 a year."

A clear sense of purpose pays, whether in corporations or cabs, Mr. Bennis concludes.

SOURCE: *The Globe and Mail*, 3 November 1992, p. B28.

📖 Waters for the World

CRYSTAL FOUNTAINS had a good business until the lights went out in the real estate industry. In the early 1990s, nobody in Canada was building malls and offices, and there was little call for Crystal's jumping water jets and musical cascades.

For president Paul L'Heureux, the darkest hour came last Christmas when, after nearly four years of poor financial results, he laid off four key workers in his 16-employee company.

"They were real good people who had worked hard for us," says Mr. L'Heureux, 37, whose father founded the decorative fountain maker 27 years ago.

Then, something remarkable happened.

The month after the layoffs, Crystal Fountains was flooded with more than $1-million of orders — and was able to recall its laid-off people.

The orders came from places where the company had little history of doing business: Thailand and the United Arab Emirates, where people were still putting up new buildings and were willing to spend $150,000 to $200,000 on fountains.

Yet this was no overnight success. After three years of hard work, and $300,000 in expenses, Crystal had changed from a company dangerously dependent on domestic customers into an exporter to the world's hottest markets.

"Customers kept saying, 'No commitment, no commitment.' We finally got the commitments," says vice-president David L'Heureux, 33. David, his brother Paul and vice-president Douglas Duff, 54, are Crystal's principal owners.

The orders confirmed a key lesson: you must be persistent to crack foreign markets. In Southeast Asia, particularly, you might make five visits before winning a deal. "Too many companies give up after their second or third tries," Paul L'Heureux says.

That burst of January orders gave Crystal momentum. The work force is now up to 21. After three years of losses and another of breaking even, it will turn a profit this year. Sales, which slipped as low as $1.7-million a year, will crest $3-million. Exports now contribute more than 90 per cent of sales, up from 10 per cent a few years ago.

That's not bad for a company once confined to its own back yard. Crystal, located in an eastern suburb of Toronto, had developed a Canadian niche for designing and engineering fountains. It not only supplied the idea — it manufactured gadgets to make the water jump, soar or play music.

Its calling card was the fountain in Toronto's Eaton Centre, a project built by developer Cadillac Fairview Ltd. But when Cadillac and other developers hit the wall in the 1990s, Crystal's owners had to look elsewhere.

First, they had to learn how to market themselves. That meant putting together a fat binder, full of photos of past projects, for architects and developers who had never seen their work.

The managers enrolled in courses on exporting, many of them offered by governments for free or for token fees. They ended up in one valuable, 13-week workshop funded by Ottawa, in which they tapped the expertise of export consultant Philip Allanson.

"They're a model because they listened and then they applied what they heard," says Mr. Allanson of Allanson Gautier and Associates of Toronto.

It was Mr. Allanson who warned them not to expect a quick buck. "If there is no long-term management commitment, you'll never make it in export markets. It takes at least a year to two years before you see a real return."

They also linked up with specialists like Al Wahba, who covers the Middle East for Ontario International Corp., a provincial agency that helps exporters. As a small company, Crystal couldn't pursue prospects all over the world. Mr. Wahba directed them to the United Arab Emirates, where public fountains were in demand. Crystal has a number of projects there now.

Mr. Duff, who spent three months of one year on the road, has found Canadian embassies and their trade commissioners helpful in arranging contacts and meetings.

He tries to plug into local partners — ideally with some complementary expertise — who know their home markets and customs. For example, Mr. Duff often asks who built the swimming pools in hotels where he stays. In Bangkok, he flicked through the yellow pages for swimming pool contractors, then visited ones that sounded promising.

He warns would-be exporters to shed the attitudes of the developed world in dealing with Third World clients. When he found, for example, that many Asian clients don't like to pay big consulting fees, the bids were repackaged.

Crystal receives payment through irrevocable letters of credit issued by foreign banks. The partners like this method: payments are more assured than when dealing with hard-pressed contractors in Canada.

They passed up an enticing $1.1-million project in Turkey because they couldn't be confident of the financing.

Crystal is more fortunate than many prospective exporters. In its good years, it had built up enough retained earnings to finance its export push. Now the overseas projects are throwing off cash for continuing efforts.

Still, Paul L'Heureux says, bankers often showed little appreciation of what the company was doing. He sees a painful paradox: "To become an exporter, you have to spend money. But all the time we were being told to cut our spending."

The partners live different lives than before the recession. Paul L'Heureux is on the road so much he never bothers to unpack his shaving equipment. At the moment, he's on a five-week trip to the Middle East.

There is the danger that as the Canadian economy recovers, companies that discovered exporting during the recession will shift attention away from foreign markets again. Mr. L'Heureux vows this won't happen with Crystal. No more than 20 per cent of sales will come from a single market.

And, he adds: "From now on, at least one person in this company will be thinking at least one year ahead."

SOURCE: Gordon Pitts, *The Globe and Mail*, 19 September 1994, p. B4. Reprinted with permission from *The Globe and Mail*.

📖 Reality Nights

SITTING under white fluorescent lights amid the steady hum of a half-dozen photocopiers, Tom McNeely Jr. frantically types on a computer.

At 11:45 at night, Mr. McNeely, a freelance graphic designer, is pushing hard to meet a deadline in Kinko's The Copy Centre on Toronto's downtown University Avenue.

"This place is crucial to me," says Mr. McNeely, 36, as his fingers fly over the Macintosh keyboard. The copy shop has been his base of operations since he lost his job with a publishing company in 1992.

Kinko's, with its state-of-the-art printers, copiers, fax machines, computers and courtesy phones, is an office for those without an office — the generation of young entrepreneurs who, like Mr. McNeely, face an inhospitable economy and are daunted by the overhead costs of setting up shop.

Although it has a wide array of customers, Kinko's core clientele consists of people with non-traditional work schedules and who are not part of mainstream business.

They include students, musicians and desktop publishers, who rely on Kinko's for one-stop shopping in publishing tools. "They can create a document, bind it, copy it or fax it," says Tammy Gentry, a spokeswoman for Kinko's Service Corp., the parent company based in Ventura, Calif.

These clients prefer Kinko's over other copy shops because they can use the equipment any time — the shops are open 24 hours a day — and it can be much cheaper than investing in office space and the latest technology.

In Toronto, Vancouver and other North American cities, Kinko's outlets are alive and bustling when most businesses, aside from the odd laundrette or doughnut shop, are sleeping. The copy shop attracts night owls with a hunger for success.

Such is Mr. McNeely, who has a small design studio at home but hikes over to Kinko's six nights a week for four-hour work sessions, where he uses the latest graphics programs such as Quark Express, Adobe Photoshop and Illustrator 5.0.

He spends $200 to $500 a month on things like photocopies (9 cents a page for black-and-white, $1.49 for a colour copy) and in-shop computer rentals ($12 an hour, or $6 an hour between midnight and 7 a.m.). If he were to buy a computer loaded with all the software Kinko's offers, it would set him back between $5,000 to $10,000.

"In my field, some people would sneer at what I'm doing, but I'm happy. My overhead is low and my turnaround is good. I'm focused on my business." Mr. McNeely even meets some of his magazine clients at Kinko's so they can see his work space.

With grey walls, grey carpets and airy layout, the shops have a clean, sterile look, not unlike a doctor's waiting room. There are some splashes of colour — from fluorescent writing on clear plastic signs that hang from the ceiling, to Renaissance art posters on the walls.

The ambience has changed since 1970, when 24-year-old Paul Orfalea, a recent college graduate whose curly hair inspired the childhood nickname of Kinko, opened his first store in California. It was just a reproduction centre where consumers could make copies and bind reports. And it was so small, the store's sole copier had to be wheeled into the street to make room for customers.

Today, the stores range in size from 3,500 to 20,000 square feet. There are more than 700 in the United States, seven in Canada (four in Toronto), two in Japan and one in the Netherlands. Worldwide, the company has 15,000 employees.

Kinko's is run by a co-operative group of 120 owner-operators, who do not release worldwide revenues, profits or the cost of starting up an operation. One manager estimates the startup cost is under $500,000.

At 8:30 on a Thursday night, the crowd at Kinko's on Toronto's Bloor Street is decidedly eclectic.

There is Anne Liebeck, 74, who has been a regular for five years. "When you get to my age you start to lose friends," she says with a smile. One friend has just died so she is sending copies of his obituary to organizations and other acquaintances.

The prices are reasonable for high-volume copying. "Why pay 25 cents at the convenience store?"

Over the years, many regular customers have become Ms. Liebeck's friends. "I've spent at least one night in here and I remember someone brought in New Orleans music — Muddy Waters I think it was. With the whir of the copy machine, it was wonderful, delightful."

Tony Hightower, 26, a musician and freelance graphic designer who works for Rivet, a neighbourhood magazine, uses Kinko's for its computers. The attraction for him is predictability, not atmosphere.

"It's almost like McDonald's. It's clean, it's antiseptic, you know exactly what you're going to get."

Mr. Hightower does acknowledge the emergence of a Kinko's subculture. It consists mostly of young artists or students in their 20s and early 30s, who are wrestling with the direction of their lives. They spend time in Kinko's, "making what they perceive to be is their mark."

At two in the morning, the streets are misty and quiet on Toronto's Yonge Street north of Eglinton Avenue. A taxi whizzes by Kinko's, which is empty except for two employees and two students.

Marco Nazzicone and Fraser McNaught, both 21, are in the creative advertising program at a local community college. They are close to deadline on an assignment — designing a TV commercial for hot dogs — worth 25 per cent of their final grade.

"We know it's open late and we knew there wouldn't be anyone here," Mr. Nazzicone explains, enjoying the undivided attention of two employees who can solve technical problems and suggest creative touches.

The 24-hour service also draws Owen Tennyson, a 37-year-old jazz musician, who earlier in the evening was designing posters to advertise a concert. Kinko's, he says, is ideal for artists inspired in the middle of the night.

"If I had a brainstorm at two in the morning, I'd want to be able to come here and get it down," says Mr. Tennyson, tossing a few stray dreadlocks over his shoulder.

Kinko's started its all-night service 10 years ago because its customers wanted it. A new generation has more sophisticated needs. The chain is experimenting with video conferencing, which allows callers to see and talk to each other over special phone lines. The service is available in 100 U.S. stores. Now, the Vancouver shop is working out an arrangement with BC Tel.

In Toronto, the next step may be an association of graphic designers built around the copy shop. Steve Ewins, desktop publishing manager at the University Avenue shop, figures the group could get together several times a month to swap ideas over beer. "A lot of people come in, lean over each other's shoulders and help each other out. What they have to offer is imaginative and innovative. It's also quite friendly."

SOURCE: Amber Nasrulla, *The Globe and Mail*, 23 August 1994, p. B20. Reprinted with permission from *The Globe and Mail*.

📖 Every Firm Needs One Tough Customer

DAGMAR EGERER has marketed condos in Spain, peddled Maple Leaf gold coins in Belgium and worked for a hotel chain in Lebanon and Iran.

But Ms. Egerer, now U.S. sales manager for Maax Inc., a Quebec bathtub and shower manufacturer, has rarely faced as persnickety a customer as Home Depot Inc., a U.S. building supplies retailer.

One of her jobs is to make sure Maax's bathtubs and showers show up on time at Home Depot's New England outlets. When the giant chain says the period from order to delivery is 18 days, it means 18, not 17 or 19.

The bathtubs aren't shipped to some convenient central warehouse, but to widely scattered stores as far as 900 kilometres from Maax's factory. Ms. Egerer and her colleagues perform somersaults to arrange trucking schedules.

What's more, Home Depot's obsession with defect-free products means Maax must package each fibreglass shower in a box to avoid mishaps in transit.

Maax doesn't mind the aggravation, Ms. Egerer insists. "They [Home Depot] don't want to lose a sale so they push us."

The wooing, winning and servicing of Home Depot is a big coup for little Maax, which has annual sales of $21-million (Canadian) and is located in the Beauce region, 30 minutes south of Quebec City. It has secured a toehold with the largest U.S. warehouse retailer of building materials, whose 194 monster outlets gross $5.4-billion (U.S.) in annual sales.

Home Depot, founded in 1979, have revolutionized the merchandising of building supplies the way discounter Price Club has changed the selling of general merchandise. It offers huge variety, low prices and a high level of service to the fast-growing do-it-yourself market.

The company is as hard on its suppliers as it is on itself. The merchandising office at its Atlanta headquarters posts 10 commandments for suppliers: "Ship Complete. Ship on Time," repeated 10 times.

After filling in 2½ years ago as an emergency supplier of fibreglass showers for two stores, Maax is now shipping to 34 Home Depot outlets in the U.S. Northeast, as far away as Maryland. Home Depot is its third-largest customer, accounting for 15 per cent of sales.

With Home Depot, Maax joins the ranks of masochistic suppliers who thrive on being abused by tough customers. In the United States, firms that sell to Wal-Mart Stores have to be bent on self-improvement.

Soft-hearted clients are no good for succeeding in the global competitive game, argues Michael Porter, the Harvard University professor and authority on competition. "A demanding market, rather than a welcoming or easy-to-serve one, is what underpins success," he writes in a 1991 report for Ottawa.

With today's emphasis on just-in-time delivery and customer service, suppliers are increasingly judged by their logistical capability. That means delivering long distances in the right time, quantity and quality. Dina Heym, assistant merchandiser for plumbing supplies at Home Depot's regional office in New Jersey, says "getting stuff on time" is essential for her company.

And that is how Maax landed the account. In 1990, Home Depot had just opened its first two stores in the New England region, and was buying fibreglass showers from the Glastec division of Eljer Industries Inc., a southern U.S. supplier.

But one day, Glastec couldn't deliver. Home Depot's regional plumbing supply buyer called Ms. Egerer, explaining he needed shower sets "the day after tomorrow." Since the order was for standard products, Maax grabbed goods from inventory — and wherever it could find them — and hustled them on to a trailer.

Home Depot was pleased. A month later, its buyer told Ms. Egerer he was dropping Glastec and wanted Maax as a replacement. But the Quebec company would have to adhere to the 18-day deadline (including shipping time) and provide lower defects than its predecessor.

Maax tackled the defects by boxing its fibreglass showers, even though the packaging means added cost for a low-value commodity item, priced at $196.

The delivery deadline proved tougher, putting intense pressure on traffic manager Pierrette Gosselin. Each Home Depot store orders its own showers from a product list provided by the regional office. There is no electronic data interchange — it's done by fax or phone, often through Maax's sales agent.

Once an order is taken, Ms. Gosselin reserves a delivery time with the store. The times are precise and can't be missed. Responsibility for co-ordinating deliveries falls entirely on Maax.

What happens if there's a screw-up? "I hear back from the agent, from Dagmar, from Robert Transport [the hauler], from Home Depot. I hear back from everyone," Ms. Gosselin says.

To complicate matters, Maax fills every truck before it's sent out to minimize transport costs. An order might include shipments to two Long Island, N.Y., outlets and to one in Connecticut. One Long Island store may set a delivery time for midnight while the other, only 20 kilometres away, may insist on 10 hours later. Ms. Gosselin has to juggle to minimize truckers' down time.

Adaptability is also the rule on the factory floor, a beehive of activity where the lung-searing smell of resin is pervasive. The bulk of the products and frequent changes in models have discouraged much automation (Maax has only one robot). But Placide Poulin, president and major shareholder, says the just-in-time demands of customers make it harder to manage inventories, forcing more flexible production.

Take thermoforming, the process whereby a sheet of acrylic is heated and then drawn by a vacuum to form the shape of the tub or shower. The existing thermoformers require 2½ to seven hours for a mold change. With 18 models of tubs and showers available, the loss of time is immense.

So employees have ordered a new thermoformer of their own design that will be able to handle two different models at the same time and can continue operating while the molds are being changed.

This eagerness to please is paying dividends. Home Depot recently agreed to stock Maax's higher-end acrylic tubs and showers, as well as its lower-value fibreglass lines. It wasn't an easy sell, because acrylic is a luxury for do-it-yourselfers.

The stores already carried acrylic products from another supplier. But last May, a Home Depot buyer requested a "real good price" on a five-foot acrylic whirlpool tub. Ms. Egerer came up with a number and the chain ordered a thousand.

With this big order, Maax could bargain harder with its own suppliers for inputs such as whirlpool pumps.

In time, Maax would like to manufacture in the United States to overcome high transportation costs and to expand markets beyond the Northeast. Mr. Poulin is on the acquisition trail.

Meanwhile, Ms. Egerer is looking ahead to next year, when she will service three Home Depots in Virginia, 1,000 km away. "I'll find a way of going there. You don't say no to Home Depot," she says.

But there is a risk of becoming too dependent on one account that could suddenly be lost. Ms. Egerer is comfortable with Home Depot's 15 per cent of sales, but at 20 per cent, she'd start to feel vulnerable.

Maax's answer is to expand the business elsewhere at the same time. Already strong in Quebec, Maax is working to increase market share in

Ontario and abroad. It sells to Hong Kong and Saudi Arabia and is close to a deal in France.

But after dancing to Home Depot's tune, these long-distance forays may not seem all that intimidating. "They've got to be learning," says George Dellon, Maax's agent to Home Depot in Metropolitan New York. "They're interfacing with the premier building material business in the world. They're getting an education second to none."

SOURCE: Alan Freeman, *The Globe and Mail*, 29 September 1992, p. B24. Reprinted with permission from *The Globe and Mail*.

11 *Questions*

1. Why do you shop where you do, for clothes, food, gas, books, music, and so forth? How do these businesses compare to the competition in your area for service, selection, convenience, knowledge, and benefits?
2. Why do you visit particular service providers (barber, doctor, dentist, auto mechanic, etc.) to obtain the services you need? How do these businesses or professionals compare to the competition in your area for personal service, knowledge, and benefits?
3. Do you travel out of your way to obtain a product or service? If so, why? If not, interview someone close to you who does. What does that business or professional provide that is so special that it causes you to spend extra time travelling to spend your money?
4. Analyse the companies profiled. What customer benefits did they add?
5. Research and do a profile of your primary and secondary target customers. Use the resources of the library and Statistics Canada to research the market size and demographics.
6. Create a plan that will make your business customer driven.

GROWING
PAINS

Before you start your business, you will have completed a business plan. This plan will tell you how you will be successful and, as your business grows, what new skills and resources you will need. Growing your business, the subject of this chapter, is all about achieving a new kind of freedom and a new kind of control.

It is also about creating an organizational structure that is responsive to change. As your business grows, the organization and reporting relationships will no longer be simple. The challenges of today's entrepreneur are to nurture the organization and to encourage market responsiveness, innovation, and proactivity. The new entrepreneurial organization must have the freedom to listen and to change.

To be prepared, you should begin thinking now about the day when your business starts to grow. For example, you may need more people to assist you, and you will undoubtedly need more money to help you through the expansionary stages. As your business expands and the number of your employees increases, you will need to know how to treat people, how to communicate and work with them. The growth of your business will most definitely affect the amount of time you have for yourself and your family. Time management takes on a new meaning to the business owner during the period of growth.

There are three major issues that you may need to confront as your business expands:

1. Your own growth as the employer.
2. How to treat people who work for you with dignity and respect.
3. How to deal with growth in the family-owned business.

▮▮ *Entrepreneurs Cannot Be Loners*

We once thought that entrepreneurs were loners who did it all themselves. In today's economy, that is simply not the case. Go back to the Entrepreneurial Questionnaire in the introduction of this book. Do you like to work alone? Most of you will say that you like to work with others. This is a key personality trait that you will need to open and operate a successful business.

Entrepreneurs are driven by a vision — their dream of a special kind of business they want to create. The growth of the business starts with the freedom to let go and share this vision — a vision which is very personal. For many entrepreneurs who have taken personal ownership of their ideas, finding this new freedom to allow others to believe and contribute to their vision is a difficult task.

An entrepreneur must allow others to help plan and set direction for the future. Setting goals and the methods to achieve them can no longer be an individual exercise. If a business is going to be successful, the goal setting must be carried out by everyone. People must set goals together or they will not be committed to achieving those goals. Growth involves the freedom to allow others to take ownership in the planning of the business.

Choosing your team is one of the most important decisions you will have to make, both during the initial start-up and later when your business expands. You will be looking for employees and associates who complement your personality characteristics and compensate for your personality weaknesses. Because you need to work with people who take ownership of your vision, the traditional employee mentality is no longer in the equation. In the traditional team, business owners thought of their members as employees, but your new team does not have to take the form of an employee/employer relationship. Get your creative juices moving. Think about such new relationships as joint ventures with other individuals or companies, subcontracting, and creating informal partnerships or associations.

Successful entrepreneurs fully understand that they have two priorities:

1. Operate a business that thrives on change. As Leo Buscaglia says, "To become the willing ally of change is to assure ourselves of life."* By embracing change, we can assure ourselves of life in the small business.

2. Operate a business that is customer driven. As Tom Peters writes, "We must become figuratively and literally attached to the customer."** Customers drive business, money does not drive business.

You will be looking for players that are excited by change and those who appreciate the value of a customer. The bottom line is that all of your associates, partners, or employees must recognize that the customer pays the bills. Your goal in selecting your people is to have a team that offers customers total respect and dignity. To ensure that you meet this goal, you must form an organization with a climate that fosters a sense of pride, respect, and dignity for each member. People drive business, and entrepreneurs must learn how to drive people.

As the employer, you must lead by example. Entrepreneurs are highly motivated and tend to drive themselves, especially during the

---

* Leo F. Buscaglia, *The Way of the Bull* (New York: Ballantine Books, 1983). © 1973 Charles B. Slack Inc.

** Thomas J. Peters, *Thriving on Chaos: Handbook for a Management Revolution* (New York: Knopf, 1987).

start-up phase. They are blessed with the internal drive which ignites them to action. But after the start-up honeymoon is over, entrepreneurs must ask whether they can maintain this level of enthusiasm, and more importantly, whether they can motivate others to be just as excited as they are. Entrepreneurs must learn how to keep themselves motivated and how to spark enthusiasm in other stakeholders. Thus, the leadership issue for new owners will gradually change from motivating the self to learning how to motivate others. If others are motivated, the entrepreneur will maintain the freedom to create, which is the true love of the Type E personality and the lifeblood of today's successful business.

Even in respect to creativity, however, the entrepreneur must recognize his or her own limitations and look to others to fill his or her creative circle. Chips Klein, owner of Chipco Canada Inc., a Toronto communications company, points out that the entrepreneur cannot be all things in an expanding business. It will become increasingly important to delegate responsibility and to institute controls that ensure the practices that have been agreed upon are being followed. Success lies in finding the right people with the right personalities to fill the right jobs. Klein identifies four basic creative types:

- *Explorers* are people with the ability to recognize opportunity and explore new markets. They have vision to seize the potential of a product, service, or business idea. They are alert and sensitive to changing market trends and can invent something completely original to fill a market need.

- *Artists* are then in position to do the "creating." They add substance to the opportunity by translating the concept to concrete ideas on paper. This fleshing-out can be accomplished by either drawing a design or plan, building prototypes or devising strategies to carry the pure idea to its next stage.

- *Judges* have an honest, realistic view of what should be kept and what should be discarded. They recognize which part of the idea, business or service has immediate potential and which part or parts should be put on the back burner for later development.

- *Coaches* (or generals) can marshall the troops and resources to make the idea, business or endeavour succeed. All the nitty-gritty details of today's business world fascinate these types. And like generals, they thrive on mustering the troops and inspecting each tiny operation.

SOURCE: Excerpt from Chips Klein, "How to Be All Things," *The Globe and Mail*, 11 April 1994, p. B4.

The entrepreneur may embody one or two of these characteristics, but not all. In order for these personality types to function in harmony, the entrepreneur must assemble a balanced team, recognize where each member would be best suited, clearly define their tasks and objectives, and above all, respect them.

As the business continues to grow, the entrepreneur must constantly check to make sure that his or her vision is aligned with the vision of all those people who are involved with the business. People are the driving force of a business, and for a business to be successful, everyone must believe in the same vision. The owner must ask, "Do the new stakeholders have the same vision of where the business is going or do they have a different vision?" While the first challenge of the entrepreneur is to allow others to share and buy into the business vision, the entrepreneur must also maintain a "vision check."

❙❙ *How to Treat People*

Part of the entrepreneur's personal growth is learning to treat people with respect. This process begins at the recruiting stage. Be sure that your vision is their vision. Don't forget — vision is the driving force. This will help you clarify the qualities you are looking for in a person. Before making your final decision, take at least a dozen interviews with people who have the education and experience on paper that you are looking for. Time and money spent up front is preventative. Preventative action is always less costly in the long run. Spend time with each person. A long interviewing process sends a clear message to the applicants that who you hire is important and that their personality must fit with the other players. You are selective and not desperate to fill the position. The entrepreneurial personality, motivation, and experience indexes in the introduction of this book will give you some ideas about the strengths and weaknesses in others that you are willing to live with.

The most successful entrepreneurs have surrounded themselves with successful people who complement their own strengths but most importantly fill the voids of the entrepreneur's weaknesses. Know yourself completely before you try to know your players.

The most important asset of any business is its people. People are the customers, people are the players. The products or services you provide are tools that may change, but the people must remain fixed to provide your business with the only stability possible. The market will change, the economy will change, but the people should not change. Once you have hired your team, how do you keep them functioning at full potential? Focus on a very simple rule: *Treat them as you would like to be treated.*

- *Treat employees with dignity and respect.* Booker T. Washington said, "No race can prosper until it learns that there is as much dignity in tilling a field as in writing a poem." Respect is defined as feeling or showing esteem, deference, or honour to another. The janitor in your business must receive the same respect as you give your vice-president. The on-line machine operators must receive the same respect as you give your accountant. Before you can give anyone else respect, you must first respect yourself. Work on respect for yourself until it is perfected. When you feel worthy of yourself, then you will respect the worthiness of others.

- *Listen to your players.* Listening means hearing what they say, considering what they say, and interacting with them. Look them in the eye and focus on what they are saying and how they are saying it. Pay attention to your body language as they are speaking. Sit up straight or stand up straight to let them know they have your full attention. Body language communicates more than words.

- *Involve everyone in everything.* Decisions are not a managerial privilege. Decisions must never be made without the inclusion of all players, starting with the on-line workers, and including supervisors, managers, and executive. No one wants to be treated simply like a spoke in the wheel. Instead, they want to help steer the bike — they want to be included in the decision-making process. Every person wants to go home at night with a feeling that they made a significant contribution to the organization.

- *Train, retrain and cross-train your players.* Invest in your most valuable asset, your people. Give them every opportunity to grow, reinforce what they have already learned, share new visions, and teach new skills. Make a commitment to have each person involved in a training program at least once a year. Cross-train so everyone has an understanding of the functions, responsibilities, frustrations, and challenges of the other person's tasks. Managers need to know the workings of the front-line players just as importantly as front-line players need to know the functions of management. Knowledge fosters understanding, respect, and tolerance. Derek Bok, president of Harvard University, said, "If you think education is expensive, try ignorance."

- Create a climate where each person has *responsibility, accountability, and authority.* To have one without the others can be likened to attempting a tennis match without a racquet. Every time you assign a task, stop and ask yourself whether you are passing on responsibility, accountability, and authority or whether you have set a person up for failure and set yourself up to hear nothing but excuses.

- *Don't major in minors.* Human behaviour lends itself well to the 90–10 rule. Ninety per cent of what you read in the newspapers is on 10 per cent of the pages. Likewise, most people spend 90 per cent of their time dealing with 10 per cent of the issues. Most people in business spend 90 per cent of their time on activities that only bring in 10 per cent of the income. In order to focus on the important issues and tasks, you must first be aware of what is not important. Assess every activity and every meeting. Every day, you must ask yourself, and teach your players to ask, Is this a major or is this a minor?

- *Be family oriented.* Make family an important part of your life and allow your employees to do the same. Respect family time and family needs. Show genuine interest, learn about your players' families, and include families in company social events. Encourage players to bring their children into the work environment on a quiet day so families can all have a link to the vision.

I I *Family Succession*

Family-owned businesses experience growing pains when the children enter the business and begin to assume control and to prepare for eventual ownership. Dissension wracks many successful family companies. Over 70 per cent of family businesses fail in the second generation.

There are many reasons for this. Building the business in the first place may have taken so much time that parent and child were unable to develop a normal bond. Or perhaps insufficient time was taken to properly groom the successor in business practices and management principles.

Of the second-generation businesses that are successful, a high percentage fail in the third generation. It is too often the second generation who expand the business and increase the debt load. The debt load is what the third generation cannot cope with. If a recession begins early in the succession, there is an added element of disaster to contend with.

Succession requires strategic planning, and it must begin early, sometimes as much as 10 to 15 years ahead of the retirement of the founder(s). (If there are no heirs, then the timely sale of the business is another option.) If left to chance or fate, emotions will rule and slowly destroy the business. Every family business deserves better than a demise. The plan must include a written will and adequate insurance. Advice should be sought from trustworthy estate and business management consultants, and personal goals should be established. Finally, following the procedures outlined below will help to ease the pains of succession:

1. Give all children the opportunity to work in the business part-time from an early (pre-teen) age. This allows them to share their parents' world, and experience with clerical or stock-room work allows them to see the company from the bottom up. It also allows employees the opportunity to get to know the children and will reduce the jealousy most staff have for the boss's family.
2. Train each child in more responsible functions of the business — not just the cushy jobs, but the less attractive work also. This practical experience allows the child to gain the respect of employees.
3. Decisions about education must be made by the time each child reaches their late teens. When it becomes clear who is interested in joining the family business, a plan must be written that specifies what, if any, post-secondary formal education each child wants and needs, and where they will fit into the business until they progress to the full capacity of taking over the reins.

4. The goals of the business must be written and written clearly. The founder, management team, and prospective successor must be clear on the future route of the business.

5. The difficult transition begins when the child joins the business full-time. The founder may have a hard time delegating responsibility when the business grows and an even greater difficulty delegating to his or her own child. The child should not be expected to live in the shadow of the founding entrepreneur, but instead must be allowed to function within the business as an individual and to contribute accordingly.

6. Through all of this planning, many families make the fatal mistake of dividing the ownership shares of the business equally amongst their children, even if some children never have an involvement in the business. Most consultants and psychologists agree that uninvolved children should receive some other compensation from the parents' estate, and control of the business should be left to those involved on a day-to-day basis.

SMALL BUSINESS NOTES

Why Small Businesses Grow

WHY do small and medium-sized businesses grow? According to the people who run them, three factors stand out: good management, good labour and good marketing.

In a 1992 survey run by John Baldwin of Statistics Canada, almost 1,500 small and growing businesses were asked to rank the factors important to their success. On a five-point scale, zero meant the factor wasn't applicable; five meant it was crucial.

Management skills ranked highest with a 3.34 score. Since managers filled out the surveys, this is not a complete surprise. Skilled labour and marketing ability came next with 2.93 and 2.87 respectively.

The survey results might end the perennial debate over whether small businesses' main financing problem is access to capital or cost of capital. The score for both was about the same.

The ability to adopt technology — from a variety of sources — came in at 2.51, just over the halfway point on the scale.

Ranking last as a contributor to commercial success was government assistance. Politicians who preen about their prowess at helping companies might remember that.

SOURCE: Bruce Little, "Management Skills Rank High," *The Globe and Mail*, 7 March 1994, p. B6.

📖 That Word Again

"EMPOWERMENT is a too-often misused word. People have to decide to become empowered. You can help them by having good communications, a trusting environment where they're included, where their ideas are wanted. And boy, when that happens, their creativity just oozes forth."

SOURCE: Stephen J. Frangos, quoted in *The Globe and Mail*, 4 January 1994, p. B14.

📖 St. Patrick Would Approve

BRITISH MANAGEMENT GURU Charles Handy says tomorrow's organizations will look like shamrocks. (Mr. Handy has Irish roots.) The first leaf "is the core of a business organization, which is very tight, very hard working and very well paid. In fact, by the year 2000, only half the work force will have full-time core jobs. The rest will be self-employed or unemployed."

The second leaf is the self-employed "contract partners" in an organization such as lawyers, accountants or computer experts. They will work out of their own offices or homes and pay their own expenses.

The third leaf is what he calls "the hired help," who work much like casual labourers today — being called on for their services when needed and having a number of employers at the same time.

"The secret to working in the new world will be the ability to sell your skills to a number of buyers. The days of the lifetime job are over and the era of the skilled self-employed worker has begun."

SOURCE: Canadian Press, as appearing in *The Globe and Mail*, 7 March 1994, p. B6.

Discreet Moves

SPEED is the name of a hot new Hollywood action flick. It also describes the breathtaking growth pace of the Montreal company whose software stars in the movie.

Discreet Logic Inc. was born three years ago in a modest space on Montreal's trendy Boulevard St-Laurent. Armed with just $27,000 in seed money, its founders — alumni of its better-known rival down the street, Softimage Inc. — planned to generate high-end computer graphics software that the film and video industry would snap up.

Those plans have come to life dramatically. Discreet's annual sales will hit a staggering $22-million by the end of July.

Its minimalist open-concept offices, decked with modern art and an espresso bar, now accommodate 30 employees. Fifty more will be hired in Montreal by this time next year. Add in sales reps, and total employment will reach 100 in 1995.

But chief executive Richard Szalwinski knows he can't revel forever in dazzling sales, steady profits (the company will make up to $3.5-million this year) and rising celebrity from hit movie roles.

"We're concerned about growing too fast and repeating the mistakes other companies have made," says Mr. Szalwinski, 45, the laid-back former Softimage sales and marketing man who founded Discreet with Diana Shearwood and Simon Mowbray.

Discreet must work to avoid what Mr. Szalwinski calls "hitting the wall" — the all-too-common plight of companies that can't sustain growth and support all the overhead they've added.

He also knows that while the sales surge may seem surprising, it only reflects the software mania in the entertainment market. "It's exploding," says David Wright, who follows software firms for Montreal brokerage Marleau Lemire. "Movies, television, video games are all using this technology."

By garnering coverage in trade magazines and appearances at crucial trade shows, Discreet has cracked markets like Moscow, Paris and, of course, Hollywood. Buyers pay $300,000 to $900,000 for a "solution" — jargon for the package of Discreet's Flame software that runs on the powerful supercomputers it buys from California-based Silicon Graphics Inc.

Sitting at a terminal, movie makers can generate digital images such as the outer-space pictures for the movie *Coneheads* or the highway hole that confronts the racing bus in *Speed*. They can add them to film or video pictures for a realistic, seamless total effect.

Customers, such as Centre de Montage Électronique of Montreal, which creates special effects for commercials and TV shows, like Flame software because it integrates all the functions they need to perform. "This is really the equipment of the future," says executive director Muriel Kearney.

All very nice, but what does Discreet do now? "You get to a size where you have to put in controls, such as on costs, so you can manage your business properly," says Mr. Wright of Marleau Lemire. "Some companies do it well, others don't."

Toronto-based Alias Research Inc., another overnight star in entertainment software, had the problem. It grew fast, suffered painful financial and management problems and had to restructure and haul in new senior executives.

Softimage may have avoided such problems by becoming part of U.S. mass market software giant Microsoft Corp. earlier this year. "It's difficult to know what would have happened if they didn't do that deal," muses Mr. Szalwinski, sporting the software industry's equivalent to the pin-striped suit: monochromatic black T-shirt and slacks.

Discreet is working on several strategies. First, it wants to evolve from a single-product company. That is why it has set up a company in Boston, a high-tech hot spot with an abundance of skilled engineers.

The U.S. branch has five employees who are developing a software-based product to be launched next April, destined for a market broader than entertainment. Beyond those details, Mr. Szalwinski is, well, discreet.

Discreet also plans to protect itself by prowling for that essential element of a young firm: capital. It hopes to align with a strategic partner in the industry or find an outside financier. It could also sell shares to the public to raise money, although that's the least desirable option.

"An initial public offering scares us," admits Mr. Szalwinski, who worries that it would shift the company's focus to profit and stock price and away from product.

The company could also be taken over — there has been interest from U.S. and European companies. That doesn't scare Mr. Szalwinski, who believes such overtures simply lend credibility.

New capital would go to building its own distribution network in Europe and Asia, instead of working through third-party agents who sell not only Flame but also products of other companies. An international sales force would consume precious management time and resources, but the reps would focus exclusively on Discreet.

Although a young company, Discreet has gone through several phases. Of the founders, Ms. Shearwood, 40, works with Mr. Szalwinski as communications director, but Mr. Mowbray, 27, has moved on to a California production house.

And the company has another challenge: a messy legal fight with Softimage over patent rights to Flame. The company that served as the model and the training ground for Discreet has become its legal foe.

The tussle has impact on both sides. Softimage says sales were hurt when the dispute led to termination of its deal to distribute Discreet's product. Last year, Discreet had to pull out of an important trade show to save money for the legal fight. And now, Softimage has the deep pockets of Microsoft behind it.

Mr. Szalwinski tries to play down the case. His bigger battle is keeping ahead in a sector that is evolving as fast as a runaway bus. He is determined not to crash.

SOURCE: Ann Gibbon, *The Globe and Mail*, 27 June 1994, p. B8. Reprinted with permission from *The Globe and Mail*.

📖 Looking for Mr. Wright

LIFE CHANGED at Virtek Vision Corp. the day last winter when Norman Wright wheeled his black Cadillac into the parking lot.

Until then, Virtek was a laid-back collection of researchers with a string of impressive patents in laser-guided manufacturing. But the University of Waterloo spinoff hadn't cracked the big leagues of industrial markets.

Enter Mr. Wright, a veteran high-tech manager recruited as Virtek's new president. He quickly turned the researchers' unfinished engineering projects into a $500,000 sale to Seattle-based aerospace giant Boeing Co.

"I agreed to a six-week delivery schedule, knowing we had never done that here," says Mr. Wright, 59.

That was the first step toward the new president's ultimate goal — turning what amounted to a laboratory engineering project into a thriving technology company with global sales.

Many startups stumble trying to take that step. But the Waterloo-based company's four founders realized they had to surrender some management authority and their collegial research culture to reach the next stage.

"The hardest part for a research company is merely to survive," says Thomas King, a co-founder and Virtek's former general manager who stepped aside for Mr. Wright. "It was really an act of tenacity to keep the company going."

In Mr. Wright's five months as president, Virtek has raised $760,000 through a private placement, increased staff to 30 from five and built a manufacturing line that turns out two of its "machine vision" systems a day.

Virtek, he says, must be sophisticated enough to pitch its systems to large customers like Boeing — and financially stable enough to win a stock exchange listing.

Before joining Virtek, Mr. Wright had been executive vice-president at Alias Research Inc., a Toronto-based software company where he had been part of a financial turnaround. But he was ripe for a change — just as Virtek's research-oriented founders were feeling ill-equipped to attract the cash and sales they needed.

Andrew Wong, Mohamed Kamel, Robert Nally and Mr. King had met in the mid-1980s at the University of Waterloo's Pattern Analysis and Machine Intelligence Laboratory. They developed technology for "machine vision," which involves using lasers to guide tools in manufacturing, eliminating the need for flimsy paper patterns and mylar templates. The group spun Virtek off from the university in 1988.

The company's strength lies in its software, which the founders say makes off-the-shelf parts, such as galvanometers, lasers and cameras, more accurate when they're assembled into computer-based systems.

Virtek financed its research through government grants and contracts from companies such as General Motors Corp. and Lockheed Corp. of Calabasas, Calif., but never broke through the $500,000 mark in annual sales. Mr. King ran the business while the others spent evenings writing proposals, formalizing contracts, going over finances and trouble-shooting in research and development.

Last year, the group decided their technology could compete with any other on the market. They chose to focus on four industries in which they had concentrated their research: aerospace, leather, construction and packaging.

Although the products are diverse, the principles are the same: Manufacturers want precision cutting of materials and maximum yield.

Kaufman Footwear of Kitchener, Ont., now cuts leather for shoes and boots with Virtek's systems; Ethan Allen Interiors Inc. of Danbury, Conn., turns out furniture. Boeing will use machine vision to fabricate composite parts for the new 777 passenger jet.

But to compete globally, the partners needed a seasoned executive at the helm. A head-hunter led them to Mr. Wright, who was receptive to their offer of an equity interest and management control. "Being No. 2 in Alias, I was looking forward to running my own show," he says.

The British-born executive had the credentials: a degree from the London School of Economics and a stint in Harvard Business School's Advanced Management Program. He had done some management consulting, as well as the Alias turnaround.

But he was taken aback when he arrived at Virtek with its empty office space, trailing wires and rented desks. He saw the need to transform the clutter into a state-of-the-art sales and manufacturing shop.

He immediately increased staff by hiring Alias's former investor relations director, a chief financial officer and four customer support people. He opened a U.S. marketing arm with a staff of two in Boston.

Once Virtek had won the order from Boeing, he had to figure out how to fill it. "A lot of things weren't finished. We had to put a lot of pressure on engineers and R&D. There wasn't much in the way of deadlines, not much discipline."

Workers scrambled to put the manufacturing facility in place and new furniture replaced the rented desks.

The corporate culture changed too, as the informal academic style gave way to a business-like environment. Mr. Wright pointed out the need for schedules, cost controls, discipline. It helped that he promised Boeing it could have six of Virtek's LaserEdge systems by June.

"That forces everybody to get very focused. We haven't missed any of our deadlines," Mr. Wright says.

The founders have given him full authority in running the business. Dr. Wong, 58, and Dr. Kamel, 45, continue to work in their University of Waterloo lab. Mr. Nally, 43, is a technology consultant and Mr. King, also 43, is vice-president in charge of operations.

"I was trying to administer accounting, raise funding, make sales," Mr. King says. "Now I can focus more on product development."

Mr. Wright is looking to international markets to boost the company's sales to $5-million this year — and $20-million in five years. (The systems sell for $50,000 to $80,000 apiece.) Ninety-five per cent of sales, he predicts, will come from exports. "The U.S. will be huge."

Half of those sales, he figures, will come from the relatively low-tech leather industry, which will be automating more. Aerospace should provide 30 per cent, with housing construction and packaging making up the rest.

He accepts that success or failure now rests squarely on his shoulders. "You're really creating something almost from scratch. You can't blame anybody else. It really puts to the test your experience and values."

SOURCE: Carolyn Leitch, *The Globe and Mail*, 9 May 1994, p. B2. Reprinted with permission from *The Globe and Mail*.

📖 Impatient Owner Gets Hard-Nosed Manager

DAVID PIGGOTT is an impatient innovator who sometimes finds his hands are tied. A manufacturer of big industrial drilling machines, he is keen to constantly improve his products — and to make the changes on the next machine that goes out the door.

Yet Mr. Piggott, the founder and majority owner of Compustep Products Corp., often finds himself overruled. The company's new president, Joseph Lipsett, has decreed that the pace of change must not be so rapid that salespeople and customers become confused — or that unsold machines are made obsolete.

"I don't want to slow down the innovation. I just want to slow down the availability to the marketplace," Mr. Lipsett explains to the man who hired him.

Surprisingly, Mr. Piggott agrees: "I can't go on making changes with the company becoming as big as it is. People can't keep up with me."

This give-and-take goes on daily as the two men forge a working relationship. It is a confrontation both welcome. Mr. Piggott, who was formerly president and is now vice-president for manufacturing, is that rare owner-manager who has accepted gracefully that he doesn't have all the answers.

That's one reason he set out about a year ago to find a working partner.

Over the past decade, Mr. Piggott, 54, had turned his metal machining shop into a manufacturer of drilling machines for industry, with annual sales of $3-million. He had built up equipment, capital and some customers.

"But I needed help," he now admits. "I was running the plant, doing the design, dealing with customers. It was tearing me to pieces.

"I know what my strengths and weaknesses are. My strengths are out at the back with the nuts and bolts."

So he turned to Toronto-based management consultants Ernst & Young to help in his search for a chief executive who would also be willing to invest in the company.

"He's pretty realistic — it's one of the reasons for his prior success," says Ernst & Young partner Peter Farwell, who is director of the firm's high-technology practice.

Mr. Piggott wasn't looking for a big brother. He needed a working partner. The successful candidate had to be willing to move to Peterborough, a 90-minute drive northeast of Toronto, and had to be an entrepreneur.

"I met a lot of polished executives scared to death of running a little company," Mr. Piggott says. "They don't know what it's like to run out of cash. They don't even understand the concept."

After a six-month search, the firm recruited Mr. Lipsett, 53, a seasoned computer industry manager with an MBA.

He had all the credentials. He was looking for a new adventure after hiring a president to run his own small computer systems company in Toronto.

The two struck a deal by which Mr. Lipsett will remain a minority shareholder for now, but the process is in place to make him an equal partner over time. And Mr. Piggott says he has no qualms about eventually ceding control to someone else.

The most difficult part "was finding someone I liked," Mr. Piggott says. "It takes an enormous emotional trust."

But such adjustments come easier for someone who's been down the road before. As an engineer, Mr. Piggott found a way to turn recycled and scrap polyethylene into garbage bags in the 1970s. His Toronto company, POLY Converters Ltd., became known as PCL Industries Ltd. and eventually went public. The firm, which diversified into other businesses after Mr. Piggott left, was recently wound down.

After selling his stake, Mr. Piggott opened a machine shop in Mississauga. He soon decided he didn't want to pay workers $18 an hour just to drill holes in steel products. He built his first computer-controlled drilling machine in 1984.

Customers liked the product and began to ask for bigger versions. They wanted to save time and increase accuracy in drilling large, crude pieces of steel used in products such as railroad box cars, truck frames and heat exchangers used in oil refineries and industrial air conditioning.

The machines are controlled by personal computers running Microsoft Corp.'s standard DOS (disk operating system) and Compu-step's software.

Looking for cost savings, Mr. Piggott relocated his company to Peterborough in 1988. By 1991, he figured that his drilling and milling machines were ready for a wider world market. He began trucking the massive machines — some 25 metres long — to trade shows and advertising in industry journals.

But his engineering background had not prepared him for marketing. "I knew how to make a product but I didn't know how to sell it." Meanwhile, he was being run ragged trying to balance his time between the shop floor and the front office.

Mr. Lipsett's arrival last September brought immediate changes. He brought staff in one weekend to brighten the offices with a coat of white paint, and the grimy furniture has been replaced. "At least if a customer comes in he has a clean chair to sit on."

Now the two men are trying to crank up the cash flow. Mr. Lipsett reorganized the sales team and is looking for distributors to sell machines around the world. He uses telemarketing and direct mail to reach prospects, as well as trade shows and trade journals.

The founder himself is learning a new style of management. "I am not polished in my ways and means of handling customers and bank documents," Mr. Piggott says. "He [Mr. Lipsett] is always revamping my documents."

The partners are also grappling with Compustep's future direction. The company could keep adding "all kinds of fancy-ass things I haven't even dreamed of," Mr. Piggott acknowledges. But he believes its niche lies in lower-priced machines that handle large, rough pieces of steel for heavy industry.

Competitors, such as Wisconsin-based giant Giddings & Lewis Inc., make high-precision machines, priced at millions of dollars, used in fashioning aircraft parts and other sophisticated tasks. The smallest Compustep machine sells for $200,000 (U.S.), and most are priced from $350,000 to $450,000.

Many customers make heat exchangers and the company will continue to serve that market. But the product can also be used in making wood-chipping equipment, frames for injection-moulding machines and paper-cutting technology.

"We have a product and we're looking for a market," Mr. Lipsett says. "That is not the right way to go, but entrepreneurs do that all the time."

Mr. Piggott talks of building sales to $50-million a year. Potential rivals would have to think twice before taking on that big a company in its market.

In pursuing these goals, he's glad to have Mr. Lipsett and his sales skills. "He's as hard-nosed a guy as I ever met in front of a customer," Mr. Piggott says admiringly.

SOURCE: Carolyn Leitch, *The Globe and Mail*, 31 January 1994, p. B6. Reprinted with permission from *The Globe and Mail*.

A Mother's Journey: From Legal Briefs to Children's Jeans

AS THE MOTHER OF THREE GIRLS, Cindy Eeson grew frustrated trying to find quality children's clothing at reasonable prices. So, she decided to try her hand at manufacturing.

"I went into it as a mother because I wanted better designs," says Ms. Eeson, 41, a lawyer who worked at Petro-Canada in Calgary before starting a family in 1982.

"I wanted something to keep me tied to my children — that's where my creative energies were going — not divorced from them like corporate law."

Ms. Eeson followed the path of many working women who change direction when they become mothers and pursue part-time careers that accommodate family needs. Starting a home business is a logical choice, especially when the product or service revolves around children.

Kids Only Clothing Club Inc., born in the basement of Cindy Eeson's home, is now five years old and sales are expected to hit $9.5-million this year.

The merchandise is made in Calgary and sold exclusively through a network of part-time consultants who stage home parties. Each guest buys an average of $102 worth of merchandise.

Direct selling, made famous by Avon, Tupperware and Mary Kay Cosmetics, has proved to be a convenient way to buy children's clothing for time-stressed parents who can't work in trips to the local mall.

Kids Only is growing quickly — a nice predicament during a recession. But the company has little control over its distribution network and finds it hard to plan for expansion.

In last fall's selling season, average sales per consultant almost doubled to $11,000 from $5,800 a year earlier. With orders far higher than expected, Ms. Eeson had to scramble to find local manufacturers to help out. Delivery deadlines, normally two weeks, ballooned to six weeks.

"We're in an industry that is traditionally done in Montreal or Toronto — and we're in Calgary," she says. "The labour force is nonexistent here and we don't have the same resources."

Sorting out such problems means long hours but Ms. Eeson still tries to maintain a balance between work and family life.

She sees her children off to school in the morning, then gets back for dinner, bringing paperwork to do after they go to bed. She can't avoid working on weekends but stays away from the office.

A year ago, husband Ralph Eeson, 45, gave up his own law practice to join the company. He was a senior partner at law firm Code Hunter in Calgary, specializing in oil and gas securities.

"People were surprised when I left," he admits. "Cindy asked me to join her early on and I said 'Get the business up to $3-million first.' A year later, she said 'I think we're there' and I had to put my money where my mouth is."

While making a comfortable living as a lawyer, he was working 80 hours a week and faced the prospect of burnout. Life is still hectic, he says, but now he is "building equity for the future."

Cindy looks after design and marketing. Ralph handles production and finance. (Born in Rhodesia and educated in Britain, he has a master's degree in business administration as well as law.) The three girls, ages 8 to 12, model outfits in catalogues and corporate videos.

Kids Only clothes, made of 100-per-cent cotton, are versatile and practical. Borrowing an idea from maternity wear, Ms. Eeson designed pants with a wide elastic waistband and adjustable buttons. Pants also have iron-on knee patches and cuffs of four to six inches to accommodate growth spurts.

The spring line features "convertible" jeans, with legs that snap off on a hot day to make a pair of denim shorts.

The company puts out two lines a year — spring and fall — in vivid colours designed to mix and match. Prices range from $30 for pants to $50 for dresses and jumpsuits.

From the start, Ms. Eeson vowed to avoid impersonal retail stores and sell exclusively through stay-at-home mothers like herself. The company now has about 600 consultants across Canada, mainly in suburban and rural areas. There are none in the city of Toronto, for example.

One successful Kids Only consultant is Cheryl Labbett, 36, of Oakville, Ont. She has a network of 22 recruits who pay her commission of 5 to 8 per cent of their sales. She keeps 25 per cent of the price of clothes she sells herself.

A mother of two young girls, Ms. Labbett finds it hard to separate business and family demands. Last fall, she worked four hours a day in her home office and did two to six parties a week.

"I have to fight the urge to wander downstairs at 11:30 p.m. in my nightie," she says.

But the work is worthwhile for Ms. Labbett, who hopes to develop a six-figure annual sales volume. Kids Only's top consultant, also in Ontario, took in $60,000 in total sales last fall alone. (Spring volume is usually 25 per cent lower.)

Ms. Eeson is still puzzling over why sales shot up last fall. She thinks it was a combination of better styling and fabrics, plus more incentives for sales consultants. And despite a slow retail climate, she says, "Women will buy for their children first before they buy for themselves or their homes."

During the fall rush, the Eesons had a tough decision to make. They were approached by a German company that wanted to sell Kids Only merchandise through consultants in Germany.

Kids Only could barely supply its Canadian sales force, and suddenly it was being pushed into exporting. Still, the opportunity seemed too good to turn down.

"We wanted to do a licencing agreement, but they liked Canadian-made goods and wanted everything made here," Ms. Eeson says.

The Germans were persistent. They had applications from 200 would-be sales consultants, plus market research showing they could sell the merchandise in Germany for twice the Canadian retail price.

Finally, the Eesons agreed to reserve 10 per cent of the company's production for export, enough to supply 70 consultants in Germany. The contract has been signed and shipments will start going overseas soon.

The next problem is finding more space for operations. Last fall, the company turned out 200,000 garments from a facility of about 3,800 square metres.

Every small business has to pace its growth, but for Cindy and Ralph Eeson it's crucial to balance work and family demands. The challenge is tough when both parents work for the same demanding company.

"Ralph has worked seven days a week for the last five months," says Cindy, who recently gave up twice-a-year trips across Canada to meet the sales force. "If you added up both our hours, it's pretty horrendous."

Still, she is determined to keep her family time — evenings and weekends — sacred and not let work interfere.

"You have to be able to look at a child at the dinner table and focus on them 100 per cent," she says. "You can't talk about work all the time. You have to be able to turn it off."

SOURCE: Ellen Roseman, *The Globe and Mail*, 17 January 1994, p. B4. Reprinted with permission from *The Globe and Mail*.

The Glare of Going Public

LYNNE STETHEM has had a whirlwind year. Her software development company has gone public, opened offices overseas, made two acquisitions and raised $2.2-million in a private placement of shares.

But fast growth in a public company puts new pressures on Ms. Stethem, 46, who now meets with investment dealers several times a month. The demands on her time are much greater than anticipated.

"Satisfying the expectations of the investment community becomes a major consideration," she says. "I wasn't prepared and had to adjust."

Her company, Angoss Software Corp. (which stands for A New Generation of Software Solutions), is a study in how entrepreneurs' lives can change as their businesses seek outside funding.

Ms. Stethem finds her management style under scrutiny as Angoss, like many young companies, has tapped capital markets to fuel its growth. Its shares are traded over the counter and will soon be listed on the Alberta Stock Exchange. The current price is $1.50, up from 65 cents in February.

In one sense, British-born Ms. Stethem is still very much a rarity — a woman heading a software company in the male-dominated computer industry. Married with two school-aged children, she has to juggle domestic responsibilities.

"I get jolly well tired of managing a multinational public company by day and doing the ironing when I get home at night," she jokes.

Ms. Stethem hopes Angoss will grow through acquisitions to $100-million in annual sales in the next four years — a goal those who work with her think is not beyond her reach.

"She's a lady of incredible substance, drive and determination, the Margaret Thatcher of software," says Lawrence Lavery, a Chicago-based software consultant who works exclusively with Angoss products.

Graduating from university with an arts degree, Ms. Stethem had no definite career plans. She worked at a British market research firm, which brought in a computer to collate data.

"I had no interest in computers, but we drew straws to see who would go for training and I drew the short straw. I was not amused."

Soon, she grew intrigued by on-line data processing and got a job with a large ticket agency, which was computerizing its box office. Later, she came to Canada for what she thought would be a temporary stay.

Hired by T. Eaton Co. as a systems analyst, she spent five years moving up through the ranks. In 1978, she married Nicholas Stethem, a military analyst, and started a family.

Working from home as a computer consultant, she discovered SmartWare, a practical office automation tool. In 1984, she set up CS Computing Services Inc. to sell solutions for companies built around SmartWare. In 1988, CS topped $1-million in sales.

But in 1989, SmartWare's developer was taken over by a California company and the product was allowed to languish. This presented an opportunity to Ms. Stethem, who wanted to move from consulting into software development.

Last January, she signed a deal with Informix Software Inc. of Menlo Park, Calif., to market, develop and support SmartWare. In the process, she acquired a huge base of 500,000 business users in North America and Europe. (About 95 per cent of sales are outside Canada.)

To pay for the acquisition, Ms. Stethem found a German company that agreed to buy part of her company, but later reneged. In desperate need of capital, she was introduced to Gornitzki Thompson & Little, a Toronto merchant banking firm that works with owner-operated businesses, in which it takes minority stakes.

GTL put up bridge financing, then helped negotiate a new deal with Informix at a better price. In February, CS Computing merged with Eastmont Gold Mines Ltd., a shell company in which GTL had an interest, and was renamed Angoss Software Corp.

Most companies do an initial public offering of shares by filing a prospectus with a provincial securities commission. Angoss, however, engineered a reverse takeover of an inactive public company.

Going public this way cost Angoss just under $100,000 in legal and accounting fees, a fraction of what an IPO can cost. But it diluted Ms. Stethem's ownership, putting her in a 40-per-cent minority position but with voting control.

A reverse takeover of this kind offers speed and assurance, GTL principal John Thompson says. Companies can wait so long for regulatory approval of an IPO that they have to cancel if the market turns unfavourable.

Investment dealers often lose interest in the firms they underwrite. But GTL, with a 10- to 15-per-cent equity position, takes an active role in promoting Angoss and enhancing the value of its shares.

On the negative side, a reverse takeover means taking on new shareholders and weakening the owner's control, says Mara Collins, a corporate finance lawyer with Toronto law firm Goodman and Carr.

Also, the shell company may have undisclosed liabilities, such as taxes owing or shareholder claims, that must be shouldered by the new owner. "And there is no one to provide a meaningful indemnity against the risk," she points out.

Angoss is now spending $50,000 for a listing on the Alberta exchange, so that investment analysts outside Canada can follow it on computer screens. It hopes to move to the Nasdaq Stock Market next year.

But Ms. Stethem had to do some fancy footwork when Angoss's third-quarter results showed a loss of $357,000 or 2 cents a share on revenue of $524,000. European sales are always slow in the summer, she explains, and many buyers held off acquiring the software, waiting for an upgrade that was late in arriving.

Mr. Thompson says a public company has to learn not to promise more than it can deliver. "There's always a problem with software. In this business, it takes longer and costs more than they ever expect."

Meanwhile, Ms. Stethem's schedule is non-stop. Last week, she was in San Francisco, nailing down yet another software acquisition. She recently hosted a three-day meeting of software developers in Toronto and heads to England next week for a similar event. The highlight is a session where users suggest product improvements.

To raise its profile, the company will launch a $1.2-million campaign in computer magazines in January. Ads will feature a character called Angus from Angoss, who writes a tongue-in-cheek computer advice column.

Ms. Stethem hopes to grow along the lines of Cognos Inc., a large Ottawa-based public company that shares the same market niche. But unlike Cognos, she has never received any federal funding.

"We built our products and paid to build them with revenues as we went. That's why the products are so practical," she says.

IBM and Microsoft grew arrogant and stopped listening, but not little Angoss. "Staying close to users and responding to their needs — it's a point of pride with us."

SOURCE: Ellen Roseman, *The Globe and Mail*, 29 November 1993, p. B8. Reprinted with permission from *The Globe and Mail*.

📖 No Magic Formula for Transferring Family Firm

IN 1951, Bill Kitchen opened a store catering to home builders and contractors. Younger brother Howard joined in 1959 and the pair parlayed the business into eight Lansing Buildall stores in the Toronto area, also selling to the do-it-yourself crowd.

In recent years, Bill Kitchen, now 66, has been planning to pass the business on to the next generation.

The successful transfer of a family firm is the exception rather than the rule, says Toronto family-business consultant David Gallagher. Most don't make it because of problems ranging from family squabbles to failure in grooming a successor to replace Dad.

There is no magic formula because each family's dynamics differ.

Lansing Buildall, which employs about 780 people, has an unusual corporate structure. The ownership is divided — Bill owns five stores and Howard owns three — but the management is the same.

Bill Kitchen's son John, 37, was appointed president in 1989 after a decade of doing various jobs with increasing responsibilities. Two daughters work for the company but did not express an interest in heading it.

Howard, 56, director of advertising and promotion, has one son in the business and one daughter who is not.

After John's appointment, outside consultants were hired to put together an organizational chart to define jobs and salaries. While everyone used to report to Bill, there are seven directors who now report to John.

As for future control of his five stores, Bill Kitchen says he intends to give his five children equal voting shares. Howard will do the same for his children and his stores.

The elder Kitchens concede that giving equal shares in the business to their children — whether they work for the company or not — could cause problems in the future. Some family businesses have been blown apart by this.

But Howard Kitchen says it's important to keep communication lines open among family members. Those working for the firm hold regular meetings, with the minutes distributed to non-active family members. There is also a yearly family meeting.

Mr. Gallagher warns there are "seven deadly sins" family firms must avoid if they want to survive to the next generation.

- *Intergenerational conflict:* Parents and children disagree on how to manage the business, because of each generation's different values and different stages of life.
- *Sibling rivalry:* The children of the owner vie for control of the business.

- *Business and owner obsolescence:* Companies refuse to update their products or management strategies.

- *Autocratic disorganization:* The founder is the boss and that's that. It can work in the beginning when the business is small, but as it grows you have to delegate.

- *Procrastination and secrecy:* The entrepreneur delays declaring a successor among the children and doesn't get advice.

- *Non-family management turn-off:* When the owner's children enter the business, non-family managers find it unpleasant to work for the boss's kids, and they leave.

- *The myth of fair is equal:* Many families leave equal shares in a business to be fair to all children, including those who may not be competent to run the company, instead of compensating them in other ways.

Dealing with succession planning is no easy task and should begin 10 to 15 years ahead of time, Mr. Gallagher says. Here are some suggestions to help families cope:

- Improve communications through regular meetings so that family members can learn the business history and finances. Outsiders, such as psychologists and consultants, can be invited to explain family behavioural patterns.

- Establish an independent board of directors — often the business owner's peers — to offset "tendencies of the imperial president" to avoid seeking advice on succession planning.

- Appoint a non-family chief operating officer as a buffer between the owner and the children. There is too much stress if an owner needs to tell a child he or she isn't doing well.

- Enroll in a family-business management course. The Centre for Entrepreneurship at the University of Toronto has a 12-week course for CEOS and other family members. Humber College in Etobicoke, Ont., is offering six family-business seminars starting May 1.

- Join a family-business organization, such as the Toronto-based Canadian Association of Family Enterprise (CAFE), a non-profit group with chapters across Canada.

SOURCE: Shirley Won, *The Globe and Mail*, 8 February 1993, p. B6. Reprinted with permission from the author.

❚❚ *Questions*

1. What is driving and motivating each of the entrepreneurs profiled?
2. Do the entrepreneur and the employees of the profiled companies have an aligned vision of the future of the company?
3. Do you want to hire employees or create a team of associates/ partners for your new business? What type of people do you want on your team?
4. Write a list of guiding principles on how you will manage and lead your team.
5. Do you have the skills to expand your business? What skills do you need to learn? What skills do you need on your team?
6. Think about the future. What will your team look like five years from now? Understand that you do have a choice — you can choose to remain small and never expand.
7. How do you intend to cope with the changes in freedom and control when your business expands?
8. Why do over 70 per cent of our family businesses fail in the second generation?
9. If you plan to operate a family-owned business, devise a plan for succession that includes steps for coping with the emotions and skills of each member of your family.

EDUCATION

Much has been written in the 1980s and early 1990s about education and what the market needs are. Towers Perrin and the Hudson Institute of Canada researched and published a report in 1991 entitled *Workforce 2000*, which cites the lack of basic writing and verbal skills, not lack of experience, as the biggest single reason for Canadian companies turning down Canadian job applicants and hiring from abroad. Canadian economist David Crane states that "unless it has the capacity to create new wealth based on ideas and knowledge, Canada will face a long period of economic decline and growing inability to support the very things we value as a society: our commitment to sharing, as reflected in our health-care system, social programs, child care, regional development equalization payments," and so on.* Nuala Beck, in her book *Shifting Gears*, urges changes to the educational system to meet the needs of today's marketplace and urges an increase in funding to education. The question then becomes, "What exactly needs to be changed?"

In the past, many of Canada's leading entrepreneurs left school at an early age. They were hindered by the teaching methods, frustrated with much of the information they were expected to memorize, and generally could see no reason for being in school. This does not mean that they stopped learning. On the contrary, entrepreneurs constantly educate themselves. They have an unquenchable thirst to learn when the subject has meaning for them. Entrepreneurs learn by doing, and their best teacher is experience — their own, as well as that of other entrepreneurs who are willing to share their mistakes and lessons. But they do avail themselves of the formal educational system when it is absolutely necessary.

The simple truth is that our formal educational sector has not prepared us for the "change economy." Entrepreneurs are agents of change, and as such they need the skills to deal with change. Ask yourself, when was the last time you took a course in creative thinking? How about team building or goal setting? Canada's educational system must devote much more attention to the needs of the entrepreneurial community. After all, entrepreneurs will be the real heroes of the 1990s.

We, as Canadians, can no longer allow our entrepreneurs to "drop out" of our schools. Education is everyone's business. We are all stakeholders and benefactors of education. Today's children are tomorrow's leaders, and today's entrepreneurs are tomorrow's employers! Gradually, our educational institutions have been addressing this problem. By the early 1990s, for example, programs were starting to link successful businesses directly to education. Businesses are becoming actively involved stakeholders, while students and the education system are gaining direct insight into market needs. We encourage you to promote and encourage this process. Small business, the engine of the 1990s,

---

* David Crane, *The Next Canadian Century: Building a Competitive Economy* (Toronto: Stoddart, 1992).

needs to take a leadership role in the education and training of future generations.

Remember, skills and abilities can be learned. The Conference Board of Canada in 1992 produced a pamphlet called "Employability Skills Profile," which outlines what critical skills are needed in today's market. These skills have been included in exercise 7.1: Rate Your Entrepreneurial Skills and Abilities. This exercise will help you determine what skills you will need to be successful in the 1990s.

❙❙ *Exercise 7.1*

RATE YOUR ENTREPRENEURIAL SKILLS AND ABILITIES

On a scale of 1 to 10, rate yourself for the following:

Accountability for Actions	. . . . . .
Adapting to Change	. . . . . .
Brain storming	. . . . . .
Communication — verbal	. . . . . .
Communication — written	. . . . . .
Comprehension	. . . . . .
Compromising	. . . . . .
Computer Skills	. . . . . .
Concentration	. . . . . .
Co-operation	. . . . . .
Creative Thinking	. . . . . .
Dealing with Lack of Job Security	. . . . . .
Decision Making	. . . . . .
Determination	. . . . . .
Diagnosing Problems	. . . . . .
Diplomacy	. . . . . .
Goal Setting	. . . . . .
Knowledge of Other Languages	. . . . . .
Lateral Thinking	. . . . . .
Leadership Skills	. . . . . .
Management Skills	. . . . . .
Listening	. . . . . .

Marketing Skills . . . . . .
Meeting New People . . . . . .
Memory Skills . . . . . .
Morals and Ethics . . . . . .
Multicultural Understanding . . . . . .
Negotiating Skills . . . . . .
Patience . . . . . .
Persistence . . . . . .
Planning . . . . . .
Positive Attitude . . . . . .
Problem-Solving Skills . . . . . .
Researching . . . . . .
Self-confidence . . . . . .
Self-motivation . . . . . .
Team Building . . . . . .
Teamwork Skills . . . . . .
Willingness to Learn . . . . . .
Working Independently . . . . . .
Working on Multiple Projects . . . . . .
Written Plans and Goals . . . . . .

SMALL BUSINESS NOTES

Still Male-Dominated

THE LOW NUMBER of women engineering graduates in Canada is the subject of considerable debate. Some say it is because the engineers' culture is hopelessly macho. Others blame it on socialization and schooling.

Most countries face the same dilemma — although many to a lesser degree than Canada. Throughout the industrial world, an average of

3.5 per cent of female university graduates are engineers, compared with 20.4 per cent of male graduates.

Canada's overall performance in graduating engineers is quite low. But we do relatively well getting students into post-secondary education — 30 per cent of the working-age population has some such training. Students here have a greater access to liberal arts programs than in many places.

SOURCE: *Canadian Social Trends* (Statistics Canada), as appearing in *The Globe and Mail*, 12 October 1993, p. B18.

📖 School's a Gas in Chemical Valley

GRADE 7 students at Ardrossan Junior High School are in the middle of a science lesson. At least they would be, if the boys and girls would only hold hands.

"This is a tricky part," says Janet Karolat, a research chemist with Dow Chemicals Canada Inc., as she transforms a line of 13-year-olds into the chemical formula for ethane gas. "You have to hold hands with the guys."

The eyeballs roll. A few faces flush with embarrassment. The hands are finally linked, and the ethane compound is formed.

This is education in Alberta's Chemical Valley, east of Edmonton, where engineers and researchers are regular visitors to classrooms. They're not there to entertain or talk about careers. Their job is to teach science.

Dow Chemical and another big local employer, Sherritt Gordon Ltd., believe it isn't enough to complain about low numbers of math and science students. They bring the subjects alive by sending their people into the schools. This business-education partnership gets deeply involved in the learning process.

On a sunny spring morning, Ms. Karolat and colleague Sandra Waters, an engineer, are teaching a unit on underground salt mining. They explain how Dow uses the caverns to store ethylene gas, a building block in the polyethylene produced at its Fort Saskatchewan plant.

Next week, a team of Sherritt Gordon employees will show up in a

Grade 8 science class, describing how nickel is refined and turned into the dollar coins.

"I think it heightens the kids' awareness of science," Mrs. Waters says. "And I think it gives them a chance to see what their dads or moms are doing."

The program allows local schools to draw on one of Canada's densest clusters of technical and engineering expertise. Dow employs 1,100 people full time at its sprawling petrochemical operations in Fort Saskatchewan; Sherritt Gordon has another 1,000 at its nickel refinery and fertilizer plant.

The companies see their involvement in schools as a blend of good works and blatant self-interest. They want to help develop the highly skilled knowledge workers they'll need in the future.

"There's a concern that people are not going into science any more, and Sherritt is very dependent on science and technology," says chemical engineer Laurie McIntosh, who co-ordinates Sherritt Gordon's classroom work. "I really liked science [as a youngster], but I never realized how practical it was. This gives the kids an idea."

About 45 per cent of the people who work at Dow's Fort Saskatchewan facility have post-secondary diplomas or degrees, says Doug Cattran, general manager and vice-president, Western Canada operations. "A high school graduate is no longer sufficient for us."

Besides classroom visits, the program has spawned another major initiative. Oil, chemical and pipeline companies in the area sponsor the annual Young Scientists Conference, which takes place this month. The event draws 120 students from six school boards to the Sherritt Gordon laboratories. There, they conduct a range of experiments under the guidance of the companies' employees.

The partnership began in 1986 when Dow decided it wanted to do more than just help out on Career Day. Managers also realized that sermons about Dow's corporate virtues wouldn't cut much ice. From the beginning, the aim was instruction, not indoctrination.

In talks with the local Strathcona County Board of Education, Dow decided it should complement what was already being taught. "It had to be meaningful and relate to the curriculum; otherwise the teachers wouldn't buy into it," says Edna Dach, the board's supervisor of science, mathematics and technology partnerships.

That meant lots of teacher input, says Mrs. Dach, one of the program's driving forces. In Grade 8, the partners found links between the content of the Solutions and Substances course and Sherritt Gordon's coin-making processes. In Grade 9, nothing seemed to fit; so not much has happened.

In the Grade 7 class at Ardrossan Junior High, Dow's lessons on underground caverns neatly complement course work on local geology and how the Prairies were formed by glaciers.

Sherritt Gordon joined Dow in the class visits. Smaller companies with fewer resources began to support the science conference. No one has calculated the costs of the companies' participation because it consists largely of volunteered time.

In fact, the commitment of employee/volunteers has been the critical factor in the program's high marks. They get a morning off work to make the presentations, but preparation is usually done on their own time.

"Instead of writing a cheque, Dow gave them the people," said Brenda Kenchington, a voice communications co-ordinator. Although she manages Dow's telephone system, she teaches the same classes on salt mining or ethylene as chemists or engineers.

"I got involved because I thought maybe I could give something back to the school system," Ms. Kenchington says. "I found out I probably got more out of it than the kids did."

Classroom presentations are informal and hands-on, complete with product samples and displays of company operations. Dow maintains a faculty of 40 to 60 people who work in pairs; the teams provide one or two presentations in each school year. Sherritt uses only eight to 10 employees for all its teaching.

In addition to regular lesson plans, employees field questions on everything from job prospects to toxic waste disposal. Bill Tchir, a research leader for Dow, once monitored a class where a student asked, "Why do you pollute so much?" The Dow employee-teacher didn't dodge the question, but gave a just-the-facts answer.

"One of the benefits is that students see it's not monsters who run these plants," Mr. Tchir says. "There's nothing in the presentations that we give that I would describe as propaganda. We talk about safety and the chemical industry."

Still, companies such as Dow find public relations value in explaining their business. "We know there's all kinds of negative stuff around about the chemical industry," Mr. Cattran says. "We don't really think we're bad folks and we don't think we're doing bad things. We're getting exposure to a lot of young people."

The school board likes the contact with big local employers. "It opens up communication lines so we can have a better understanding of what industry's needs are," says superintendent Gordon Welch of the Strathcona County Board.

So far, measurement of the program's progress is only anecdotal. No one has actually determined whether students in Chemical Valley are taking more science classes than in the 1980s. But all the partners believe it succeeds merely by making science more accessible.

The program has spread to neighbouring school districts, such as the Sherwood Park Separate, Fort Saskatchewan Separate and Lamont County school boards.

For young people, the visits are a welcome break from classroom tedium. "You listen more," says Craig Watson, a student in Ardrossan Junior High's Grade 7 class. "If it's your teacher, you don't listen as well."

Being 13-year-olds, Craig and his fellow students squirm and fidget through the lesson on ethylene. But when the teacher asks for a recap, the answers come fast and furious. Although novices at chemical formulas, some kids draw fairly representative gas diagrams.

Then there are indirect benefits. A number of girls in the Grade 7 class are encouraged to find that there are female role models in science careers. "It's nice to know that women are working in this kind of business," 13-year-old Angela Anonson says.

SOURCE: Cathryn Motherwell, *The Globe and Mail*, 4 May 1993, p. B24. Reprinted with permission from *The Globe and Mail*.

📖 Student Power

HAL ETHERIDGE had no time for jitters when he reported for work last year as a co-op student with a Victoria high-technology firm.

"On the first day of the job, I was told, 'Here's your project. Here's the general specifications. Go and do it,' " he recalls.

Mr. Etheridge was just 20, a third-year electrical engineering student at the University of Victoria. But that didn't stop his employer, Power Measurement Ltd., from assigning him to write new software for its mainstay product.

Power Measurement, which makes digital power meters, has a reputation for throwing co-op students into the fire. It draws a regular feed of young talent from UVic, which, as a centre of co-operative studies, operates a year-round schedule of alternating school and work semesters.

The job semesters — often called "four-month interviews" — give students a valuable taste of workplace realism. The program is also a godsend for small, technology-intensive businesses scrabbling for nuggets and advantage at the leading edge of knowledge.

Few companies make better use of it than privately owned, publicity-shy Power Measurement. It has built an international reputation — and sales as high as $2-million a month — partly on the efforts of students and graduates of the UVic program.

At any time, the company employs up to six engineering and business co-op students. It often ends up hiring them. About 25 of its 75 permanent employees are graduates of co-op learning. Eighty per cent of its design team came straight out of UVic's engineering co-op program.

"The co-op style is far superior to the traditional style of engineering education," says Ron Hart, the engineering vice-president who has developed Power Measurement's breakthrough products.

"Students are better educated, they're productive a lot faster and they bring a lot more to the table. They have the academic knowledge — but also the practical experience of having worked with many different employers and seen different ways of doing things."

Mr. Etheridge is a case in point. Even before he joined Power Measurement, he had already crammed a year of full-time work into his résumé.

The heart of Power Measurement's business is a range of smart, digital meters that continuously monitor power consumption and record hiccups in the supply of electricity to vital plant equipment. That's an important tool as computers and other power-sensitive electronic equipment become pervasive in industry.

The company got its start when, as a beginning engineer with BC Tel, Mr. Hart became aware of the havoc that uneven electrical supply could cause in telephone systems. But in the mid-1970s there were no technological fixes.

A microelectronics specialist, he began dabbling at home during evenings and weekends, collaborating with his first boss at the phone company, William McMillan.

Mr. Hart first came up with a meter that could monitor direct-current services used by phone companies. U.S. giant AT&T Corp. adopted it as a standard, which kick-started Power Measurement's cash flow. That original DC meter is still being supplied to Northern Telecom Ltd. for use in China.

Mr. McMillan quit his phone company job in 1985 to market meters as Power Measurement's president. Mr. Hart continued to moonlight until 1990, when he joined his partner full time. It was during that five-year interval that the bond was forged with the University of Victoria, which was just launching its engineering co-op program.

One of the company's first students in 1987 was Bradford Forth. Now 29, he's Power Measurement's marketing manager. Another was Jacques Van Campen, who is now production manager.

At that time, Power Measurement couldn't afford staff engineers — but it could hire co-op engineers at about two-thirds of a novice's starting salary. (Today, the average industry salary for co-op engineers is $2,000 a month.) The students would work without supervision during the day on tasks that included designing circuit boards. Mr. Hart, who still held down a day job at BC Tel, met them at night to give directions for the next few days.

Mr. Forth was left to work on his own designing the innards for a new power meter and writing embedded software that would run it. "There aren't a lot of companies that would let a co-op student do work like that," he says.

This raw talent helped Power Measurement through the early years, when its products had to carve out a new market. Until Mr. Hart's innovation, there was no microprocessor-based, digital power meter with an ability to store and communicate information. The only way to check on power supply was to watch a needle on a conventional instrument dial.

But with electronics invading the factory, knowing what's going on inside power supply wires and transformers has become a major cost issue. Power Measurement, which exports 80 per cent of its sales, has benefitted.

One example: In 1990, an electricity substation exploded at the de Havilland aircraft plant in Downsview, north of Toronto. The incident was blamed on a build-up of carbon caused by overheating—the result of battery-powered forklifts being plugged in for recharging.

Further investigation showed that some of de Havilland's 40-year-old power meters had worn out. A network of Power Measurement's meters was installed to bird-dog the plant's entire power supply. In one of several early paybacks, they spotted another transformer that was also being cooked.

Power Measurement's co-op students feel fortunate to play a direct role in such solutions. "I see academics more as jumping through hoops," says Rory Dueck, 25, who just finished a work semester in Power Measurement's testing laboratory.

"But work semesters are like four-month industry samplers. They give you the practical side, where you use your brain to solve problems that actually occur in the world, not ones that have been fabricated for your 'benefit.' "

Mr. Etheridge agrees. "The student gets experience and money and a good possibility of a job after graduation. You get blooded. You know the company and they know you."

But the real bonus, he says, lies in the stuff that books don't teach— "all the interpersonal skills you have to develop to get along with your co-workers. Learning them before you get a permanent job makes you better prepared in interviews."

For the university, Power Measurement provides a work-world experience for some of the 200 engineering students who need jobs every semester. Across the campus, 27 departments have more than 2,000 students in co-op education programs. Nationally, UVic ranks third in co-op enrolment, behind the University of Waterloo and Université de Sherbrooke.

"From the students' points of view, Power Measurement is definitely one of the choice jobs to get. As a result, they get the choice students," says Audrey McFarlane, an engineering co-op co-ordinator at UVic.

She argues that any company can benefit. "Instead of filling a permanent job with a one-hour or one-day interview, you have four months to see how the person really fits into your industry and whether or not they really can do what they say they can."

Mr. Etheridge, for example, told Mr. Hart he could write simple software. On his first day, he was teamed with two other co-op students to create a Windows software program that would allow personal computers to send configuration instructions to the company's power meters.

"We just went and did it," he says. "We got feedback each step of the way from the other engineers on how we were doing, what they liked and what they didn't like. We saw it right from the beginning, right to the end."

That software is now part of Power Measurement's product line — and Mr. Etheridge is back on another co-op work assignment. He's chipping away at new software that will allow easier electronic communication with the power meters.

But this time, there's more at stake. With graduation looming, Mr. Etheridge is hoping his eight-month interview will help clinch a full-time career.

SOURCE: Robert Williamson, *The Globe and Mail*, 3 May 1994, p. B26. Reprinted with permission from *The Globe and Mail*.

📖 Waterloo Uses Its Brains

TWENTY YEARS AGO, if you asked Larry Smith what Waterloo region had going for it, he might have mentioned Highway 401, handiness to Ontario auto makers, lots of skilled labour. . . . "We would have talked about railroads 20 years ago."

Today, the University of Waterloo economics professor would say the community's main strengths lie not in its hardware but in its software — entrepreneurial talents and survival instincts rooted in the immigrants who helped settle this land-locked region in south-central Ontario a century ago.

These characteristics have served Kitchener-Waterloo well over the years, Mr. Smith says, helping to spawn auto parts and food and beverage industries that continue to be the region's backbone.

And in recent years, they have fostered high-technology research within sight of Mennonite corn fields that has spun off a host of small businesses, which have developed the research into products for world consumption.

While other communities scramble to rebuild their recession-torn economies by pushing for new highways or creating industrial parks, Kitchener-Waterloo has capitalized on its internal strengths and today boasts one of the most resilient and dynamic economies in North America, Mr. Smith says.

Indeed, the new economy that stresses flexibility, productivity and being competitive on a global scale has given rise to a new geography: highways and serviced lots are still important but, increasingly, if businesses are to survive they will need to tap the community's intangible strengths.

"It may be more important to have this culture of enterprise and adaptability than a deep water port because, whether it's making sausages or software, both of these enterprises find within the community what they need to be competitive," Mr. Smith says.

Kitchener-Waterloo's 7-per-cent unemployment rate is the lowest in Canada. Not only has employment returned to prerecession levels, it is peaking (195,300 people employed in 1993), according to a study Mr. Smith prepared last fall titled Dynamic Profile of the Economy of Waterloo Region.

And the region's gross domestic product, now close to $11-billion, has rebounded smartly from the recession, rising 8 per cent in 1992, compared with 1.2 per cent for Ontario. From 1984 to 1992, Waterloo's economic growth rate has been double Ontario's, the study says.

These numbers do not reflect a major influx of industry; in fact, the region has had to adjust to corporate retrenchment (Uniroyal Goodrich Canada Inc. recently closed a plant, shedding 1,000 jobs) much like the rest of Canada, officials say.

Long before Microsoft Corp. founder William Gates put Waterloo on the map when he extolled the university's applied mathematics, engineering and co-operative education programs, the community was benefiting from high-tech enterprises, producing software, circuit boards and industrial boards, among others.

"Waterloo is a good address to have if you're in the software, high-technology business. In some areas of the States, they tell me . . . Waterloo is better known than Toronto is," says Doug Mackenzie, the City of Waterloo's director of economic development.

The so-called Canadian technology triangle, encompassing research and development taking place in Kitchener-Waterloo, nearby Cambridge and Guelph, has generated about 14,000 jobs at 160 businesses.

Key to this has been the University of Waterloo, which has spun off 106 hi-tech companies, employing 2,134 people. Some have moved to Toronto, others as far away as California, but about half are still in the region.

Considering that most export their products, primarily to the United States, it is significant that half chose to remain, says Don Eastwood, general manager of business development at the City of Cambridge. "What they tell us is: 'The people we need are here. That's why we stay.' "

Some of the leading edge technology and work practices have rubbed off on the "old economy" industries.

There's a lesson here for other Canadian regions, Mr. Smith says. Those that rely on glitzy promotions or a new highway to attract industry may be missing the boat. "If the new economy is about anything, it's about a new way of looking at enterprise, at cultural considerations — the willingness to adapt, hustle, experiment."

Kitchener-Waterloo "is not waiting for businesses to come in for its economic prosperity. If I were looking for a place to locate my enterprise . . . I would want to place it in a community that is successful in its own right. I don't want to be a white knight."

SOURCE: Brian Christmas, *The Globe and Mail*, 26 April 1994, p. B26. Reprinted with permission from *The Globe and Mail*.

📖 How Training Primed the Pump

FOR SURJIT SAGOO, a functioning water pump symbolizes how Circo Craft Co. Inc. has overcome the sloppy practices that were once a way of life.

The company makes printed circuit boards, the core of today's electronic products. But two years ago, its processes were hardly world-beaters. Early in the production run, Mr. Sagoo would dunk the boards in a cleansing chemical bath. But the pump, which flushes water into the bath, kept breaking down.

The frustrated worker would contact the maintenance people. Several days later, if he was lucky, they would fix or replace the offending pump. Meanwhile, boards were junked, time was wasted and productivity plunged.

Things only improved when Mr. Sagoo took matters into his own hands. He formed a team of workers who discovered the culprit was the calcium in the tap water. They started using de-ionized water and the system hasn't broken down since.

The solution flowed from Mr. Sagoo's training in total quality, a problem-solving approach that encourages workers to suggest ways to do things better. "Before, we were told what to do," says the veteran operator, who carries a worn black notebook under his arm to keep track of problems. "Now, we decide ourselves how to get the job done."

Quality breakdowns aren't often associated with companies whose products operate on the frontiers of technology. Yet defects, sloppiness and complacency know no bounds. Those businesses most exposed to global competition — such as Circo Craft — must be most vigorous in seeking solutions if they are to survive.

While some critics dismiss total quality as little more than common sense dressed up in expensive 1990s psychobabble, Circo Craft swears by the approach, which, it says, pulled the firm back from the brink.

Still, introducing the process proved jarring because both managers and workers had grown cocky in their status as the Canadian leader in printed boards, those thin panels containing electronic circuits for components in cars, telephone switches and computers.

Dwayne Poteet, the U.S. executive hired from Texas Instruments Inc. to spearhead the change, quickly encountered this attitude. "When I arrived, most of the staff thought they were world class. I had to tell them that if I was on the outside looking in, I wouldn't even do business with them."

In the late 1980s, fewer customers did. Circo Craft, based on Montreal's West Island, found that markets were no longer local but global. It was being undercut by Asian firms that could make the boards for up to 20 per cent less.

In addition, the industry was restructuring and the survivors were more competitive than ever. The worldwide recession compounded the crisis.

The financial results were a stark indicator of Circo Craft's plight. It lost $5.9-million in 1991, following upon a $1.4-million loss the previous year, which was the first time in its 20-year history it had lost money. The shock jarred management into action.

As troubled companies often do, it called in a consulting firm, Montreal-based Perrier & Beaudry. The prescription was total quality, a Japanese-style approach that advocates the formation of teams that meet regularly to discuss problems in their particular area. They come up with their own solutions to saving money, responding more quickly to clients and generally making things run more smoothly.

Circo Craft embraced quality with a vigour that surprised even the consultants. "It is probably one of the most aggressive companies I've seen in terms of making this thing work," says Perrier & Beaudry president Danyelle Beaudry.

The training effort is particularly striking. The company in 1992 devoted 60 to 100 hours per worker in training. This year, the average to the end of October is 71 hours. Its goal is an average of 100 hours a year, compared with a North American average of eight hours per employee.

But this didn't come cheap: Circo Craft allocated $1-million just in 1992 to train its troops. Workers took time off the assembly line and went to classes — lots of them — to learn to work together in teams, to find out how to gather data to document the source of a problem and, of course, to resolve problems.

They learned skills beyond those needed for their own jobs, and how to work with clients or suppliers. They were videotaped on the job to determine whether — and where — they were wasting time.

At the same time, managers learned how to give employees more latitude to figure out things for themselves. This would free up time for more mid- and long-term planning and less putting out fires.

Layers of management were compressed to two from five. Often, managers' power shrank. They were called coaches now, and that took some getting used to. "Middle managers probably showed the most resistance," says human resources director Madeline Gareau.

But to Dave Rooke, who acts as a liaison between the company and its customers and suppliers, these management-level changes were necessary. "The new culture is to let the operations people solve the problem," he says. "The people at the top maintain the vision."

Despite its success, total quality has yet to be fully embraced at Circo Craft. At last count, 60 per cent of the 900 employees have participated in at least one team. Membership is voluntary.

Mr. Poteet acknowledges there is resistance. Some employees feel they've seen it all before. "They're waiting for us to go back to the old way." Others don't feel comfortable opening up in a group setting.

Supporters say the proof lies in improved financial results. Despite the training cost — plus the expense of hiring temporary workers while permanent staff was off to class — Circo turned the previous years' losses into a $3-million profit in 1992. And it did it without raising prices.

Cycle time — the period between receiving an order and getting the product delivered — was cut by 30 per cent. Sales per worker rose to more than $121,000 in 1992 from $93,000 in 1990.

And the teams saved lots of money, too. In the Kirkland, Que., plant's drilling room, where layers of a circuit board are drilled together, a team headed by Agostino Cappiello extended the life of a drill, saving $5,750 a year.

Circo Craft claims that such improvements could not have been made without the hefty training investment. As Mr. Poteet maintains: "Our profitability is almost directly linked to our investment in training."

The training also helped overcome a certain rigidity that was reflected in an inability to respond to clients other than the most important customer, Northern Telecom Ltd. In 1992, Northern Telecom accounted for 49 per cent of Circo Craft's $94-million in sales.

The attitude was: "If an approach was okay for Northern Telecom, it was okay for everyone else," Mr. Poteet says.

These days, other customers encounter more flexibility. When they make inquiries, they are directed to the Circo Craft plant that is handling their business. (There are four — in Kirkland, Granby and Pointe Claire, Que., and, most recently, Puerto Rico.)

"Before, the customer could not relate to a given face," Mr. Poteet says. "Now, he or she can often deal with the person right on the shop floor."

To keep the faith, incentives are crucial. "Once a project is completed, a team is taken out for lunch or dinner, or they get gifts like pins or pens," says Mr. Cappiello, head of the drill team.

Managers insist total quality is no passing fancy, to be abandoned after a string of good results. Says Ms. Gareau: "We tell employees that if we maintain productivity and competitiveness, then we'll be here tomorrow."

SOURCE: Ann Gibbon, *The Globe and Mail*, 16 November 1993, p. B26. Reprinted with permission from *The Globe and Mail*.

📖 High Tech's Class Act

SIXTH GRADER Matthew Rempel slips a note to his classmate Lindsay LeBlanc: "Why don't you get a new pair of boots?"

"Why should I?" Lindsay snaps back.

"Because they're always getting caught on the seat in the lobby," Matthew replies.

"Why don't you get a new brain?" Lindsay retorts.

Getting a new brain — or, more precisely, a new attitude toward technology — is what learning is all about for students at Birds Hill Elementary School.

On this winter's day, the classroom is Northern Telecom Ltd.'s Winnipeg factory, which makes telephone switching equipment. And the notes being passed? They are actually electronic messages, conveyed along the factory's internal E-mail system.

The sixth graders have just finished a shift on the Northern Telecom assembly line where they helped install computer chips on to integrated circuit boards of their own design. Then they tested the boards to make sure they worked.

A day at Northern Telecom is a core component in an innovative learning approach pioneered by Birds Hill school, a kindergarten to Grade 6 facility with 500 students in a northern satellite of Winnipeg.

Like many North American schools, Birds Hill and its staff recognize the need for its children to adapt to a changing workplace. But few are as single-minded about providing hands-on experience in new technology and problem-solving.

Birds Hill, although part of the public River East School Division, marches to its own drummer. "We call it education entrepreneurialism," says teacher Norman Lee, the program's prime mover. "We're saying there is a marketplace called education. What an entrepreneur does is look at the marketplace and sees that there are needs not being met out there."

To achieve its goals, Birds Hill has enlisted an army of "stakeholders" from its school community. These include parents who participate in a busy lineup of plant tours, workshops and after-four classes. Winnipeg businesses such as Northern Telecom have signed on as volunteer "mentors" for these knowledge workers of the future.

Set on the windswept prairie north of Winnipeg, Birds Hill school doesn't look like an education innovator from the outside. The architecture is modern elementary school. The community is primarily upper middle class.

But inside the brick walls, something different is going on. The school is spectacularly well-equipped with information technology, thanks to the generosity of its business contacts. The computer laboratory contains scores of donated personal computers, as well as a mini-robotics lab.

In one corner sits a $50,000 Digital Equipment Corp. mini-main-frame, given by the manufacturer. It could run the local school board's entire data base. Birds Hill plans to use it for a big electronic bulletin board.

The school's regular bulletin boards promote activities not normally found in public schools. On one evening, there is a meeting of Science Moms, in which community mothers will be given math and science primers. The idea is to help them, in turn, encourage their daughters to pursue careers in technology and science.

Another feature is Engineering After School, where students can work with civil, electrical and mechanical engineers who volunteer their time. Then there is Parent Technology Group, in which parents organize tours to local high-tech sites and provide workshops on technology.

This approach is the brainchild of Mr. Lee, 46, who about a decade ago was having second thoughts about his own career. In the mid-1980s, he returned from a teaching exchange in Germany and was "dumped" into Birds Hill as a resource teacher.

He found that his new principal, Roberta Vyse, shared his views on education. He helped develop the school's new mission statement: "To encourage students in a compassionate and sensitive way to deal with the technological, environmental and social issues in a rapidly changing world."

Mr. Lee began to bang on corporate doors to line up clients for his mentorship program. The business community was receptive. Today the school has links with 23 Winnipeg firms, mostly in high-tech and biomedical industries. The program gives Grades 5 and 6 pupils a chance to learn firsthand from practicing professionals in fields from journalism to telecommunications.

As a resource teacher, Mr. Lee passes half his official work day helping Grades 4 to 6 students upgrade math and reading skills. The rest of it is spent as a technical and computer adviser. But most of his waking hours, including many evenings and weekends, are devoted to networking with other teachers, parents, and businesses.

For companies, the motivation is both self-interest and service. "By 1996 or 1997, Northern Telecom says it could hire every graduate in electrical engineering in Canada," explains Mr. Lee. "They alone could use every single person who graduates. This is part of their grassroots program to develop more science and technological expertise."

Northern Telecom product engineer Tim Broschuk volunteers an estimated 150 hours a year to working with Birds Hill children. "The kids are really our future customers," he says.

But Mr. Broschuk is also the father of a seven-month-old daughter. "We have to take action. We're here to help them put more tools in their tool box."

Parents like the results. Accountant Fred Whitehouse pulled daughter Suzanne, 11, and son Jonathan, 9, out of French immersion when he learned about Birds Hill's brand of educational entrepreneurship.

Like many Canadian parents, Mr. Whitehouse didn't think his youngsters were developing the right skills in their old school. In his view, expectations were extremely low in terms of reading, language skills and mathematics.

Mr. Whitehouse says that, after moving to Birds Hill, his children have more of a desire to learn. "It's not all high-tech — they have an excellent music program as well. But over all, I think the standards are higher. If you push a little harder the kids respond."

Ms. Vyse, the principal, sees the change in the career aspirations of the children. "It's not ballerina, actress, rock star or hockey player any more. They are talking about careers that they've been exposed to through the mentorship program."

Birds Hill's approach to technology education has garnered rave reviews. It has captured several national teaching awards. Former federal science minister William Winegard, once a university scientist, has said Canada could use 10,000 more Birds Hill schools.

Its independent course has gained grudging tolerance from the local school board. But some educators are outright opposed to the approach. They argue there is more to developing young minds than simply organizing them for the workplace.

Ron Bannister, vice-president of the Manitoba Teachers Society, says society needs artists, musicians and philosophers as much as aerospace engineers, geneticists and MBAS.

He criticizes Birds Hill for single-mindedly adopting a business prescription. "There's no question business in Canada has an agenda to get into the classroom and we are resisting that. We don't want business to co-opt education."

Mr. Lee, meanwhile, is unapologetic about his goal of moving a school system that resists movement. "The way you get schools to change is you end-run [the system]. You tell parents: 'Hey, do you want your kids to have a high-skilled, high-paying job? This is what's at stake.'"

But what about the children themselves? How do they feel about Birds Hill's near-obsession with technology training? Among the 11-year-olds at the Northern Telecom plant in Winnipeg, there is no evidence of overkill.

Mr. Broschuk, the product engineer, is explaining how fibre optics are revolutionizing telecommunications. "I need four volunteers to be free electrons," he says. Up pop four grinning youngsters who line up shoulder-to-shoulder. Another student simulates a digital voice signal travelling down a telephone wire.

The reaction is typical, Mr. Lee says. "If you talk to the kids while they're doing it, they're just so excited."

SOURCE: David Roberts, *The Globe and Mail*, 26 January 1993. Reprinted with permission from *The Globe and Mail*.

❙❙ *Questions*

1. Complete exercise 7.1: Rate Your Entrepreneurial Skills and Abilities. How do you plan to compensate and learn in the areas you feel weak?

2. What are the students described in the articles learning from the businesses who have linked to education?

3. Learning is a lifelong pursuit. How do you plan to continue your learning process?

4. How do you intend to participate as an active stakeholder in the education of others in the future? How will you take a leadership role?

5. Locate a business that will give you firsthand work experience, even if you have to work free in the short term. Interview the owner and report back to your group.

GOING
OUTSIDE
CANADA

Exports now account for about 26 per cent (1992) of our gross domestic product, which adds up to about $180 billion. Today, about one-third of Canadian jobs depend on the export market, and we know that our export trade will grow by leaps and bounds over the next ten years. The signing of the Free Trade Agreement (1991) and the North America Free Trade Agreement (1994) signalled the dawn of a new era in Canadian small business. These agreements alone have opened the door for Canadians to a huge single market of 370 million consumers with an annual economic output of nearly $7 trillion and 30 per cent of all global trade.

Today, our major trading partner is the United States, accounting for over 70 per cent of our export trade. But with a new economic order taking shape, the picture on into the next millenium may be quite different. The North American market is expected to grow by about 2.5 per cent per year over the next few years, compared with a yearly growth rate of 5 to 6 per cent in the Asian-Pacific region, and a corresponding growth rate of 3 to 4 per cent in the European Community. If these growth rates continue, our major trading partners may very well be outside North America. In Asia alone, the share of world income is projected to increase from 24 per cent (1989) to 35 per cent (2010).*

Has Canadian small business taken advantage of this trend to go global? The answer is a clear NO! For example, only 3 to 4 per cent (dollar value) of our manufacturing exports come from businesses with sales of less than $2 million. There are approximately 15,000 Canadian manufacturers, but only 50 large firms account for over one half of our export revenue. Our major exports are motor vehicles, lumber, and paper. Figures 8.1 and 8.2 show Canada's top-ranked export markets and our leading merchandise exports.

Figure 8.1. CANADA'S TOP 10 RANKED EXPORT MARKETS, 1991

RANK	COUNTRY	$ CDN. (*millions*)	% OF TOTAL EXPORTS
1	United States	109,614	75.25
2	Japan	7,157	4.91
3	United Kingdom	3,036	2.08
4	Germany	2,432	1.67
5	South Korea	1,889	1.30
6	China	1,886	1.29
7	Netherlands	1,724	1.18
8	France	1,422	.98
9	Belgium	1,100	.76
10	Italy	1,072	.74

NOTE: Total trade with the world in 1991: $145,659 million.

SOURCE: External Affairs and International Trade Canada, 1992 (based on Statistics Canada data).

---

* OECD Forum for the Future, Long-Term Prospects for the World Economy (Paris: OECD, 1992).

Figure 8.2. CANADA'S FIVE LEADING
MERCHANDISE EXPORTS, 1991

RANK	EXPORT COMMODITY	$ CDN. (millions)	% OF TOTAL EXPORTS
1	passenger cars	16,500	11.32
2	trucks	7,200	4.94
3	motor vehicle parts and engines	6,300	4.32
4	softwood lumber	5,000	3.4
5	wood pulp and similar pulp	4,900	3.36

NOTE: Total trade with the world in 1991: $145,659 million.

SOURCE: External Affairs and International Trade Canada, 1992 (based on Statistics Canada data).

In the new economy of the 1990s, it is likely that export trading patterns will change dramatically. Growth in the Asian, Latin American, Mexican, and Eastern European markets will offer new opportunities to Canadian small business. The global marketplace is no longer about natural resources and automobiles, industries which require mainly large businesses. The new marketplace is about information and technology industries in which small businesses can effectively compete. For example, Canada currently has about a two per cent share of the global market in the software and computer services, but we also have over 2,000 companies (mainly small) positioned to increase our world market share in this growing field. Opportunities abound for small business in the export market, and we can no longer afford to ignore opportunities. In a world of global telecommunications networks, small businesses with fax machines and computer modems are well positioned to enter the global economy.

The first step is adjusting our mind-set: we have to believe that we really can compete. Success starts with the belief that you can be a player in the new economic order. Evaluate your export readiness by completing exercise 8.1: Test Your Export Quotient. If, after completing this test, you find that you are not cut out to export, don't be too quick to pack up and quit. Even if you do not think that you are going to be involved in exporting, all Canadians must be ready to learn as much as they can about our new global economy.

▮▮ *Exercise 8.1*

TEST YOUR EXPORT QUOTIENT

		YES	NO
1.	Are you entrepreneurial?	. . . . . .	. . . . . .
2.	Do you have a reliable, service-oriented character?	. . . . . .	. . . . . .
3.	Are you a natural networker, building and maintaining relationships?	. . . . . .	. . . . . .
4.	Do you see yourself as highly organized and research-oriented?	. . . . . .	. . . . . .
5.	Do you have a sense of "mission" as a Canadian?	. . . . . .	. . . . . .
6.	Do you possess good communication skills?	. . . . . .	. . . . . .
7.	Is a sales, marketing or distribution background featured in your résumé?	. . . . . .	. . . . . .
8.	Do you excel in finance and business related subjects?	. . . . . .	. . . . . .
9.	Do you pride yourself in your strong negotiating skills?	. . . . . .	. . . . . .
10.	Are you experienced in handling complex documentation?	. . . . . .	. . . . . .
11.	Are you an avid follower of global politics?	. . . . . .	. . . . . .
12.	Do you have the ability to speak and write more than one language?	. . . . . .	. . . . . .
13.	Are you sensitive to different cultures?	. . . . . .	. . . . . .
14.	Do you consider yourself able to adopt ideas easily, even under pressure?	. . . . . .	. . . . . .
15.	Are you well-travelled or curious about other cultures?	. . . . . .	. . . . . .

TOTAL *(award 1 point for every "yes")*:   . . . . . .

EVALUATING YOUR SCORE

1–6   Although you have acquired some skills related to exporting, you need further assessment to find out if you are suited to this field.

7–10   You show a keen interest in the subject. However, you should consider increasing your knowledge, language and technical trading skills training.

11–15 You have a high rating in the critical factors that make companies and individuals successful in the exciting field of global trade.

SOURCE: Forum for International Trade Training Inc. (FITT), *Global Entrepreneurship*, 1993, module 1, p. 206.

A major factor in becoming "export ready" is increasing your cultural and geographical awareness. Did you know, for example, that over 50 per cent of Mexico's population is under the age of twenty? Did you know that Mexico City is the world's largest city, with over 20 million people? Did you know that the distance between Toronto and Mexico City is shorter than the distance between Toronto and Vancouver? We encourage you to choose a country and learn as much as you can about it. How much do you know about the culture of China, Japan, India, or Mexico for that matter? How many languages can you speak?

Here is an outline of basic cultural differences between three of Canada's trading partners.

- *Japan:* Though it is a highly advanced economic powerhouse, Japan displays many of the characteristics of a traditional society. The Japanese value hard work, practicality, and dedication. Their society is group-oriented and its members are loyal to each other and to their superiors. At the same time, many important decisions are taken on the basis of consensus, rather than as a result of a direct order by a superior. Aggressiveness is not appreciated and politeness is preferred. Age and tradition are both highly respected.

- *Mexico:* Mexico has many of the characteristics of a traditional society, but as the country undergoes rapid modernization, non-traditional elements are beginning to appear. Mexicans are highly family oriented. They value personal honour and the preservation of "face." At the same time, Mexicans view individuals as more important that schedules. They do not like to do business with strangers and prefer to get to know people before entering into business transactions with them. Two- to three-hour lunches are common in business: the social part of the lunch takes up the largest portion of the time and business is dealt with in the last few minutes.

- *United States:* The U.S. is the classic example of a non-traditional society. Americans tend to value individualism and personal achievement. They can be aggressive and outspoken. They are not easily embarrassed and like to express candid opinions on a wide variety of topics, some quite personal. They value innovation, industry, and integrity. They enjoy a good sense of humour, and strongly value freedom and independence. Above all, American business people are motivated by a "can do" sense of energetic purpose that resents delays and moves impatiently toward action.

SOURCE: Forum for International Trade Training Inc. (FITT), *Global Entrepreneurship*, 1993, module 1, pp. 209–10.

In addition to mind-set and cultural awareness, you are also going to need technical knowledge to compete effectively in the international market. You must know about laws regulating free trade, the role of forwarders, brokers, agents, and so on. You will need to know about transportation, insurance, letters of credit, and other trade instruments. To feel comfortable with this new "language" of trade, you are probably going to need some training. The best time to start is now. Your first task will be to learn how to create a market profile. A market research profile of a particular country would include information about the following topics:

- Customs and business practices
- Transportation and communications
- Networks
- Political environment
- Economic situation
- Trade statistics with Canada and other countries

Once you have completed your market profile, there are a number of other steps to be taken. These are summarized in figure 8.3. Much more detail on each of these steps is provided in the Industry, Science and Technology Canada publication entitled "Exporting for Competitiveness: Ten Steps for Small Business." If you are seriously thinking about the export market, this publication is a valuable source of information. You should also solicit the help of Canadian embassies and trade commissions, the federal and provincial governments, and non-government sources such as trade associations and banks.

Figure 8.3. TEN STEPS FOR SMALL BUSINESS — EXPORTING

Step #1	Evaluate your export potential.
Step #2	Select and research target foreign markets.
Step #3	Master the terminology of exporting.
Step #4	Choose an entry strategy.
Step #5	Determine your price.
Step #6	Promote your product or service.
Step #7	Arrange your financing.
Step #8	Get your product or service to market.
Step #9	Implement your export plan.
Step #10	Review and revise your strategy.

SOURCE: "Exporting for Competitiveness: Ten Steps for Small Business," Entrepreneurship and Small Business Office, Industry, Science, and Technology Canada, 1992, pp. 3–6.

SMALL BUSINESS NOTES

📖 A Talent for Talk

HOW DO CANADIANS EXCEL in the world? We're pretty handy with charts, diagrams, overhead projectors and all the tools of the consulting game. In fact, Canadian consultants have done better selling their services abroad than foreign consultants have done in Canada, futurist John Kettle says.

The exports aren't very big—at best, a quarter of 1 per cent of gross domestic product—and they've bounced up and down with recessions. But this is a small triumph in global services trade, where Canada otherwise has done poorly. It's also a nice niche in a post-industrial world where services play a bigger economic role.

The major contributors are our consulting engineers, who have a stellar world reputation. But we have lawyers, management experts and constitutional experts who can talk up a storm, too.

SOURCE: *The Globe and Mail*, 28 June 1994, p. 6.

📖 Liberal Promises

WHILE IN OPPOSITION, the Liberals applauded a plan by the Canadian Chamber of Commerce to launch an export-oriented, networking program for small businesses. Under this plan borrowed from Denmark and used there with astonishing success, four to five small companies in a particular industry are linked together.

"The thinking is that alone [these firms] may not be big enough to do anything, but together they can take a run at shipping to other countries," said Philip O'Brien, chairman of the Chamber of Commerce. As well, entrepreneurs are given a "mentor" from a larger company, who can pass on expertise about marketing, finance and exporting.

The chamber is ready to roll with five pilot projects by February [1994]. The costs—$100,000 per project for the services of the mentors, marketing studies and test market runs—would be split by the federal government and participants.

"The Liberals are very much aware of it and we hope they make it part of their program," Mr. O'Brien said. He said that in Denmark, 500 of these small-business networks have been established in the past four years.

SOURCE: Excerpt from Jerry Zeidenberg, "Liberal Promises Sound Good to Cash-Starved Sector," *The Globe and Mail*, 1 November 1993, p. B6.

📖 Net Results

SMALL CANADIAN BUSINESSES looking for foreign partners can now plug into an international business network with links to 35 countries. BCNet was established in 1988 to assist businesses in the 12 countries of the European Community, but has expanded to countries such as Argentina, Morocco and Australia.

Companies can gain access to the network through private business consultants, who, for a fee, submit profiles to the network's central unit in Brussels. These profiles are entered into a computer system that identifies potential partners among 13,000 other entries. If a match is found, the consultant follows up with more direct contact and negotiation.

The Canadian Chamber of Commerce is the Canadian "gateway" to BCNet. It charges consultants $375 for up to six different profiles of a company placed on the network. Consultants will determine their own final fees, depending on the package of services provided.

For more information, contact: BCNet national contact point, Canadian Chamber of Commerce, Suite 1160, Ottawa, Ont., KIP 6N4, Telephone (613) 238-4000 or fax (613) 238-7643.

SOURCE: *The Globe and Mail*, 7 February 1994, p. B6.

📖 High Hopes, Wide Horizons

THE ENTREPRENEURIAL CROWD is going global. For many fast-growing companies, the story for 1994 will be international expansion, spurred on by the North American free-trade agreement and the General Agreement on Tariffs and Trade.

A large number of Canada's owner-managers expect increased sales and profit in 1994. And, confirming the fashionable view that job growth is strongest among small business, they are talking about hiring.

These are the themes of interviews with a sampling of business owners across the country. Here are the individual outlooks:

GRACE WHITE, 35.
President, 80-per-cent owner.
Canjam Trading Ltd., Dartmouth, N.S.

BUSINESS: Exports frozen food (mackerel, herring, for example), primarily to Jamaica, and the United States and Hong Kong.

ANNUAL SALES: $6.5-million. Employees: 2.

Ms. White has mixed feelings — she's high on global expansion but has soured on aspects of doing business in Canada. She hopes to increase the company's revenue by 10 per cent in 1994 and has set her sights on South Korea, which she believes is a good match for Canjam's exports.

"We know our expertise lies in working in one country at a time until we learn all there really is to know before we move on. It's how we want to strategically grow. We've done what we want to do in Jamaica. Now we have certain goals and objectives in Korea.

"But some of the issues I'm looking at are the increased taxation and all the different costs of doing business in Canada and, in particular, Nova Scotia. There are corporate taxation, personal taxation, unemployment insurance, Canada Pension Plan — and all the different costs of having employees.

"What is business all about? It's about: How much money am I going to put in my pocket at the end of the day? I'm prepared to pay a certain percentage for the benefits of living in Canada. I just feel I'm at the saturation point.

"It's amazing that I have to think in terms of how I'm going to grow my business in terms of all these costs. Every movement up [in income] is going to be a movement that, instead of keeping me here, is going to make me look at other places to do my business."

LINDA COLLIER, 30.
President and owner.
Tri-ad International Freight Forwarding Ltd., Mississauga.

BUSINESS: Freight forwarder, importing and exporting high-tech products.

ANNUAL SALES: $3.9-million. Employees: 10.

Five years ago, Ms. Collier predicted that 1994 would be a year of strong growth. It's shaping up better than expected — she hopes to double staff and revenue in 1994.

"We recently joined forces with a very large U.S. freight forwarding company called Surfair [based in Atlanta with 32 offices and sales of

$75-million U.S.]. We have agreed to represent each other in the other's country. Our sales team will be going to the States to see their offices and basically doing a large push to promote transborder trade.

"Because Surfair is only a domestic U.S. freight forwarder, we're assisting them in opening their borders and taking on all of North America.

"I think we'll be greatly affected by NAFTA — not right out of the gate but certainly in the long run and I think very positively.

"We're planning on doing a lot of our own work in 1994. We've bought a lot of trucks and equipment, and we've gone to the government and obtained a Customs bond to have our own bonded warehouse facility."

GEOFFREY CHUTTER, 41.
President, majority shareholder.
Whitewater West Industries Ltd., Richmond, B.C.

BUSINESS: Makes waterpark equipment, such as fibreglass slides and wave-making equipment.
ANNUAL REVENUE: $13-million. Employees: 85.

Mr. Chutter, who ran for the Conservatives in the 1993 federal election, is looking farther afield now — at emerging markets in Asia.

"Our two most interesting developments in 1994 are the opening up of China as a market and the diversification program under way within our company. Whitewater has always been very active in the international market with 97 per cent of our work exported.

"We have a well-organized strategy for Asia that we have been implementing for the past eight or nine years. Japan has historically been our No. 1 customer there, but most recently we have had tremendous interest from mainland China.

"The thirst in that country for development, and certainly recreation and leisure development, remains very large. We recently shipped 45 container loads of our products into China and expect more in the near future.

"Our biggest opportunity is the continued development of new ideas and new products in the waterpark/amusement park industry — and also the full development of marketing strategy for our soft [cushioned] bathtub.

"It's ironic that the worse the economic policy, the more we profit as an exporting company. We quote all our contracts in U.S. dollars. As long as the international market feels our economy is weak, we will enjoy a very favourable exchange rate — and an improved bottom line."

MARY TIDLUND, 37.
President and part owner.
Trophy Resources Ltd., Arcola, Sask.

BUSINESS: Oil company specializing in horizontal drilling.
SALES FOR YEAR ENDED JUNE 30: $4-million. Employees: 50 full time, about 200 drilling rig hands as needed.

Ms. Tidlund's company has just beefed up its drilling capacity by acquiring another Saskatchewan company. In 1994, she hopes to build on Trophy's reputation as a leader in horizontal drilling, a technology with high costs but high output too.

"With that [new business] wrapped into our already busy schedule, we will definitely be one of the most active horizontal drilling companies in 1994.

"We're a little different than your standard oil company. We own all of our own horizontal drilling equipment. . . . We also designed a lot of our equipment, which saves money.

"Right now, 98 per cent of our production is out of the southeastern corner of Saskatchewan. But we will be expanding and we've already started in Manitoba and Alberta."

Trophy is entering 1994 on a roll, having surpassed its 1992-93 results in the first quarter of 1993-94. Ms. Tidlund expects to double staff in 1994 and triple daily oil production to 2,300 barrels by the end of the next fiscal year.

TIM CRAGO, 39.
President and majority owner.
Nortech Surveys (Canada) Inc., Calgary.

BUSINESS: Geodetic, aerial and marine surveying.
SALES: $10-million. Employees: 90 (Calgary, Halifax, the Middle East and Malaysia).

Mr. Crago will be looking for business in Russia, North Africa and South America, areas that are opening to development and require surveying services.

"I have a different view of things than other companies. I more than welcome competition to come into Canada and have it out with us, as long as I can go to their country and have it out with them. I think, in the end, Canadian expertise is going to win those battles more often than not.

"The majority of our work is overseas and, having poked around, there's a lot of opportunity there for us. The challenge is staying ahead of our competition. The geographical spread of our business is changing rapidly. The people who are out getting the chances first are going to be the winners. If you're in second, you're really in a tough spot.

"NAFTA is of great interest to us, and the United States is a big market. It's becoming easier to export to the States than to export to other provinces in Canada. We're also interested in free trade opening up access for Canadian professionals to U.S. service industries."

ERIC D'ANJOU, 26.
Vice-president and owner (with wife Evelyn Trempe).
Orage Vêtements Sports, Waterloo, Que.

BUSINESS: Manufacturer of sportswear (skiing, cycling, hiking).
ANNUAL SALES: Under $4-million. Employees: 65.

"We are a small company and still don't cover all of Canada. But we are looking for a 30-per-cent increase in sales next year.

"We're going after new markets in fall and spring clothing. We have longer spring and fall periods in Canada now, and snow is less and less important. We put a lot of emphasis on fall fashions and it has paid off. We are now selling in Vancouver, Saskatchewan, Alberta, but we are not yet in Southern Ontario. We are working on this now, probably for 1994.

"As we expand, we are using contractors more to make our clothing. A lot of these are in Ontario. In fact, there are probably more people working on our products in Ontario than there are regular customers there.

"Our biggest risk is the weather. In Montreal, we just had our first big snowstorm. The climate is changing quite a bit in the country — and we have to adjust our product to it."

J. REGIS DUFFY, 61.
President and owner.
Diagnostic Chemicals Ltd., Charlottetown.

BUSINESS: Makes specialty chemicals for use in clinical diagnostic testing.

SALES: $7.5-million. Employees: 65 (plus 20 at U.S. marketing subsidiary).

Mr. Duffy hopes to expand on exports, which represent 85 per cent of sales, and to improve revenue to $9-million in 1994. The company had a pretax profit of $400,000 in 1993, he says. "I can easily see $650,000 next year."

"We are shipping into Mexico, we're starting to ship into China. We are increasing our U.S. sales.

"I think the important thing is we give a high level of service. The large companies are always looking for people who will do specialty work for them on a fairly reliable basis."

SOURCE: *The Globe and Mail*, 27 December 1993, p. B4. Reprinted with permission from *The Globe and Mail*.

📖 Firms Team Up to Tackle East

A CONSORTIUM of Canadian companies, eager to crack some of Southeast Asia's hot markets for advanced environmental services, are pooling their knowledge and resources to chase multi-million dollar contracts.

Canora Asia Inc., established earlier this year, so far has 15 companies on board and is ready to set up its head office in Indonesia, where it says it is close to landing its first deal.

The chief appeal of Canora is that it promises small to medium-sized companies with specialized services and products a low-cost entree to the region and a chance to work on large projects that otherwise would be out of their league.

As well, it provides larger companies with a chance to make connections in new Asian markets and the opportunity to use the consortium as a farm network where they can scout for smaller, niche players that might be recruited for future export project teams.

For a minimum two-share, $20,000 stake, companies — which are sometimes competitors back home — agree to share their staff and their expertise on projects secured by Canora.

Participating companies will help draft proposals and will be invited to nominate employees to work on Canora project teams.

Team members will be selected by Curtis Whyte, a Calgary management consultant and Canora's vice-president of operations, based on their expertise and price. In return, Canora will reimburse companies for the use of their staff, plus a markup.

Canora is also prepared to be a joint venture partner, backstopping consortium members independently pursuing contracts in Asia.

The consortium will concentrate on contracts involving solid waste management, the treatment of hazardous waste and waste water, and the supply of safe drinking water.

"A group like Canora, with members from many disciplines and different sectors of the economy, gives us that much more clout, especially in a market that's right now dominated by Japanese or well-established British groups," said Roger Woeller, senior vice-president of Ottawa-based Water and Earth Science Associates Ltd., a Canora member.

With the tab running to more than $10,000 for three weeks of executive door-knocking in Asia, Canora's concept appealed to the mid-sided company that specializes in consulting work on water supply issues.

Maintaining an independent office in Asia can cost a company $250,000 a year. It can take a year or two of beating bushes in patient, market-building commitment to start landing contracts.

Partnership, said Mr. Woeller, is the best way to get the critical mass needed to get on the bidding lists for Pacific Rim projects.

The consortium can marshal a broad front of expertise to be matched to job needs, sharing expenses and creating an exclusive forum in which shareholders get to rub shoulders in what he calls "the old connections game."

Canora says two other companies from Ontario, three from Newfoundland, one from Nova Scotia, three from Quebec, two from Alberta and three from British Columbia have made at least a $10,000 down payment for a stake in the consortium.

Ten more subscribing shareholders are needed to round out the target roster of 25.

"As somebody said to me, it's so Canadian it's almost un-Canadian," said acting president Gerry Glazier, a Halifax environmental management consultant. Mr. Glazier worked for three years on a project to transfer Canadian environmental management know-how to Indonesian authorities.

In Asia, where connections are the first rule of business, the Canadians are banking that Canora's team approach can add up to marketplace advantage.

Although some of the companies in the consortium are rivals in Canada, consortium organizers say there's more than enough work to go around in Indonesia, Malaysia, Thailand, the Philippines and Singapore, where large projects are being funded by the World Bank and Asia Development Bank.

Canora projects potential billings of $114-million over the first five years and net revenue of at least $9-million.

Shareholders that don't get to work on Canora projects could share, over the long term, in possible retained earnings and dividends.

Roche Ltd., a large Quebec City engineering firm, bought into the consortium more for the prospects of networking in a Canadian-Asia business incubator than for the appeal of new work.

Pierre Brulotte, executive vice-president of Roche International and Canora's interim chairman, said Roche, with 150 of its 650 employees dedicated to environmental and resource management work, has spent $80,000 in the past two years chasing jobs in Asia. It has already teamed up with small specialty firms from Eastern Canada for projects in China and Malaysia.

Canora, Mr. Brulotte said, looks like a very cheap way to market in Southeast Asia. "Although we're bigger than most of the firms around the table, it's an opportunity for us to be part of something even bigger."

Another Canora member, Essa Technologies Ltd. of Vancouver, is typical of the environmental boutique businesses that appeal to Roche. Essa's specialties include using computer modelling to assess environmental impacts and proprietary software to support decision making. With 36 staff, it's looking to open offices in Europe and Asia next year.

"For the large infrastructure projects being proposed for Southeast Asia, we can only hope to compete for very small fractions of that work," said Essa chairman and co-founder Nicholas Sonntag.

"Getting together with a group of companies like Canora will give us a competitive advantage against some of the monolithic corporations that are bidding."

A meeting in Toronto in early January could greatly influence Canora's business plan. Mr. Glazier says he hopes to settle a memorandum of understanding with Jakarta Industrial Estate for a joint venture company to be 60 per cent owned by Canora. Jakarta Industrial is a subsidiary of P.T. Pesero and is jointly owned by the Indonesian ministry of finance and the metropolitan district of Jakarta.

If it happens, it will be a sign that Canora's connections are sparking.

Jakarta Industrial operates a 450-hectare industrial park, where 400 companies dump waste water into a river after no more than primary treatment.

Canora is proposing to design, build, own and operate a low-tech, aerobic water treatment system as a demonstration project, recovering its costs through user fees.

SOURCE: Robert Williamson, *The Globe and Mail*, 13 December 1993, p. B5. Reprinted with permission from *The Globe and Mail*.

📖 Help Wanted, Canadians Preferred

WHEN TORONTO ENTREPRENEUR David Medhurst was trying to line up Canadian suppliers of windows and doors for houses that already had buyers in Germany, he wrote 430 letters to major suppliers in Canada and received a total of three responses.

That was two years ago. Canada was in a deep recession. The construction industry was in a slump. Yet only three companies inquired further about possible export business. "It's so shocking, you can't believe it," says Mr. Medhurst, who with partner John Sobottka started Teckbau Bau Elemente und Systeme GmbH to sell precut housing panels to German contractors. "We have the orders. But we can't get Canadian companies to supply us with products."

The lack of response is more amazing given the desperate need for housing in the former east Germany. The government estimates at least one million units are needed immediately, with another 100,000 needed annually to keep pace with requirements. And that's just the eastern states. Western Germany requires 400,000 units a year on top of the two million units needed right away.

Flaking concrete apartment blocks throughout eastern Germany are testament to the former Communist government's inability to provide adequate housing for its people. The cheap concrete is deteriorating and the joints between concrete slabs have eroded to the point that air passes through in places. The former government built one million units and most will have to be torn down.

"Housing is the biggest area of opportunity for Canadians right now in Germany," says Michel Têtu, trade commissioner at the Canadian consulate in Berlin. "But there are not enough companies interested."

In fact, the number active in the housing market in eastern Germany can be counted on the fingers of two hands.

Why Canadian suppliers and contractors are not leaping at this opportunity has as much to do with the Canadian mind set as it has to do with the difficulties of entering the German market, Mr. Medhurst says.

He has faced bureaucratic hurdles that must be cleared, at a significant cost in time and money. The panels Tekbau plans to manufacture at a former plywood plant in nearby Klosterfelde are new for the German market and therefore had to meet a standard known as the Deutsche Industrie Norm (DIN) before they could be used in German housing.

Basically a sandwich of chipboard on the outside and five inches of polyurethane foam on the inside, a panel has enough structural strength to hold up a roof by itself. When used for roofing, it requires no trusses or interior support beams, which means added room at the top of the house and reduced costs. It also provides good insulation, an added attraction in environment-conscious Germany.

Jürgen Hanne, the German developer who is planning to build houses with the Tekbau panel, says using it instead of poured concrete, the usual way German houses are built, translates into savings of up to 30 per cent. It is easier to work with, takes less time to erect and costs less.

But before Mr. Hanne can use it, the product must receive its final DIN approval, which Mr. Medhurst is expecting within weeks. It has cost his company about $142,000 to pay the testing institute and 2½ years of effort to get this far. Despite prior international exposure with his Toronto firm of Medhurst Hogg Sobottka Leong and Associates Ltd., Mr. Medhurst has been surprised at the extent of the bureaucracy.

"There's enormous investment here in a regulatory environment, which you just have to battle your way through," he says. Mr. Têtu of the Canadian consulate concurs but points out: "The approvals process is like a mine field, which is a deterrent. But once you're through it's a protection, because competitors also have to make it through." Both men warn that Canadian companies planning to enter the German market must set aside time and money to get DIN approval for their products, perhaps paying a local German firm to do the legwork.

This same process might have to be repeated for other European Community countries, they warn. Despite the talk of a single European market, Mr. Medhurst has discovered that most countries still insist on their own standard and will not accept tests done elsewhere. Tekbau is repeating in Britain the same tests it did in Germany, where it also wants to market the panels.

"The EC haven't got together on technical approvals. A lot of lip service is paid to the single market," he says.

The light at the end of this bureaucratic tunnel is $20-million worth of orders for the panel this year, rising to about $100-million in 1994, Mr. Medhurst says.

Mr. Hanne, who also has a construction company in Calgary, says German developers can't keep up with housing demand, particularly in eastern Germany.

Easterners also are more open than western Germans to trying something new, such as a house built with wooden panels rather than concrete. Klaus Kapalle, the architect designing the houses, says the very fact the homes are different from those traditionally built in western Germany is a selling point in the east, where there is growing antagonism to all things west German because easterners think they got a raw deal in unification.

Mr. Hanne, like Mr. Medhurst, is amazed that more Canadian companies have not tried to enter the market, particularly when directly approached by someone already there with orders in hand.

"Canadians are not flexible," he concludes. "They don't see the opportunities. We would understand it if they were busy, but they're all starving."

Mr. Medhurst says the few companies he contacted personally were unwilling to make the minor changes needed to sell their product in Germany. For example, windows open inward in Germany, unlike in Canada where they generally open out. "The ones we talked to said 'We're not going to turn our windows around,' " he says. "The real impediment for Canadians is their mind set. We're lacking the can-do mentality."

The Canadian Construction Association and the Canadian Home Builders Association insist their members are interested in export possibilities, but they need government support to go overseas.

"We need an international trade strategy with competitive financing and general government support," says Michael Makin, spokesman for the CCA in Ottawa. "We don't have that same aggressive thrust behind us that France, Belgium, Germany and other countries have."

Of the $95-billion worth of construction work done by CCA members last year, less than 1 per cent was overseas, Mr. Makin estimates.

Banks also are a problem, he says. "There's no assistance for international work and their collateral requirements are ridiculous. In other countries, government, business and banks work together. Here, we work at cross-purposes."

John Kenward of the Canadian Home Builders Association says there is growing interest among his members in export markets.

They will get a second chance to prove that when Mr. Medhurst sends out another round of letters later this year soliciting Canadian suppliers.

SOURCE: Madelaine Drohan, *The Globe and Mail*, 22 November 1993, pp. B1, B2. Reprinted with permission from *The Globe and Mail*.

📖 Timothy's Cup Runs Over in Crowded Manhattan

THIS TOWN may think it's the trend-setting capital of the world, but when it comes to coffee, New York is on another planet.

In Manhattan, the typical caffeine jolt is a watery black brew dispensed in Grecian paper cups from sidewalk carts and delis. New Yorkers have swallowed this tepid coffee for the simple reason that it was convenient and not much else was available.

Gourmet coffee stores such as Starbucks and Timothy's Coffees have revolutionized caffeine tastes from Seattle to Toronto in the past decade, but few specialty coffee retailers have had the stomach for the gruelling Manhattan market.

"You could go crazy operating a coffee store in this town, there's too many regulations, hassles and competitors . . . it's very, very difficult," says Donald Schoenholt, president of Gillies Coffee Co. of Brooklyn, the oldest U.S. coffee roaster and wholesaler.

Lately, those difficulties have started to look like opportunities. Most major U.S. cities are overflowing with gourmet coffee shops, so New York, hassles and all, suddenly looks tempting.

Dozens of major coffee retailers are starting to target Manhattan and industry experts predict hundreds of stores will be serving espressos and flavoured coffees within a few years.

Helping to lead the way is Timothy's Coffees of the World Inc., a Toronto-based retailer that stepped into the Manhattan market in 1991. Since it arrived, Timothy's has quietly operated two midtown coffee bars to get a taste of the market. Bankers and consultants warned Timothy's president Becky McKinnon she would probably flop in cut-throat New York, but she had a plan.

After a strategic review of Timothy's 47 Canadian stores four years ago, Ms. McKinnon realized her most successful outlets were those in office towers. The bigger the tower, the larger the lineup of caffeine-needy workers. If Timothy's was going to expand, Ms. McKinnon decided, the company had to go after big city office buildings.

After some quick calculations, she realized Canada had limited potential. For example, only 25 of Toronto's towers had the 750,000 square feet of rented space that she felt was necessary to sustain her office stores. In New York, there were more than 150 such buildings.

Her instincts paid off. In the first year, the Manhattan stores exceeded her sales expectations by 25 per cent. Now the two are Timothy's biggest money makers, ringing up average annual sales of about $900 (U.S.) a square foot. Timothy's Canadian stores average about $600 (U.S.) a square foot.

That was enough to convince a handful of U.S. venture capital investors to buy $11.5-million of Timothy's preferred shares this spring to help finance a major U.S. expansion.

The company recently opened a new store in Boston and four more in Manhattan. Five more New York stores will open in the next two months and by the end of 1995, Ms. McKinnon said, Timothy's will have more than 50 outlets in this city.

She predicts the privately held company's annual sales will double to $20-million next year. If sales growth continues after that, she said she and her co-owner husband, financial analyst Ian McKinnon, may consider issuing public shares.

Not bad for a company that couldn't find a Canadian bank to back its U.S. expansion a few years ago. When Ms. McKinnon went to her bank, Canadian Imperial Bank of Commerce, in the late 1980s to negotiate financing for the U.S. expansion, she said, "they were very nervous" and turned her down.

The bank's reticence is understandable. Most Canadian lenders have bet too many loans on Canadian retailers who lost their touch south of the border.

"Zillions have been lost by Canadian retailers who saw great market opportunities in the United States, but didn't do their research and underestimated the competition," said Wendy Evans, a cross-border retail consultant.

To be sure, Timothy's runs the risk of being scalded in the New York market because competition is just starting to heat up in the city's coffee market. Several major U.S. retailers are planning to expand here and they will be looking for an edge with service, an area in which Canadians often get poor marks.

Ms. McKinnon said she has devoted a lot of time training her staff in New York, but there are still some rough edges. When a caller recently asked for Ms. McKinnon at her new Greenwich Village store, a sales clerk said he had never heard of her, even though at the time she was sitting a few feet away. When a photographer at the same store asked a clerk to help move coffee during a recent photo session, he walked away.

New Yorkers are used to plenty of attitude in stores, but Timothy's can't afford it if it wants to stay ahead of bigger competitors that are steaming into the city.

Specialty coffee consumption is one of the fastest-growing areas of food consumption in the United States and a flood of retailers are chasing the business with new coffee houses. Leading coffee retailer Starbucks Corp. of Seattle, which has 250 coffee bars across the country, plans to open 125 stores next year including, for the first time, such cities as New York and Boston. Even mass merchandisers such as Woolworth Corp. of New York are experimenting with specialty coffees. Can McDonald's McSpresso be far behind?

These retailers may be bigger and more familiar with the U.S. market, but Ms. McKinnon does have a few things working in her favour. For one thing, she is an American who was raised in nearby Philadelphia and lived in Manhattan before moving to Canada in 1969.

Ms. McKinnon also has a financial edge over some of her U.S. competitors. Most U.S. retailers steer clear of Manhattan because labour and real estate costs are prohibitive. By Toronto standards, however, New York can be a deal.

Canada's high minimum wage levels are comparable to New York's retail wages, but the big cost saver these days is real estate in the depressed Manhattan market. Ms. McKinnon estimates it costs her about $90 (U.S.) a square foot a month in total charges to rent retail space in a Toronto office tower, whereas in mid-town Manhattan rates now run at about $60 a square foot.

"Our timing was good. I wouldn't have thought New York would have been cheaper," she says.

When she decided to move into the New York market two years ago, Ms. McKinnon took it slowly. She didn't want to repeat the mistakes of the company's former owner and founder, Timothy Snelgrove.

Three years after he founded the company in 1975, Mr. Snelgrove plunged into the U.S. market with aggressive plans for stores in Cleveland, Washington, Pittsburgh, Chicago and Texas. Before all of the stores were even opened, however, Mr. Snelgrove was forced to retreat because the expansion was too much of a strain on the young company.

"The concept wasn't well developed enough. Tim didn't have the management or financial strength to weather the challenge," Ms. McKinnon said.

When she and her husband bought control of Timothy's in 1985, Ms. McKinnon's first priority was to redesign the company's stores to appeal to a more upscale market. Stores were refitted with mahogany trim, brass fixtures and espresso machines. The company also expanded its line of private-label coffees and teas.

By 1991, she was ready to export the concept to New York. The two midtown stores have given her plenty of exposure to Manhattan's retail frustrations.

The biggest challenge has been time. What takes weeks to accomplish with a new store in Toronto can take months in New York, whether it's construction, training or obtaining city approvals. The worst delays occurred with lease negotiations.

Leasing space can be a nightmare. When she first began looking for sites in 1991, New York commercial landlords were crying for tenants, but few were willing to take a chance investing in store renovations for a small unknown Canadian coffee retailer. Some landlords dragged their feet for years. Negotiations began in September, 1991, for the outlet Timothy's is opening at 120 Broadway this week.

"The landlord was paranoid that we would disappear after they spent money on renovations for the store," Ms. McKinnon says.

For the moment, it looks like Timothy's is here to stay. Now that her company has a track record in the city, office buildings are opening their doors to Ms. McKinnon.

Thanks to two years of preparation, Ms. McKinnon has already started negotiations for most of the buildings she has targeted for Timothy's stores. The planning, combined with two years of experience in Manhattan, gives her a head start against bigger competitors such as Starbucks.

"Timothy's has probably done it more intelligently than most coffee retailers," says Mr. Schoenholt of Gillies Coffee. "You have to learn to walk before you run, because you can stub your toe real fast in this town."

SOURCE: Jacquie McNish, *The Globe and Mail*, 15 November 1993, pp. B1, B6. Reprinted with permission from *The Globe and Mail*.

📖 Tiny Firm Strikes Gold in Jerusalem

LEGEND HAS IT that when Caliph Abd al-Malik's workers completed the Dome of the Rock in the year 691, the finished cupola glowed with 10,000 sheets of purest Egyptian gold.

Thirteen hundred years later, descendants of those same labourers toiling beneath the same Jerusalem sun, are covering the dome again — this time, under the eye of an electroplating consultant from Burlington, Ont.

Six weeks ago, Dalcan Services Ltd., a tiny company specializing in brush-plating, was awarded a consulting contract for the gold work on the Dome of the Rock, the third-holiest Muslim site in the world after Mecca and Medina.

With five employees, operating out of a 2,650-square-foot Burlington office, Dalcan's victory demonstrates that, in doing business globally, size is no substitute for owning a niche.

"How many people can plate 1,700 square metres of gold?" asks Garry Byrne, Dalcan's owner and president. "It frightens everybody. It takes 80 kilograms of gold bullion. How many people want to gamble on that?"

Trying to salvage gold that has been poorly plated is a complicated process, and the recovery ratio is never greater than 60 per cent, Mr. Byrne says. But for Dalcan, the risk of failure is minimal. The company has large-scale gold-plating experience; in 1986 it covered the dome of the Cathedral of the Transfiguration in Markham, Ont.

It also has perfected an on-site brush-plating process he says few companies in the world can match.

"Strangely enough, they do seem to be at the forefront of the technology," says Henry Johnston, managing director of Mivan Overseas Ltd., the Belfast company that holds the contract for restoring the entire Dome structure.

"You don't normally get such large areas to be electroplated in gold . . . Dalcan, having had the experience from the Markham [cathedral], really hasn't too many people in front of them."

Surprisingly, Dalcan considers its gold work peripheral to its overall business, the largest part of which comes from industrial clients, half of whom are in the United States.

Industrial brush-plating requires even more precision than decorative gold work, Mr. Byrne explains. Among Dalcan's clients, for example, are several newspapers — including the Ottawa Citizen and the Toronto Star — that depend on the tiny company to repair the gouges and dings that occur every time a foreign object falls into the presses.

So precise is Dalcan's technique that an indentation can be filled in so that the patched area lines up within one-tenth of a hair of the surface.

"We're the only people who can do the repair so you can't find the marks anymore," Mr. Byrne says proudly.

Dalcan keeps portable equipment in Buffalo, Chicago and Detroit, so it can service companies across North America within four days. By the time an employee is flown to the repair site from Toronto, the equipment is already waiting. And with a lifetime guarantee on all repairs, Mr. Byrne says the company's services are in such demand that it will open a second office in Chicago within the next few months.

The decorative side of the business began as a natural sideline to the ability to brush-plate all kinds of metals, Mr. Byrne says. In the early to mid-eighties, the company began gaining exposure from its gold work on various sculptures and, in 1986, landed the contract for the cathedral in Markham.

But nothing Dalcan has handled in the past — industrial or decorative — has commanded the public attention of this project.

The Dome's restoration, which is being financed by King Hussein of Jordan, is of enormous significance to Muslims, Jews and Christians around the world. The Prophet Mohammed is said to have ascended to heaven from the rock enshrined by the dome. Followers of the Old Testament believe the structure stands on the spot where Abraham was prepared to sacrifice Isaac.

Under Mr. Byrne's direction, workers employed by Mivan will mould brass sheets to the shape of the Dome and then brush-plate — a process developed by Dalcan — a 12-micron thickness of copper, four-micron thickness of nickel, and two-micron thickness of gold across the surface. (A micron is one thousandth of a millimetre, or about one-fifteenth thickness of a single coat of emulsion paint.)

In 1016, after an earthquake caused substantial damage to the dome, it was repaired with lead, and in 1963, it was covered again with gold-coloured aluminum. The decision, after thirteen centuries, to return to 24-karat gold is far more expensive. (The gold for the Dome has a current market value of about $1-million (U.S.). And the final product must be physically, as well as visibly flawless, Mr. Byrne stresses.

Using Dalcan's process, Mr. Byrne says the final layer of gold will be so uniform it will pass a test of exposure, for two hours, to nitric acid, without sustaining a mark.

It is this kind of workmanship that lets Dalcan charge top dollar, Mr. Byrne admits. While he would not reveal the exact size of the Dome contract, he did say Dalcan's annual revenue is normally $600,000 to $700,000, and that this job may double that figure.

Although he refers to the project as "a great experience," he also admits there are problems specific to working in the Middle East. The Dome, for example, is under Arab control, but everything must be done within the confines of Israeli bureaucracy, which is often complex.

"If I were doing the job in Buffalo, I would have what I needed in 24 hours. When I'm doing the job [in the Middle East], and I decide I need something, it's three weeks."

The total restoration is already six months behind schedule, containers of chemicals have been held in Israeli storage for months, and the crews responsible for erecting the brass sheets have been sent home several times, he said.

Because he is acting as a consultant only on this particular project, costs resulting from the delays are not borne by his company. However, in any future business forays in this part of the world, he says he will make sure costs of bureaucratic delays are borne by the customer.

Mr. Byrne hopes to use the work done on the Dome as a springboard into the European and Middle-Eastern markets. He is negotiating with one Israeli and one Arab electroplating expert to establish a three-way joint venture to do industrial and decorative work in the Middle East.

"We've already had inquiries from Quatar and Saudi Arabia and Bucharest. The Muslim population throughout the world is so great that if you have had anything to do with the Dome of the Rock, boy that's a boost."

SOURCE: Danielle Bochove, *The Globe and Mail*, 20 September 1993, pp. B1, B8. Reprinted with permission from *The Globe and Mail*.

▮▮ *Questions*

1. Can Canadian women compete and succeed in the export market-place? Becky McKinnon, president of Timothy's Coffees, certainly has proved that she can be successful. Review figure 8.3: Ten Steps for Small Business — Exporting. What steps did Timothy's focus on to be successful in the U.S. market?

2. Many Canadian entrepreneurs recommend that your first export market should be the U.S. Why did Becky McKinnon choose the U.S. market as Timothy's first export target? Are there any other reasons why you might want to focus first on the U.S. market?

3. The success of many of our small businesses does not necessarily depend on the exporting of high-technology equipment and services. In many cases, it makes little difference whether you are high tech, low tech, or no tech; you can still be a successful exporter. Review our case studies and make a list of the kinds of products and services that are being exported. Start creating your own list of export opportunities.

4. We have provided you with many examples of owners of small businesses who are optimistic about the opportunities in the new global economy. Make a list of their market niches. Where are they doing business? Why? Get your creative juices moving. What would you like to export? Why?

5. In many cases, small businesses are not financially strong enough to penetrate a foreign market. As a result, they have to create partnerships, alliances, joint ventures, and so on. What was Canora's market niche and strategy to penetrate the market in Southeast Asia? What kinds of partnerships and alliances did our other successful entrepreneurs create? Why?

Recommended Reading

Russell Acknoff. *The Art of Problem Solving*

James Adams. *The Care and Feeding of Ideas: A Guide to Encouraging Creativity*

Teresa Amabile. *Growing Up Creative: Nurturing a Lifetime of Creativity*

Janet Attard. *The Home Office and Small Business Answer*

Roger Axtell. *The Do's and Taboos of International Trade*

Mark Bacon. *Do It Yourself Direct Marketing*

D. Wesley Balderson. *Canadian Entrepreneurship and Small Business Management*

Nuala Beck. *Shifting Gears: Thriving in the New Economy*

Dale Beckman. *Small Business Management*

Peter Urs Bender. *Secrets of Power Presentations*

Wendy Binggeli. *After the Idea, What Comes Next?*

William Brannen. *Successful Marketing for Your Small Business*

Deaver Brown. *The Entrepreneur's Guide*

William D. Bygrave. *The Portable MBA in Entrepreneurship*

Gerald Byers. *Marketing for Small Business*

Colin Campbell. *Where the Jobs Are: Career Survival for Canadians in the New Global Economy*

Cy Charney. *The Instant Manager*

Herb Cohen. *You Can Negotiate Anything*

William Cohen. *The Entrepreneur and Small Business Problem Solver*

James Cook. *The Start-up Entrepreneur*

David Crane. *The Next Canadian Century*

Jeff Davidson. *Marketing on a Shoe String*

Roger Dawson. *The Secrets of Power Negotiating*

Sandra L. Dean. *How to Advertise: A Handbook for Small Business*

Edward De Bono. *The Use of Lateral Thinking Lateral Thinking*

William Delaney. *Why Small Businesses Fail*

Forum for International Trade Training (FITT). *Global Entrepreneurship*

David Foot. *The Over Forty Society — Issues in Canada*

Charles Ford. *Think Smart, Move Fast*

Mike Fuller. *Above the Bottom Line*

Douglas Goold. *How to Get What You Want from Your Bank*

Douglas Gray. *Marketing Your Product: A Planning Guide Have You Got What It Takes? The Entrepreneur's Complete Self Assessment Guide*

Paul Hague. *Do Your Own Market Research*

Paul Hawken. *Growing a Business*

Spencer Johnson. *Yes or No*

Gregory Kishel. *Your Business Is a Success: Now What?*

Ron Knowles. *Canadian Small Business — An Entrepreneur's Plan*

Barbara Lambesis. *101 Big Ideas for Promoting a Business on a Small Budget*

Jay Levinson. *Guerrilla Marketing: Secrets for Making Big Profits from Small Business*

Harvey MacKay. *Swim with the Sharks without Being Eaten Alive: Outsell, Outmanage, Outmotivate and Outnegotiate Your Competition*

Linda McAllister. *I Wish I'd Said That*

Norman Maier. *Problem Solving and Creativity in Individuals and Groups*

Peter Malkowsky. *The Basics of Import/Export*

Og Mandino. *The Greatest Salesman in the World, Part 1*
The Greatest Salesman in the World, Part 2
The Greatest Miracle in the World

Lyle Maul. *The Entrepreneur's Road Map to Business Success*

Ed Mirvish. *How to Build an Empire on an Orange Crate or 121 Lessons I Never Learned in School*

Paul and Dan Monaghan. *Why Not Me?*

Paul Moody. *Decision Making*

John Naisbitt. *Megatrends*

Thomas Peters. *A Passion for Excellence: The Leadership Difference*
    Excellence in the Organization
    In Search of Excellence: Lessons from America's Best-Run Companies
    Thriving on Chaos: Handbook for a Management Revolution
Michael E. Roch. *Ethics, to Live By, to Work By*
    Dynamics of Supervision
Marvin G. Ryder. *Marketing Insights: Contemporary Canadian Cases*
Mike Schatzki. *Negotiation — The Art of Getting What You Want*
Edna Sheedy. *The Entrepreneur's Guide to Growing Up*
Walter Staples. *Think Like a Winner*
Tapon, Francis, et al. *Learning for Success in Business*
Iain Williamson. *Successful Small Business Financing in Canada*
Maridee A. Winter. *Mind Your Own Business, Be Your Own Boss*

R E A D E R   R E P L Y   C A R D

We are interested in your reaction to *Issues in Canadian Small Business* by Ron Knowles and Debbie White. You can help us to improve this book in future editions by completing this questionnaire.

1. What was your reason for using this book?
    - ❏ university course
    - ❏ continuing-education course
    - ❏ personal development
    - ❏ college course
    - ❏ professional
    - ❏ other interest _____

2. If you are a student, please identify your school and the course in which you used this book.

3. Which chapters or parts of this book did you use? Which did you omit?

4. What did you like best about this book? What did you like least?

5. Please identify any topics you think should be added to future editions.

6. Please add any comments or suggestions.

7. May we contact you for further information?

Name: _____

Address: _____

_____

_____

Phone: _____

(fold here and tape shut)

MAIL ➤ **POSTE**

Canada Post Corporation / Société canadienne des postes

Postage paid
If mailed in Canada

Port payé
si posté au Canada

**Business
Reply**

**Réponse
d'affaires**

0116870399   01

0116870399-M8Z4X6-BR01

Heather McWhinney
Publisher, College Division
HARCOURT BRACE & COMPANY, CANADA
55 HORNER AVENUE
TORONTO, ONTARIO
M8Z 9Z9